China–ASEAN Relations and International Law

CHANDOS
ASIAN STUDIES SERIES:
CONTEMPORARY ISSUES AND TRENDS

Series Editor: Professor Chris Rowley,
Cass Business School, City University, UK
(email: c.rowley@city.ac.uk)

Chandos Publishing is pleased to publish this major Series of books entitled *Asian Studies: Contemporary Issues and Trends.* The Series Editor is Professor Chris Rowley, Cass Business School, City University, UK.

Asia has clearly undergone some major transformations in recent years and books in the Series examine this transformation from a number of perspectives: economic, management, social, political and cultural. We seek authors from a broad range of areas and disciplinary interests: covering, for example, business/management, political science, social science, history, sociology, gender studies, ethnography, economics and international relations, etc.

Importantly, the Series examines both current developments and possible future trends. The Series is aimed at an international market of academics and professionals working in the area. The books have been specially commissioned from leading authors. The objective is to provide the reader with an authoritative view of current thinking.

New authors: we would be delighted to hear from you if you have an idea for a book. We are interested in both shorter, practically orientated publications (45,000+ words) and longer, theoretical monographs (75,000–100,000 words). Our books can be single, joint or multi-author volumes. If you have an idea for a book, please contact the publishers or Professor Chris Rowley, the Series Editor.

Dr Glyn Jones
Chandos Publishing
Email: gjones@chandospublishing.com
www.chandospublishing.com

Professor Chris Rowley
Cass Business School, City University
Email: c.rowley@city.ac.uk
www.cass.city.ac.uk/faculty/c.rowley

Chandos Publishing: Chandos Publishing is an imprint of Woodhead Publishing Limited. The aim of Chandos Publishing is to publish books of the highest possible standard: books that are both intellectually stimulating and innovative.

We are delighted and proud to count our authors from such well-known international organisations as the Asian Institute of Technology, Tsinghua University, Kookmin University, Kobe University, Kyoto Sangyo University, London School of Economics, University of Oxford, Michigan State University, Getty Research Library, University of Texas at Austin, University of South Australia, University of Newcastle, Australia, University of Melbourne, ILO, Max-Planck Institute, Duke University and the leading law firm Clifford Chance.

A key feature of Chandos Publishing's activities is the service it offers its authors and customers. Chandos Publishing recognises that its authors are at the core of its publishing ethos, and authors are treated in a friendly, efficient and timely manner. Chandos Publishing's books are marketed on an international basis, via its range of overseas agents and representatives.

Professor Chris Rowley: Dr Rowley, BA, MA (Warwick), DPhil (Nuffield College, Oxford) is Subject Group leader and the inaugural Professor of Human Resource Management at Cass Business School, City University, London, UK. He is the founding Director of the new, multi-disciplinary and internationally networked *Centre for Research on Asian Management* and Editor of the leading journal *Asia Pacific Business Review* (www.tandf.co.uk/journals/titles/13602381.asp). He is well known and highly regarded in the area, with visiting appointments at leading Asian universities and top journal Editorial Boards in the US and UK. He has given a range of talks and lectures to universities and companies internationally with research and consultancy experience with unions, business and government and his previous employment includes varied work in both the public and private sectors. Professor Rowley researches in a range of areas, including international and comparative human resource management and Asia Pacific management and business. He has been awarded grants from the British Academy, an ESRC AIM International Study Fellowship and gained a 5-year RCUK Fellowship in Asian Business and Management. He acts as a reviewer for many funding bodies, as well as for numerous journals and publishers. Professor Rowley publishes very widely, including in leading US and UK journals, with over 100 articles, 80 book chapters and other contributions and 20 edited and sole authored books.

China–ASEAN Relations and International Law

Zou Keyuan

Chandos Publishing
Oxford · Cambridge · New Delhi

Chandos Publishing
TBAC Business Centre
Avenue 4
Station Lane
Witney
Oxford OX28 4BN
UK
Tel: +44 (0) 1993 848726
Email: info@chandospublishing.com

Chandos Publishing is an imprint of Woodhead Publishing Limited

Woodhead Publishing Limited
Abington Hall
Granta Park
Great Abington
Cambridge CB21 6AH
UK
www.woodheadpublishing.com

First published in 2009

ISBN:
978 1 84334 438 4

British Library Cataloguing-in-Publication Data.
A catalogue record for this book is available from the British Library.

Typeset by Macmillan Publishing Solutions.
Printed in the UK and USA.

For my family

Contents

About the author

Zou Keyuan is Harris Professor of International Law at the Lancashire Law School of the University of Central Lancashire (UCLan), United Kingdom. He specializes in international law, in particular law of the sea and international environmental law. Before joining UCLan, he worked in Dalhousie University (Canada), Peking University (China), University of Hannover (Germany) and National University of Singapore.

He has published over 50 referred English papers in more than 20 international journals including *Asian Yearbook of International Law, Asia-Pacific Journal of Environmental Law, Chinese Journal of International Law* and *Columbia Journal of International Affairs*.

His recent books include *Law of the Sea in East Asia: Issues and Prospects* (London/New York: Routledge, 2005), *China's Marine Legal System and the Law of the Sea* (Leiden/Boston: Martinus Nijhoff, 2005) and *China's Legal Reform: Towards the Rule of Law* (Leiden/Boston: Martinus Nijhoff, 2006).

He is member of Editorial Boards of the *International Journal of Marine and Coastal Law* (Martinus Nijhoff), *Ocean Development and International Law* (Taylor & Francis), *Journal of International Wildlife Law and Policy* (Taylor & Francis) and *Chinese Journal of International Law* (Oxford University Press), and Advisory Board of the *Chinese Oceans Law Review* (Hong Kong: China Review Culture Limited).

He has also acted as reviewer for *Singapore Yearbook of International Law* (National University of Singapore), *China: An International Journal* (National University of Singapore), *China Review: An Interdisciplinary Journal on Greater China* (Chinese University of Hong Kong), *Chinese (Taiwan) Review of International and Transnational Law* (Academia Sinica, Taiwan), *Ocean Yearbook* (Dalhousie University), *Issues and*

Studies (National Chenchi University, Taiwan) and *Coastal Management* (Taylor & Francis).

He is Academic Advisor to the China National Institute for South China Sea Studies and External Assessor for the Australian Research Council and Hong Kong Research Grants Council. He is member of the Commission on Environmental Law, IUCN and Associate of the Centre for Asia-Pacific Initiatives of the University of Victoria, Canada.

Part I
Introduction

1

History and development of contemporary China–ASEAN relations

History of interchange

China's relations with Southeast Asia have a long history. 'Southeast Asia has had deep historical and cultural bonds with both India and China because they were not only geographically close, but also traded with each other at least for 2500 years; the Southeast Asian realm enjoyed an intermediate locational vantage.'[1] History records that the first Chinese settlements in Southeast Asia, such as in Singapore, began in the middle of the fourteenth century.[2] During 1405–33, the great seafarer in Chinese history, Zheng He of the Ming Dynasty (1368–1644), led the biggest ocean-going fleets of the time, sailing to Southeast Asia and the Indian Ocean. His fleets brought Chinese culture and products to Southeast Asia and even helped the locals maintain social order by quelling piracy in the Southeast Asian seas.[3] Although the relations between China and Southeast Asia in the past had generally been friendly and mutually beneficial, equality between China and Southeast Asian nations based on the tributary system created by China was questionable in accordance with modern international law, though in practice the system benefited both sides. It is commonly acknowledged that Chinese influence over Southeast Asia is considerable: many Chinese have migrated to Southeast Asia over the centuries, as economically, this is a vibrant region in close communication with China's coastal provinces, the powerhouse of China's own economic development.[4]

Nevertheless, after the founding of the People's Republic of China (PRC), the relations between China and Southeast Asia encountered ups and downs from the 1950s to the 1970s. China and Indonesia had a honeymoon period lasting from the early 1950s until the coup d'état led by Suharto, which cruelly suppressed the Indonesian Communist Party in 1967. China attended the Asian-African Bandung Conference, which put forward the famous 10 principles of peaceful coexistence and friendly cooperation. In the Sino-Burmese Joint Declaration in June 1954, China and Myanmar agreed to the Five Principles of Peaceful Coexistence to guide the development of their bilateral relations. They also solved the border problem by signing a border settlement agreement in the early 1960s. Vietnam maintained close ties with China as a communist comrade during the 1950s and 1960s.

When China began its notorious Cultural Revolution (1966–76), the relationship between China and many Southeast Asian countries deteriorated to various degrees. China even severed its diplomatic ties with Indonesia. A Southeast Asian specialist in China examined the early period of PRC–Southeast Asian relations and listed several reasons for the deterioration of bilateral relations. First was the disturbance from China's extra-leftist radicals, carrying out the so-called revolutionary diplomacy based on social systems and ideology, and trying to export 'revolution' to other countries, particularly its neighbouring countries. Second was the influence from the Sino-centralism, as China appointed itself the leader of the Third World. Third was China's miscalculation of its international status.[5] Thus, China's provocative diplomacy and domestic radicalism damaged its ties with Southeast Asia.[6] The improvement and positive development of China–ASEAN (Association of the Southeast Asian Nations) relations became possible only after China carried out the new policy of economic reform and decided to open itself to the outside world in 1978.

Establishment and evolution of ASEAN

Southeast Asia is commonly recognised as a land of diversity in terms of political systems, levels of economic development, religion and culture. However, the Southeast Asian nations were able to establish a regional organisation, named ASEAN, which is a miraculous achievement in the development of civilisation, particularly in comparison with the establishment of the European Union, which is much less diverse.

It is said that one of the hidden purposes of the establishment of ASEAN was to contain the spread of communism to Southeast Asia, mainly from China and Vietnam in the 1960s. Because of this, ASEAN was viewed by its neighbours as an unfriendly entity: Moscow regarded it as another instrument of the other side of the Cold War, while Beijing regarded it as a tool of American imperialism being used to contain the PRC. Even Vietnam regarded ASEAN as a barrier to its unification.[7] However, while there might have been various reasons to establish ASEAN, the main goals as pronounced in the Bangkok Declaration, the founding document of ASEAN, are to 'accelerate the economic growth, social progress and cultural development in the region through joint endeavours in the spirit of equality and partnership in order to strengthen the foundation for a prosperous and peaceful community of South-East Asian Nations' and to 'promote regional peace and stability through abiding respect for justice and the rule of law in the relationship among countries of the region and adherence to the principles of the United Nations Charter'.[8]

At the beginning, the operations of ASEAN were not really smooth. The five original founding member countries, namely Indonesia, Malaysia, the Philippines, Singapore and Thailand, held their first summit nine years after the establishment of the organisation in 1976 when ASEAN adopted the Declaration of the ASEAN Concord as well as the Treaty of Amity and Cooperation in Southeast Asia (TAC). Only since then, ASEAN has been developing rapidly. New members were admitted into it: Brunei Darussalam joined on 8 January 1984, Vietnam on 28 July 1995, Lao PDR and Myanmar on 23 July 1997, and Cambodia on 30 April 1999. As of 2008, ASEAN has 10 members.

On the 30th anniversary of ASEAN in 1997, its leaders adopted the ASEAN Vision 2020 and agreed on a shared vision of ASEAN as a concert of Southeast Asian nations.[9] In 2003 they decided to build an ASEAN Community with three indispensable pillars, namely ASEAN Security Community (ASC), ASEAN Economic Community and ASEAN Socio-Cultural Community. The ASC aims to ensure that countries in the region live at peace with one another and with the world in a just, democratic and harmonious environment based on the strong foundation of ASEAN processes, principles, agreements and structures. 'The members of the Community pledge to rely exclusively on peaceful processes in the settlement of intra-regional differences and regard their security as fundamentally linked to one another and bound by geographic location, common vision and objectives. It has the following components: political development; shaping and sharing of norms; conflict prevention; conflict resolution; post-conflict peace building; and implementing mechanisms.'[10] The ASEAN Regional Forum (ARF),[11] which was established in 1994, can play an active role in maintaining peace and security in East Asia.

The goal of the ASEAN Economic Community 'is to create a stable, prosperous and highly competitive ASEAN economic region in which there is a free flow of goods, services, investment and a freer flow of capital, equitable economic development and reduced poverty and socio-economic disparities in year 2020'. 'The ASEAN Economic Community shall establish ASEAN as a single market and production base, turning the diversity that characterises the region into opportunities for business complementation and making the ASEAN a more dynamic and stronger segment of the global supply chain. ASEAN's strategy shall consist of the integration of ASEAN and enhancing ASEAN's economic competitiveness.'[12] The ASEAN Free Trade Area (AFTA) was launched in 1992, with an aim to promote the region's competitive advantage as a single production unit. According to some data, as of 1 January 2005, tariffs on almost 99 per cent of the products in the Inclusion List of the ASEAN-6 (Brunei Darussalam, Indonesia, Malaysia, the Philippines, Singapore, and Thailand) had been reduced to no more than 5 per cent. More than 60 per cent of these products had zero tariffs. For the newer member countries, namely Cambodia, Lao PDR, Myanmar and Vietnam (CLMV), tariffs on about 81 per cent of the products in their Inclusion List had been brought down to the 0–5 per cent range.[13] The ASEAN member states also agree to cooperate in other areas of economic development such as agriculture for the purpose of formulating a single market in the near future.

The ASEAN Socio-Cultural Community 'envisages a Southeast Asia bonded together in partnership as a community of caring societies and founded on a common regional identity' and 'foster[s] cooperation in social development aimed at raising the standard of living of disadvantaged groups and the rural population, and shall seek the active involvement of all sectors of society, in particular women, youth, and local communities'.[14] Many ASEAN programs on various issues such as social welfare, HIV/AIDS, sustainable employment and media exchange attempt to achieve that purpose.

The most remarkable achievement in the development of ASEAN is the adoption of the ASEAN Charter in November 2007. Reaffirming the building of the ASEAN Community, the charter establishes the ASEAN Community Councils for political security and economic and socio-cultural affairs.[15] Though the charter repeats some purposes and objectives enshrined in the ASEAN Vision 2020, what is different is that the charter has turned those political promises and commitments into legal ones, thus making it obligatory for the ASEAN member states to fulfill them. The development of ASEAN itself inevitably has an immense impact on the development of the China–ASEAN relations.

Modern relations between China and ASEAN

There are generally three layers of interaction and interchange between China and ASEAN. The first layer is the relationship between China and ASEAN as an international organisation (relations between a nation state and an international organisation); the second is the relationship between China and ASEAN members through ASEAN (the ASEAN collectivity) and the third is the relationship between China and individual ASEAN member states (state-to-state bilateral relations). Anyone who wishes to study the China–ASEAN relations has to look into these three layers, though students can place emphasis on one layer or the other at their discretion, depending on the needs of their study.

Since China carried out its significant economic reform and pragmatic diplomacy when Deng Xiaoping came to power in the late 1970s, China has gradually improved its relations with Southeast Asia. In November 1978, Deng Xiaoping visited Malaysia, Myanmar, Singapore and Thailand. After this, China stopped its support to communist parties in Southeast Asia. Despite the embargo imposed on China by the West after the 1989 Tiananmen Square human disaster, the relations between China and Southeast Asia continued to improve. In 1990 China resumed its diplomatic ties with Indonesia and established such ties with Singapore. In September 1991, Brunei Darussalam became the last ASEAN country to establish diplomatic ties with China. By this time, therefore, all ASEAN members had diplomatic relations with China. China–Vietnam relations were normalised in the early 1990s as well.

China's contact with ASEAN also began in 1991 when Qian Qichen, the Chinese foreign minister, attended the opening of the 24th ASEAN Ministerial Meeting (AMM) in Kuala Lumpur, and China was granted the status of an ASEAN Consultative Dialogue Partner. The two sides established two joint committees on science and technology and on economy and trade in 1994. In July 1996, the status of China as an ASEAN Consultative Dialogue Partner was elevated to that of a full Dialogue Partner. The ASEAN Heads of Missions in Beijing also established the ASEAN Committee of Beijing (ACB) to promote ASEAN–China relations.[16] In December 1997, then-President Jiang Zemin and ASEAN leaders held their first ever summit and issued a joint statement in which they announced their decision to establish a twenty-first-century-oriented partnership of good neighbourhood and mutual trust between China and ASEAN (see Table 1.1).

Table 1.1 **Chronology of China–ASEAN summits**

Date	Summit
16 December 1997	China attended the first China–ASEAN summit in Kuala Lumpur, Malaysia. At the meeting, then-Chinese President Jiang Zemin delivered a speech on 'Establishing Good-Neighbourly Partnership of Mutual Trust Oriented to the Twenty-First Century'. The two sides issued a Joint Declaration, establishing guidelines for their relationship and common policies of good neighbourly partnership.
16 December 1998	The then-Chinese Vice President Hu Jintao attended the second China–ASIAN summit in Hanoi, Vietnam. Leaders of the two sides agreed to maintain friendly relations between China and ASEAN countries in various fields, at different levels and through various channels within an all-around dialogue cooperation framework. They also reached consensus on appropriately dealing with differences to boost their partnership.
28 November 1999	The then-Chinese Premier Zhu Rongji attended the third China–ASEAN summit in Manila, the Philippines. He offered China's advice on strengthening the good neighbourly partnership of mutual trust with ASEAN in the twenty-first century. ASEAN countries praised China's achievements in its development and spoke highly of its support and assistance to them in the Asian financial crisis.
25 November 2000	The fourth China–ASIAN summit was held in Singapore. At the meeting, the then-Chinese Premier Zhu Rongji spoke highly of the relationship between China and ASEAN, and offered advice on cooperation between the two sides in politics, human resource development, construction of infrastructure projects on the Mekong River, advanced technology, agriculture, trade and investment.
6 November 2001	The then-Chinese Premier Zhu Rongji attended the fifth China–ASEAN summit in Seri Begawan, Brunei Darussalam. The two sides agreed on the establishment of the China–ASEAN FTA over the following 10 years, and senior officials were authorised to begin negotiations on relevant agreements as soon as possible.

Table 1.1 Chronology of China–ASEAN summits (cont'd)

Date	Summit
4 November 2002	At the sixth China–ASEAN summit in Phnom Penh, Cambodia, the then-Chinese Premier Zhu Rongji and ASEAN leaders signed the Framework Agreement on China–ASEAN Comprehensive Economic Cooperation, and decided to establish the China–ASEAN FTA by 2010.
8 October 2003	Chinese Premier Wen Jiabao attended the seventh China–ASEAN summit in the Indonesian resort island of Bali. During the summit, ASEAN and China agreed to establish 'a strategic partnership for peace and prosperity'.
29 November 2004	Chinese Premier Wen Jiabao attended the eighth China–ASEAN summit in Vientiane, Laos. At the summit, Wen delivered a speech on the appraisal of China–ASEAN cooperation, China's policy towards ASEAN countries, principles for cooperation and proposals for further cooperation.
12 December 2005	At the ninth China–ASEAN summit in Kuala Lumpur, Chinese Premier Wen Jiabao put forward five initiatives to ensure more vigorous and fruitful growth of relations between China and ASEAN, including forging stronger bonds of friendship, putting in place a planned framework for relations and vigorously promoting personnel exchanges.
14 January 2007	At the 10th China–ASEAN summit in Cebu in the central Philippines, Chinese Premier Wen Jiabao and leaders of the 10 ASEAN member countries witnessed the signing of the China–ASEAN Agreement on Trade in Services.
20 November 2007	The 11th summit between ASEAN and China (10+1) was convened in Singapore. Chinese Premier Wen Jiabao and leaders of the 10 ASEAN member countries attended the summit. The Chinese premier hailed the Strategic Partnership for Peace and Prosperity between China and ASEAN, calling for expanding the China–ASEAN cooperation for mutual benefit and win–win progress. Both sides agreed to include 'environment' as the 11th priority area of cooperation between ASEAN and China.

Source: mainly based on *http://news.xinhuanet.com/english/2007-11/21/content_7116936.htm* (accessed 5 July 2008).

In February 1997, the ASEAN–China Joint Cooperation Committee (ACJCC) was formed and an all-round dialogue structure consisting of five parallel mechanisms was established. Thus, China and ASEAN established their regular institutional mechanisms for the development of their relations. The top cooperation mechanism is the '10+1' Summit Meeting. Below it are five operating mechanisms: the China–ASEAN Senior Official Political Consultation Mechanism, the China–ASEAN Joint Committee on Cooperation, the China–ASEAN Joint Committee on Economic and Trade Cooperation, the China–ASEAN Joint Science and Technology Committee and the ASEAN Committee in Beijing. The China–ASEAN Joint Committee on Cooperation acts as a coordinator for all the committees at the working level.

Some Chinese scholars divided China–ASEAN relations into two phases. The first phase from China's recognition of ASEAN in 1975 up to 1991 was a 'getting in touch' phase. The time when China's Foreign Minister Qian Qichen attended the 24th ASEAN Conference of Foreign Ministers in 1991 'witnessed the establishment of formal relations between the two sides'. The second phase was marked by the signing of the China–ASEAN Framework Agreement on Comprehensive Economic Cooperation on 4 November 2002.[17] Following this division, the current China–ASEAN relations encompass a new era of cooperation and common development based on the signing of the historic Joint Declaration of the Heads of State/Government of the Association of the Southeast Asian Nations and the People's Republic of China on Strategic Partnership for Peace and Prosperity at the ASEAN–China Summit on 8 October 2003 in Bali, in which both China and ASEAN member states declared they would develop their bilateral relations into a strategic partnership with comprehensive cooperation. Also in 2003 China acceded to the TAC, thus becoming the first non-ASEAN country to join the treaty. Internally, China set up the China–ASEAN Association, which was founded in August 2004 under the Chinese People's Association for Friendship with Foreign Countries in Beijing. Its mission is to promote cooperation and communication between China and the different ASEAN countries in the fields of politics, culture, business, technology and sports, among other fields.[18]

In the overall China–ASEAN relations, the most rapidly developed area is the economic cooperation. Therefore, the China–ASEAN relations have often been characterised as economic cooperation at first hand. Based on this cooperation, the two sides have expanded cooperation to other areas. As manifested by recent developments in the bilateral relations between China and ASEAN, a comprehensive cooperative framework has been gradually evolved and formulated, thus extending such relations from economic to political, security and legal relations and touching on as many areas as possible for cooperation between the two sides.

During the Asian financial crisis in 1997, China maintained the value of its currency, which helped Southeast Asia countries stabilise their financial systems and was appreciated by those countries. China was among the first to rush in with an offer of aid – US$1 billion in standby credit.[19] The crisis, on the other hand, helped Southeast Asia realise the necessity to establish a regional economic integration system so as to prevent such a crisis from occurring in the future. Economic integration began first within ASEAN and was then expanded to include other countries in Asia. As discussed in Chapter 4, China and ASEAN concluded the 2002 Framework Agreement on Comprehensive Economic Cooperation, which China initiated and ASEAN endorsed for the benefit of both sides. According to the agreement, an ASEAN–China Free Trade Area (ACFTA) will be established by the year 2010 for Brunei Darussalam, China, Indonesia, Malaysia, the Philippines, Singapore and Thailand, and by 2015, for the newer ASEAN member countries, Cambodia, Laos, Myanmar and Vietnam. Based on this Framework Agreement, the two sides further signed the Trade in Goods Agreement and the Dispute Settlement Mechanism Agreement in 2004 and the Trade in Service Agreement in 2007. It is reported that the two sides will sign another agreement on investment in the near future. All these agreements are discussed in Chapter 4 in some detail.

Besides economic cooperation centred on the ACFTA Framework Agreement, sub-regional economic cooperation is also under way. Two remarkable sub-regional cooperation mechanisms include the Greater Mekong Sub-Region Cooperation, which has been sponsored by the Asian Development Bank and involves Mekong River riparians as well as other ASEAN countries, and the relatively new Pan-Beibu Gulf (Gulf of Tonkin) Economic Cooperation, which was initiated by Guangxi, China, in 2006, and warmly welcomed by ASEAN countries. The discussion on the economic and environmental cooperation along the Mekong River can be found in Chapter 5, while a brief discussion on the Pan-Beibu Gulf economic cooperation is contained in Chapter 4. In other areas of economic cooperation, China and ASEAN signed MOUs or political documents on agriculture, information and communications technology (ICT), transport, port development and tourism, among others. It is well anticipated that with the deepening of economic cooperation between the two sides, more and more areas will be covered for cooperation under the ACFTA Framework Agreement. Closer economic cooperation between China and ASEAN is mutually beneficial, providing each with an additional source of economic growth and catalysing the process of economic integration in the whole East Asian region.

Cooperation in the political and security fields has also been undertaken between China and ASEAN. China attended the ARF established by ASEAN in 1994, which has the objectives 'to foster constructive dialogue and consultation on political and security issues of common interest and concern; and to make significant contributions to efforts towards confidence-building and preventive diplomacy in the Asia-Pacific region'.[20] Since 2004 China has co-hosted several ARF conferences on security policy, trans-national crimes including terrorism, drug control and natural disaster relief.[21] It also expressed its willingness to work with ASEAN for its accession to the Protocol to the Treaty on Southeast Asia Nuclear Weapons-Free Zone (SEANWFZ).

Since the September 11 terrorist attack, the world has confronted non-traditional security issues, which have become subject matters to be dealt with in the China–ASEAN cooperative framework. In November 2002, ASEAN and China signed the Joint Declaration on Cooperation in the Field of Non-Traditional Security Issues, which initiated full cooperation between ASEAN and China for dealing with such issues and listed the priority and form of cooperation.[22] Following this declaration, a non-traditional security issue MOU was adopted in 2004 to combat trafficking in illegal drugs, people smuggling including trafficking in women and children, sea piracy, terrorism, arms smuggling, money laundering, international economic crime and cyber crime. Chapter 7 discusses several important non-traditional security issues particularly terrorism, sea piracy, illegal human trafficking and drug trafficking. As shown in that chapter, there are other non-traditional security issues which are not mentioned in the Joint Declaration or the MOU, but also need to be dealt with, such as pandemic (e.g. SARS) and natural disaster.

A major political and security issue that has adversely affected the development of China–ASEAN relations from time to time is the South China Sea issue, which is discussed in Chapter 8. There are maritime and territorial disputes in the South China Sea, in particular, in and around the Spratly Islands, which has been claimed by five countries and six parties (Brunei Darussalam, China, Malaysia, the Philippines, Taiwan and Vietnam). Such multiple claims cause tensions among the claimants, on the one hand, and make cooperation difficult, on the other. Under international law, states should resolve their disputes through peaceful means. While a resolution cannot be reached at present, countries concerned should seek cooperative measures to defuse tension and to conduct joint programs. In accordance with relevant norms and rules in international law, in 2002 ASEAN countries and China signed the Declaration on the Conduct of the Parties in the South China Sea,[23] which acted as a milestone in resolving their territorial and jurisdictional disputes by peaceful means, without resorting to threat or the use of force, and pledging to explore or undertake cooperative activities in the South China Sea. The 11th China–ASEAN High Rank Official Consultation held in Shanghai on 29 April 2005 deliberated the implementation of the Plan of Action to Implement the Joint Declaration of China–ASEAN Strategic Partnership and agreed to hold the first working group meeting to implement the Declaration on the Conduct of the Parties in the South China Sea.[24] However, despite the declaration, incidents concerning competing territorial and/or maritime claims in the South China Sea continue to occur. On the other hand, it should be noted that the declaration is only a political document without a legally binding force. It is uncertain whether ASEAN and China would sign a legal document governing the South China Sea issue in the future. Finally, it should be noted that in comparison with the extent of cooperation in the economic area, cooperation in the political and security areas is not pro-active enough.

Another area where economic development and non-traditional security issues overlap is sustainable development and environmental protection, which is dealt with in Chapter 6. Many environmental issues that are caused by economic development such as pollution and depletion of natural resources and that concern the survival of human beings are treated as non-traditional security issues. One example is China's hydropower projects on the Lancang River, which are likely to have extensive environmental effects on lower river basin of the Mekong River. Another example is the current overarching problem of climate change and global warming, which would ultimately destroy the Earth if no adequate measures are taken by mankind. However, as is evident from the development of the China–ASEAN relations, cooperation in the area of environmental protection is just a beginning, but it is believed that such cooperation will be further enhanced with the deepening of the relationship between the two sides. At the 11th China–ASEAN Summit held in November 2007, both sides agreed to include 'environment' as the 11th priority area of cooperation between ASEAN and China.[25]

Future prospects

China–ASEAN relations will continue to develop more and more in the future. The interchange in the last 17 years has laid a solid foundation for such a development. Economically, China has set forth a target of US$200 billion annual trade with ASEAN countries by 2010 and of steady progress in the development of a China–ASEAN FTA. This goal was reiterated by Hu Jintao in a speech made before the joint session of the Philippine Congress on 27 April 2005.[26] A 2005 data from the Chinese customs shows that for the first time ASEAN had become China's fourth trade partner in 2005 in the first two months, and trade volume between the two sides reached US$16.63 billion.[27] Moreover, China–ASEAN cooperation has stimulated other Asian countries to co-operate with ASEAN countries. After China, India, Japan and South Korea also signed similar agreements with ASEAN, particularly in the area of economic cooperation.

However, there are some challenges and difficulties in the development of the China–ASEAN relations. In the economic sector, since ASEAN and China both try to attract more foreign direct investment (FDI) from other countries, they lack mutual trade dependence, mutual investment flow, economic infrastructure and cohesion.[28] Though ASEAN ranked among China's top 10 export markets, it accounted for only 7.2 per cent of total exports, which was much lower than 21.1 per cent of the export to the United States and 18.1 per cent to the European Union.[29] Another challenge to the China–ASEAN economic cooperation is the concern raised regarding the economic capacity of some ASEAN countries, which would impede the full realisation of FTA benefits.[30] Nevertheless, despite the challenges and difficulties, China and ASEAN countries will further improve their economic relations based on the agreements they have signed and will be able to overcome any impending difficulties.

In comparison with economic development, cooperation in the political and security areas is more challenging. As indicated in the negotiation history for the Declaration on the Conduct of the Parties in the South China Sea, the parties overcame several difficulties and finally reached the consensus on the need of the declaration. During the implementation of the declaration, new challenges and difficulties arose in addition to the existing ones. The South China Sea remains a thorny issue in the China–ASEAN relations, because of which, ASEAN countries have worries about China's possible expansion to Southeast Asia. It reminds Southeast Asia of the possible comeback of 'China threat,' which they experienced in the 1950s and 1960s when China spread communism to

Southeast Asia. However, after the Cold War, China's relations with Southeast Asia improved very significantly and a strategic partnership has been established between China and ASEAN. Still, ASEAN countries are wary of China's motives and moves. The South China Sea could be a right indicator to observe China. As commented, '[m]any Southeast Asian observers have seen this dispute as a litmus test for a newly-strong China's relations with its smaller neighbours – whether China would use its formidable military power to attempt to intimidate the other claimants, or settle the matter peacefully through good-faith negotiations'.[31]

The China threat perception will always exist due to its geographical and demographic advantage of being a big country with 25 per cent of the world's population. Some ideological considerations are also obviously behind this perception, as China is still a communist country. As is rightly pointed out, '[a]ll superpowers are potential threats to stability because superpowers end up using their power to achieve strategic ends'.[32] The West began to talk about the China threat after the Tiananmen Square human disaster; this talk intensified after the collapse of the Soviet Union in December 1991.[33] China seemed to be a new potential rival to the United States. China may not be a great economic threat to Southeast Asia, since China and ASEAN reached a win–win situation from concluding the comprehensive economic cooperation agreement, but there is still a question mark whether China would be a threat to Southeast Asia in political and strategic terms. Nevertheless, Chinese leaders gradually realised that 'much of China's external environment was shaped by the world's perception of China and that China needed to counter the China threat argument through its moderate behaviour and a good explanation about its foreign policy strategy'.[34]

In order to diffuse the China threat perception, China recently added a new term to its diplomatic strategy: 'peaceful rise'. The term was first introduced by Zheng Bijian, the former executive vice president of the Central Party School, in his speech at the Boao Forum in November 2003, and was later endorsed by the Chinese top leaders Hu Jintao and Wen Jiabao, as a national development strategy, particularly relating to China's link to the international arena.[35] The term implies that China pursues its soft power in the world by mainly using its economic leverage and seeking a peaceful environment for its economic development. Clearly, the doctrine of 'peaceful rise' counterbalances the prevailing jargon "China threat" in the Asia-Pacific region. To appease its neighbours, on many occasions, China has reiterated that it will never seek to become a hegemon. However, although China's gesture embodies good intention, its rise, whether peaceful or not, still scares its neighbours, as its military capability is expanding with the pace of its economic growth. For China, peaceful rise is really a good term, favourable for its development, but for its neighbours, particularly ASEAN countries, China has already become their 'peaceful' rival, but not a threat, in competing for markets and investment to some extent.

In response to China's rise, ASEAN countries have adopted a strategy of engagement with some hedging elements. Hedging means keeping open more than one strategic option against the possibility of a future security threat.[36] 'Engagement rests on the assumption that including China in regional activities will reduce tensions and bring about political convergence' such as partnership.[37] It is argued that 'while hedging and engagement are the principal Southeast Asian strategies toward China, the hedging involves a significant component of what may be termed "low-intensity balancing"[38] with the United States against China along with efforts to maintain a working relationship with Beijing'.[39] This at least partially explains why most ASEAN nations, especially the original ASEAN-5 – Indonesia, Malaysia, the Philippines, Singapore and Thailand – still maintain robust relations (including military relations) with the West and the United States even though China–ASEAN relations has improved considerably since 1991.[40] It is noted that the Philippines and Thailand are major non-NATO allies. The ASEAN Plus Three (APT) mechanism established under the ASEAN general framework contains more or less some elements of balancing China by introducing other important regional players – Japan and South Korea – to regional cooperation. The APT cooperation began in 1997 and was institutionalised in 1999 when the leaders from 13 countries issued a Joint Statement on East Asia Cooperation at their third APT Summit in Manila. The APT Unit was established at the ASEAN Secretariat in December 2003.[41] At the 11th APT Summit held in November 2007, the Second Joint Statement on East Asia Cooperation and the APT Cooperation Work Plan (2007–17) were adopted. However, there is no substantial document to be signed among the participating states, and the mechanism largely remains as a talk shop in comparison with the bilateral cooperation between China and ASEAN.

Historically, China might not have been a threat to Southeast Asia for centuries: 'the old Southeast Asian kingdoms and principalities regarded powerful imperial China as a source of prosperity and lucrative trade rather than an expansionist threat'.[42] However, in modern times and under a different international order, uncertainties and probabilities have increased. No one can predict what the future exactly will be. Although it seems that the future of China–ASEAN cooperation is bright, China should be aware of ASEAN's suspicions of and even distrust in China's behaviour. It therefore needs to make more efforts in the long run, diffusing and even eliminating the unfavourable elements which would hamper the smooth development of the relations between the two sides. On the other hand, it should be noted that certain concerns of ASEAN with the rise of China are reasonable as ASEAN countries are smaller than China. Southeast Asia does not want to see any big power including China and the United States to dominate the region.[43]

ASEAN attempts and, in practice, has so far tried successfully to play a central role in Asian regional integration. It calls itself the 'heart of a dynamic Asia'.[44] As commented, 'ASEAN's diplomatic leadership has not only yielded political dividends but also changed the chemistry of the region significantly and enabled cooperation to emerge in many new areas. ASEAN has helped the region to become more aware of its historical patterns of cooperation'.[45] ASEAN intends to maintain its centrality in regional cooperation and integration as is pledged in the 2007 ASEAN Charter to 'maintain the centrality and proactive role of ASEAN as the primary driving force in its relations and cooperation with external partners in a regional architecture that is open, transparent and inclusive'.[46] However, it is doubtful whether in the long run ASEAN could continue to be the driver for regional cooperation and integration under the circumstances that changes occur over time. The recent proposal made by Australia in 2008 to establish the 'Asia-Pacific Community' could be one.[47] Another challenge is from Northeast Asia: it has been reported that from September 2008, China, Japan and South Korea will hold their trilateral summit independently of the APT framework. This has caused worries in the Southeast Asian region that 'ASEAN+3 may turn into 3+ASEAN and this is a signal that ASEAN is losing its driver's seat in East Asian cooperation mechanisms'.[48] It is believed though that ASEAN members will respond to upcoming challenges adeptly and timely.

More reliance on international law is one of the steps that ASEAN recently took. The adoption of the ASEAN Charter indicates that the ASEAN member states realised the importance of using international law in enhancing the status of ASEAN in the region as well as in the world. For the first time in ASEAN history, a fundamental legal document with legally binding force has been adopted. Cooperation based on rules and norms of international law will be more reliable, stable, predicable and enforceable than that merely based on political statements. More legal documents have also been signed between China and ASEAN as discussed in this book. Moreover, Chapters 2 and 3 examine, respectively, the Asian approaches and contributions to international law and the general legal framework of the China–ASEAN cooperation. It should be noted that there is a general trend of globalisation of the rule of law principle. In December 2007 the United Nations General Assembly adopted a resolution on 'the rule of law at the national and international levels', reaffirming that international law including the UN Charter is the indispensable foundation of a more peaceful, prosperous and just world and that the advancement of the rule of law at the national and international levels is essential for the realisation of sustained economic growth, sustainable development, the eradication of poverty and hunger and the protection of all human rights and fundamental freedoms.[49] It is well perceived that both China and ASEAN will continue to uphold the basic principles of international law to further develop their relations and co-operation. Also, it is hoped that this book can render a humble support to the advancement of the rule of law in the world community, particularly in East Asia.

Notes

1. Ashok K. Dutt, 'An Introductory Framework: Southeast Asia', in Ashok K. Dutt (ed.), *Southeast Asia: A Ten Nation Region* (Dordrecht: Kluwer Academic Publishers, 1996), p. 1.
2. John Cole, *Geography of the World's Major Regions* (London: Routledge, 1996), p. 352.
3. Wang Li, 'Zheng He's Voyage and Solution of Pirates Issue', in Nanjing Zheng He Study Association (ed.), *Chinese Heading for the Sea* (Beijing: Sea Tide Publisher, 1996) (in Chinese), pp. 311–9.
4. Martin Stuart-Fox, 'Southeast Asia and China: The Role of History and Culture in Shaping Future Relations', *Contemporary Southeast Asia*, vol. 26 (1), 2004, p. 117.
5. Chen Qiaozhi, 'Examination of China's Diplomacy towards Southeast Asia for the Last Half Century', in Li Yiping and Zhuang Guotu (eds.), *International Relations of Southeast Asia since the Cold War* (Xiamen: Xiamen University Press, 2005) (in Chinese), pp. 123–7.
6. Lai Hongyi, 'China's Evolving Relations with Southeast Asia: Domestic and Strategic factors', in Lai Hongyi and Lim Tin Seng (eds.), *Harmony and Development: ASEAN-China Relations* (Singapore: World Scientific, 2007), p. 17.
7. Rodolfo C. Severino, 'ASEAN Beyond Forty: Towards Political and Economic Integration', *Contemporary Southeast Asia*, vol. 29 (3), 2007, pp. 408–9.
8. The ASEAN Declaration, made in Bangkok, 8 August 1967. Text is available at *http://www.aseansec.org/1212.htm* (accessed 28 July 2008).
9. Text is available at *http://www.aseansec.org/1814.htm* (accessed 31 July 2008).

10. 'Overview: Association of Southeast Asian Nations', available at *http://www.aseansec.org/64.htm* (accessed 28 July 2008).
11. The participants in the ARF as of 2008 include Australia, Canada, China, European Union, India, Japan, Democratic Republic of Korea, Republic of Korea (ROK), Mongolia, New Zealand, Pakistan, Papua New Guinea, the Russian Federation and the United States, in addition to the ASEAN member states.
12. 'Overview: Association of Southeast Asian Nations', available at *http://www.aseansec.org/64.htm* (accessed 28 July 2008).
13. 'Overview: Association of Southeast Asian Nations', available at *http://www.aseansec.org/64.htm* (accessed 28 July 2008).
14. 'Overview: Association of Southeast Asian Nations', available at *http://www.aseansec.org/64.htm* (accessed 28 July 2008).
15. Article 9 of the ASEAN Charter. Text is available at *http://www.aseansec.org/21069.pdf* (accessed 28 July 2008).
16. Song Dexing, 'Repositioning the Sino-ASEAN Relations and Their Important Characteristics in the Transitional Period of Centuries', *China Diplomacy* (in Chinese), 2000, no. 2, p. 28.
17. Zhang Haibing, 'China and Southeast Asian Cooperation: New Developments and Challenges', in John Wong and Lai Hongyi (eds.), *China into the Hu-Wen Era: Policy Initiatives and Challenges* (Singapore: World Scientific Publishing, 2006), p. 542.
18. 'The China–ASEAN Association', available at *http://en.chinaasean.org/news/2005/07/11/16531221067595.html* (accessed 5 July 2008).
19. Michael R.J. Vatikiotis, 'Catching the Dragon's Tail: China and Southeast Asia in the 21st Century', *Contemporary Southeast Asia*, vol. 25 (1), 2003, p. 69.
20. 'The ASEAN Regional Forum', available at *http://www.aseanregionalforum.org/AboutUs/tabid/57/Default.aspx* (accessed 29 July 2008).
21. For details, see 'Introduction to ARF', available at *http://www.fmprc.gov.cn/chn/wjb/zzjg/gjs/gjzzyhy/1136/t410566.htm* (accessed 30 July 2008).
22. Joint Declaration of ASEAN and China on Cooperation in the Field of Non-Traditional Security Issues, made at the 6th ASEAN–China Summit, Phnom Penh, Cambodia, on 4 November 2002, available at *http://www.aseansec.org/13185.htm* (accessed 29 July 2008).
23. Text is available at *http://www.aseansec.org/13163.htm* (accessed 28 July 2008).
24. 'The 11th China–ASEAN High Rank Official Consultation held', *People's Daily* (in Chinese), 30 April 2005, p. 3.
25. Chairman's Statement of the 11th ASEAN–China Summit, Singapore, 20 November 2007, available at *http://www.aseansec.org/21105.htm* (accessed 29 July 2008).
26. Qin Jize, '14 agreements signed in Manila', *China Daily*, 28 April 2005, p. 1.
27. 'ASEAN becomes China's 4th trade partner', 12 April 2005, available at *http://www.chinadaily.com.cn/english/doc/2005-04/12/content_435584.htm* (accessed 5 May 2005).
28. Zhang Haibing, supra note 17, p. 549.

29. Data from the Ministry of Commerce website, cited in Zhang Haibing, ibid., p. 550.
30. Zhang Haibing, supra note 17, pp. 551–552.
31. Denny Roy, 'Southeast Asia and China: Balancing or Bandwagoning?', *Contemporary Southeast Asia*, vol. 27 (2), 2005, p. 309.
32. Michael R.J. Vatikiotis, supra note 19, p. 74.
33. Lai Hongyi, supra note 6, p. 23. For general reference, see Herbert Yee and Ian James Storey (eds.), *The China Threat: Perceptions, Myths and Reality* (London: RoutledgeCurzon, 2002).
34. Lai Hongyi, supra note 6, p. 26.
35. For more details, see Bo Zhiyue, 'Elite Politics and the "Peaceful Rise" of China', *EAI Bulletin*, vol. 6 (2), 2004, p. 1 and 10.
36. Denny Roy, supra note 31, p. 306.
37. Denny Roy, ibid., p. 310.
38. As explained in the case of low intensity balancing the state attempts to maintain a constructive relationship with the targeted state. See Denny Roy, ibid., p. 306.
39. Denny Roy, ibid., p. 306.
40. Sheng Lijun, 'China's Peaceful Rise and Its Political and Security Implications for Southeast Asia', in Lai Hongyi and Lim Tin Seng (eds.), supra note 6, p. 36.
41. For details, see 'ASEAN Plus Three Cooperation', available at *http://www.aseansec.org/16580.htm* (accessed 30 July 2008).
42. Michael R.J. Vatikiotis, supra note 19, p. 66.
43. Amitav Acharya, 'Seeking Security in the Dragon's Shadow: China and Southeast Asia in the Emerging Asian Order', IDSS Working Paper No. 44 (Institute of Defense and Strategic Studies, Singapore), March 2003, p. 18.
44. Zai Kun, 'ASEAN's Important Role', available at *http://www.zaobao.com/special/newspapers/2008/07/liaowang080729c.shtml* (accessed 30 July 2008).
45. Kishore Mahbubani, *The New Asian Hemisphere: The Irresistible Shift of Global Power to the East* (New York: Public Affairs, 2008), p. 270.
46. Article 1 (15) of the ASEAN Charter.
47. John Chan, 'Australian call for "Asia-Pacific Community": A sign of growing tensions', 27 June 2008, available at *http://www.wsws.org/articles/2008/jun2008/rudd-j27.shtml* (accessed 30 July 2008).
48. To Thi Thuy, 'China, Japan and South Korea: Time for Trilateralism?', *RSIS Commentaries 82/2008*, 5 August 2008, p. 3.
49. UN Doc A/RES/62/70, 8 January 2008, p. 1, available at http://daccessdds.un.org/doc/UNDOC/GEN/N07/467/97/PDF/N0746797.pdf?OpenElement (accessed 30 July 2008).

2

Asian approaches and contributions to international law

Introduction

With the rise of China and India, the question arises whether these new powers would change the existing international order, including legal order. Over the last decade, China's economic growth has continued to rise with the increase in its annual GDP at the rate of more than 9 per cent. In 2006 its GDP growth was 10.7 per cent.[1] 'China is now the third largest producer of manufactured goods, its share having risen from four to 12 percent in the past decade'.[2] Although India lags behind China in terms of its economy, it has recently attained a high level of economic growth as well. Its economic growth rate in 2006 was 9.2 per cent.[3] Demographically, China and India are among the largest countries in the world with the total population of over 2.3 billion. Politically, China is one of the five permanent members of the UN Security Council, while India has recently gained its status as a global nuclear power. It is believed that this trend of Asian ascendancy will continue in the next century as well. The world political landscape will thus inevitably change in response to the rise of Asia, and so will the global legal order. As is predicted, 'Asia will alter the rules of the globalizing process' and 'Asian giants may use the power of their markets to set industry standards, rather than adopting those promoted by Western nations or international standards bodies'.[4] Although these comments focus more on the economic sector of globalisation, the Asian influence over the global legal order will possibly far exceed the realm of the World Trade Organization (WTO).

On the other hand, it is a well-known fact that despite their recent remarkable economic growth, both China and India are categorised as developing or Third World countries at least at present. In comparison with developed or First World countries, they are still poor. This is one of the reasons why China and India, despite being signatories to the Kyoto Protocol, do not have emission reduction targets. Therefore, these two countries will influence the development of international law as rising global powers as well as fast developing countries.

Both China and India have realised their importance and indispensability in the development of the future international order including the international legal order, which is evident in the statement that 'they are two major powers in the formulation of the multi-polar international order and their simultaneous developments will exert an active influence over the future international system'.[5]

The picture of the rise of Asia would not be complete without the mention of the contributions from other Asian countries such as Japan, South Korea and Association of Southeast Asian Nations (ASEAN) member countries. They will also influence the development of international law in various ways. Thus, the thread running through the Asian influence on and/or contributions to the development of international law is twofold: from the practice of an individual Asian state and from the collective endeavours of all Asian states, mainly through multinational mechanisms or organisations such as ASEAN.

Existing contributions of Asian countries to international law

There are four main driving forces behind the development of modern international law: (1) independent movements in Asia, Africa and Latin America, which became a great influencing force; (2) the development of international economic relations; (3) the establishment of international organisations and (4) the development of science and technology.[6] With decolonisation, more and more nations have gained independence and have become members of the United Nations. As of August 2008, the United Nations has 192 members, the majority of which are developing countries.

It is unfortunate that the attempt of developing countries during the 1970s to establish a new international economic order has come to no fruition because the current world economic order is directed towards and maintained by the developed countries, centred on the regulations of the WTO, World Bank and other West-created international organisations. But the contributions of developing countries, including Asian nations, to the development and codification of modern international law cannot be ignored despite the fact that international law is a creation of the Western civilisation. The Third World countries 'aligned themselves to take concerted action and play an important role in the international legal structure in pursuance of their interests'.[7] However, it is impossible to list each and every contribution from these countries, including the Asian nations, to every aspect of international law. For the purpose of illustration, it is wise to choose one of the branches of international law as an example – the law of the sea.

We know that the law of the sea is the oldest and the most well-developed branch of international law. Its main contents have now been incorporated into the 1982 United Nations Convention on the Law of the Sea (the LOS Convention), which came into force in 1994. The LOS Convention guarantees global marine legal order and is of utmost significance for maintaining world peace, justice and progress. According to the convention, the ocean space is divided into several maritime zones: internal waters within the baselines of a coastal state, the 12-nautical-miles territorial sea measured from the baselines, the exclusive economic zone (EEZ) and continental shelf, and the high seas and international seabed area. Different maritime zones have different legal regimes. Internal waters and territorial sea are under the sovereignty of the coastal state; the EEZ and continental shelf are subject to the coastal state's jurisdiction and sovereign rights; and the high seas and international seabed area can be defined as one of the global commons which are open to all nations in the world in accordance with international law.

The most significant contribution of the developing countries, including Asian nations, to the development of the law of the sea is the legal concept of common heritage of mankind (CHM). During the 1958 Geneva Conference on the Law of the Sea, Prince Wan Waithayakon of Thailand mentioned that 'the sea is the common heritage of mankind'.[8] Arvid Pardo, then-Maltese ambassador, later elaborated this concept in a memorandum dated 17 August 1967 from the Permanent Mission of Malta sent to the UN Secretary General, stating that 'the time has come to declare the sea-bed and the ocean floor a common heritage of mankind'. According to him, the following principles should be drafted in a treaty: (a) the seabed and ocean floor are not subject to national appropriation, (b) they should be explored complying with the purposes and principles of the UN Charter and with the aim of safeguarding the interests of mankind and (c) they should be reserved exclusively for peaceful purposes in perpetuity.[9] The concept of the CHM was finally incorporated into the negotiation text of the Third United Nations Conference on the Law of the Sea in May 1975, and was later formally written in the LOS Convention. Article 136 of the convention provides that: 'The Area and its resources are the common heritage of mankind'.[10] Article 137 establishes the legal status of the Area and its resources, and Article 140 sets out the economic objectives of the CHM. The adoption of the CHM concept in the LOS Convention marked the establishment of the concept as a formal legal principle. There are five accepted principal elements which characterise the CHM: 'First, the common heritage cannot be appropriated – it could be used but not owned; second, the use of the common heritage required a system of management in which all users must share; third, it implied an active sharing of benefits, including not only financial benefits but also benefits derived from shared management and exchange and transfer of technologies; fourth, the principle of common heritage implied eventual reservation for peaceful purposes; and finally, it implies transmission of the heritage substantially unimpaired to future generations'.[11] Although the 1994 Agreement Relating to the Implementation of Part XI of the LOS Convention made significant changes to the legal regime for the international seabed area, the CHM provision remains unchanged.[12]

Other contributions of developing countries to the LOS Convention include, inter alia, the legal regimes for the EEZ, archipelagic waters and transit passage through straits used for international navigation. The contributions of Indonesia and the Philippines as archipelagic countries and of Malaysia and Singapore as littoral countries of the Straits of Malacca and Singapore in establishing the legal regimes for archipelagic waters and transit passage are remarkable, as manifested in the official records of the Third United Nations Conference on the Law of the Sea.

Most Asian countries have ratified the LOS Convention. For example, China ratified it in 1996 and India in 1995. In addition, both China and India are pioneer investors in the international seabed. China possesses a major portion of mining area of 75,000 km^2, which is located in the C-C fault zone in the east Pacific Ocean basin.[13] By participating in the activities of the International Seabed Authority, these two countries can influence its law/regulation making pertaining to deep seabed mining.

The latest contribution from Asian countries to the development of the law of the sea is the conclusion of the Regional Cooperation Agreement on Combating Piracy and Armed Robbery against Ships in Asia (ReCAAP) in 2004 among 16 Asian countries including Bangladesh, Brunei, Cambodia, China, India, Indonesia, Japan, Laos, Malaysia, Myanmar, the Philippines, Sri Lanka, Singapore, South Korea, Thailand and Vietnam. The agreement mandates these states to prevent and suppress piracy and armed robbery against ships.[14] This was the first specific international legal document concerning the crackdown of piracy in the sea. Therefore, it becomes a model law for other regional legal arrangements. A similar agreement is reported to be concluded for the western Indian Ocean.[15]

Finally, the famous Five Principles of Peaceful Coexistence are worth discussing, as they are an Asian input in international law. These principles include: (1) respect for each other's sovereignty and territorial integrity, (2) non-aggression, (3) non-interference in each other's internal affairs, (4) equality and mutual benefit and (5) peaceful coexistence. These five principles first appeared in the Agreement Between the Republic of India and the People's Republic of China on Trade and Intercourse Between Tibet Region of China and India signed on 29 April 1954.[16] Since then, these have been reiterated in China's foreign policy documents as well as in agreements, declarations and joint statements signed between China and other countries that are willing to incorporate those principles into the relevant documents. According to some source, from 1954 to 1995, more than 150 such documents were signed.[17] Thus, in China's view, these principles have become universally applicable among the states and are thus accepted as the fundamental principles of international law.

Although it is reasonable for China to say that by creating the Five Principles of Peaceful Coexistence, it has contributed to the development of contemporary international law, we may argue that these principles have been over-emphasised to some extent. If we compare these with other established principles of international law, particularly those embodied in the UN Charter, we observe that only the fourth principle of 'equality and mutual benefit' contains some new elements, because by combining equality with mutual benefit, it emphasises on equality in economic relations. It has been argued that these five principles bear little significance since they only manifest the existing basic principles of international law.[18] In response to this argument, a Chinese authority in international law justifies the Chinese approach by stating that (1) the combination of five important principles in international law has formulated a systematic integration, which constitutes the basis of international law; (2) the expression of mutual respect for sovereignty and territorial integrity both stress the respect for sovereignty and territorial integrity and emphasise the concept of mutuality so as to manifest the principle that sovereignty is not absolute, but relative; and (3) the connection between equality and mutual benefit results in the combination of legal and economic equalities, making equality substantial rather than formal.[19] However, it is time to re-consider whether it is necessary for China to still obsessively stick to these principles, as the fifth principle of 'peaceful coexistence' implies passive attitude towards international cooperation and development of international friendly relations. After the Cold War, what has become more important and necessary is not only 'coexistence' but also active cooperation and integration, without which global issues such as terrorism and global warming cannot be effectively tackled and solutions cannot be found.

Notably, these five principles have always been highly regarded in China, despite changing times as well as changes in political and diplomatic environment after the founding of the People's Republic of China (PRC) in 1949.[20] Compared with the zeal of the Chinese, Indians no longer seem to stress on these principles specifically. At present, the only country in Asia, other than China, which still adheres to these principles is Myanmar.[21] However, in the documents signed between China and ASEAN, these principles are specifically mentioned in parallel to other fundamental principles of international law such as those embraced in the UN Charter and the Treaty of Amity and Cooperation in Southeast Asia (the TAC).[22]

Asian perspectives of international law

In the literature on international law, there is an approach called the Third World Approach to International Law (TWAIL), which, according to some legal scholars, 'indicated colonial international law for legitimizing the subjugation and suppression of Third World peoples', 'emphasized that pre-colonial Third World states were not strangers to international law' and 'laid great stress on the principles of sovereign equality of states and non-intervention'.[23] Thus, TWAIL contains three objectives: 'the first is to understand, deconstruct, and unpack the uses of international law as a medium for the creation and perpetuation of a racialized hierarchy of international norms and institutions that subordinate non-Europeans to Europeans. Second, it seeks to construct and present an alternative normative legal edifice for international governance. Finally, TWAIL seeks through scholarship, policy, and politics to eradicate the conditions of underdevelopment in the Third World'.[24] Although there is no unified definition of TWAIL, the Third World view on international law has been clearly expressed to the world community.

Mao Zedong, the founder of the PRC, put forward the 'Three Worlds' doctrine in the early 1970s. According to him, the world was divided into three worlds: the United States and the then–Soviet Union belonged to the First World, developed European countries and Japan to the Second World and countries of Asia, except Japan, of Africa and of Latin America to the Third World.[25] He believed that the Third World countries should unite with the Second World countries to fight against the hegemony of the First World. The term 'Third World' in TWAIL was simply borrowed from the Three Worlds doctrine. When this doctrine was released, the Chinese international law scholars tried to put its theory into international law. The remarkable debate was whether anti-hegemony was a principle of international law.[26] However, after China began its economic reform and open-door policy in 1978, the 'Three Worlds' doctrine was no longer stressed upon. Instead, China developed a foreign policy centred on pragmatism. Since then, the Chinese use the term 'developing countries' more frequently than 'Third World countries'.

While TWAIL is only an approach to international law reflecting the state practice of the Third World, what is more important in developing countries is state practice per se as well as the attitudes of these countries towards international law. One of the fundamental concepts in the formulation of nation states is 'sovereignty', which is defined as the 'supreme, absolute, and uncontrollable power by which any independent state is governed'.[27]

China's attitude and practice is thus critical. Of the five principles discussed before, the principle of sovereignty ranks first. According to China, sovereignty can be interpreted as independence and includes the internal powers of independence (such as legislation, establishment of national system, etc.) as well as its external powers (such as freedom to deal with international affairs, participation in international conferences and signing treaties).[28] Strict adherence to the principle of inviolability of sovereignty has become a distinctive feature of foreign policy of the PRC and is treated as the basis of international relations and the cornerstone of the whole system of international law.[29] Thus, China's external powers are inherent in its principle of sovereignty; therefore, China does not allow any violation or infringement of its sovereignty and independence, which is justifiable if we look back at the bitter Chinese history when the weak China was bullied by the Western powers in the nineteenth and the early twentieth centuries.

Sovereignty guarantees complete independence in political, economic and other areas. When a state is independent, it can exercise jurisdiction over its controlled territory as well as over its citizens. Based on these essential elements of sovereignty, aggression and intervention are illegal in China's view. Chinese scholars are of the opinion that although some forms of intervention were allowed in traditional international law, such as intervention by rights and humanitarian intervention, modern international law has prohibited all forms of intervention.[30] In practice, China strongly opposes any intervention from other countries. This is well illustrated by its stand in the Taiwan issue.

The Taiwan issue is a result of the Chinese civil war in the late 1940s, in which the Nationalist government retreated to Taiwan after defeat, while the Communists established the PRC in the mainland. During the Korean War, America sent troops to Taiwan and blockaded the Taiwan Strait to prevent the PRC from liberating the Taiwan Island. Since then, the Taiwan issue has remained the biggest and the most complex bone of contention in the Sino-American relations despite diplomatic ties established between China and the United States in 1979. China strongly opposed the Taiwan Relations Act passed by the US Congress and regarded it as intervention into China's domestic affairs. A leading Chinese international law scholar writes: 'the Taiwan Relations Act is merely another version of the Mutual Defence Treaty signed between the United States and Taiwan on 2 December 1954. As such, the Act violates the principles of the Shanghai Communiqué and unduly interferes with Chinese internal affairs'.[31] China was also against any intervention by big powers. The recent example is the Kosovo crisis in 1999, when China strongly criticised the NATO intervention into Kosovo. In China's view, 'NATO's action violated the principle of non-interference in the internal affairs of a sovereign country. Second, the principle of finding a peaceful solution to international disputes has been violated. Third, NATO's action is also a violation of the group security in the United Nations'. Thus, 'the Kosovo crisis shows that in the eyes of the United States, national sovereignty and equality no longer have substantial importance'.[32]

Another important aspect of sovereignty is territorial integrity. The territory of a state includes the land and its subsoil, the territorial sea as well as the airspace. Since the founding of the PRC, China has maintained a very strong position on its territorial integrity. In China's view, Taiwan, Hong Kong and Macao are Chinese territories, although they are under different jurisdictions. In the early 1950s, China reiterated that 'Macao is Chinese territory. The Chinese people have never forgotten Macao, nor have they forgotten that they have the right to demand the recovery of this territory from the hands of Portugal'.[33] Similarly, China stated that 'Hong Kong has been Chinese territory since ancient times. . . . the whole of Hong Kong must return to the domain of the motherland'.[34] As a result of China's persevering efforts, Hong Kong was handed over to China in 1997 and Macao in December 1999 under the principle of 'one China, two systems'. Chinese scholars supported the governmental policy in this regard and justified its rightness.[35] China's next step is aimed at the recovery of Taiwan by similar means to achieve the final Chinese reunification.

Although China emphasises the principle of sovereignty and territorial integrity, it has realised that in the contemporary era, sovereignty is no longer absolute, such as in global warming and human rights areas. According to Chinese scholars, China's adamant efforts in defending its sovereignty are not its endorsement of the doctrine of absolute sovereignty. China has never considered sovereignty as an illimitable power.[36]

After the bombing of the Chinese Embassy in Belgrade in May 1999, China sharply criticised the Western approach to human rights, considering human rights to be superior to sovereignty in international affairs. As Chinese international law scholars perceive, this approach of the superiority of human rights is untenable in international law both in theory and in practice. The efforts of the United Nations to enhance human rights do not change the nature of human rights as a matter of domestic jurisdiction. The principle of state sovereignty is fundamental to international law and international relations, and is applicable to all branches of international law including the international human rights law. The international society today consists of sovereign states and nation states, and the principle of human rights cannot replace or be used against the principle of state sovereignty.[37] ASEAN member states have differences of opinion concerning the protection of human rights. This is evident in the recent discussions on how to establish a human rights body within ASEAN in accordance with the ASEAN Charter, which will be discussed in Chapter 3.

A related subject is the controversy over the legality of humanitarian intervention. For China, 'international intervention does not have a legitimate political basis and violates the Charter of the United Nations and international law'. It is designed to 'promote the interests of an intervening state rather than those of the people of the target state'. Thus, it 'causes more harm than good'.[38] Some Chinese legal scholars even blame the Untied States for causing a crisis in international humanitarian law by invading Iraq and mistreating the Iraqi prisoners of war (POWs); the fact that the United States does not bear any liability in international law makes international humanitarian law ineffective.[39] However, in recent years some subtle change has been observed in China's position on sovereignty and humanitarian intervention. It now considers intervention acceptable 'under exceptional circumstances, such as when a national government practices racist policies, kills its people en masse, or collapses only to leave slaughtered people in its wake'.[40] Furthermore, China supports international intervention sponsored and/or authorised by the United Nations. In recent years, it has started sending its troops to join the UN Peacekeeping Forces.

India takes a similar stand on 'intervention' and views the term as implying 'the use of force by a state or organization/entity inside another sovereign state without the latter's concurrence and in violation of the sovereignty of that state'.[41] It regards unilateral intervention as 'a crime specifically forbidden under Chapter I, Article 2(4) of the UN Charter'[42] and the sovereign-state system as 'still the only viable form of organization of the world. The central objective of the international community to deal with human rights violations should be to prevent circumstances from arising in which the state is not built or managed in accordance with the principles of the equality, liberty, and fraternity of all human beings living therein'.[43] ASEAN countries have long adhered to the principle of non-interference and non-intervention as core values of the so-called ASEAN way of dealing with their matters. Thus, humanitarian intervention is 'another exception to the general prohibition against one state using force against another'.[44]

Interestingly, the recent approach – 'the responsibility to protect' – is also derived from sovereignty. It is argued that 'State sovereignty implies responsibility, and the primary responsibility for the protection of its people lies with the state itself. Where a population is suffering serious harm, as a result of internal war, insurgency, repression or state failure, and the state in question is unwilling or unable to halt or avert it, the principle of non-intervention yields to the international responsibility to protect'.[45] Nevertheless, this approach has changed the essentials of the original sovereignty principle and has expanded the scope of international jurisdiction. No doubt, this functional expansion of sovereignty will benefit big powers which have the capacity to intervene, rather than small and weak developing countries. The history of international intervention is witness to the fact that big powers have always intervened in small and weak states.

Resort to international judiciary

International judiciary is an indispensable component of the international law body. It has been designed to settle international disputes, though in recent years its functions have been expanded to cover the areas of human rights protection as well as punishment for international crimes. Asian countries have varying attitudes towards international judiciary due to different cultural and social backgrounds. Some Asian countries accept compulsory jurisdiction of the International Court of Justice (ICJ), while others do not. However, despite their diverse legal and cultural backgrounds, these countries share identical viewpoint on the dispute settlement mechanisms under the LOS Convention.

China has always advocated bilateral negotiations as the most practical means of dispute settlement between states. In practice, China has resolved several of its bilateral disputes with other countries through negotiation and consultation, such as border disputes and dual nationality, among other issues. Recent examples are the handover of Hong Kong and Macao to China by the United Kingdom and Portugal, respectively, after negotiations between China and these two countries. The 'one country, two systems' model for the settlement of international disputes can be regarded as one of the contributions of China to international law.

So far as judiciary is concerned, China's attitude is very conservative. Thus far no dispute between China and any other state has been brought to the ICJ or other international tribunal(s). During the Sino-India border conflict in 1962, China refused India's proposal to submit the dispute to international arbitration by stating that 'the Sino-India border dispute is an important matter concerning the sovereignty of the two countries, and the vast size of more than 100,000 square kilometres of territories. It is self-evident that it can only be resolved through direct bilateral negotiations. It is never possible to seek a settlement from any form of international arbitration'.[46] However, after the 1980s, it changed its policy by consenting to arbitration in treaties that it ratified to, but confined this only to economic, trade, scientific, transport, environmental and health areas. Some conventions require the contracting states to accept compulsory judicial dispute settlement procedures. For instance, the LOS Convention makes it obligatory for its state parties to select at least one of the compulsory procedures: special arbitration, arbitration, the ICJ and the International Tribunal for the Law of the Sea (ITLOS). Upon ratification of the convention, China did not state which mechanism it had accepted. Therefore, it was deemed to accept the mechanism of arbitration.[47]

Meanwhile, China's perception of the role of international courts in dispute settlement is also passive. In treaties in which it is a party, China has usually made a reservation about the clause of judicial settlement by the ICJ. On 5 September 1972, China declared not to recognise the statement of the former Chinese government on Acceptance of the Compulsory Jurisdiction of the International Court of Justice. In fact, it refused to settle any dispute with other countries through the ICJ.[48] On the other hand, as a UN Security Council member, it has nominated judges of Chinese nationality to the ICJ as well as to other international courts. Since these courts are comprised mainly of judges from the West, developing countries, including China, are doubtful about the impartiality and justice the international judiciary can maintain. As for the ITLOS, China declared on 7 September 2006 under Article 298 of the LOS Convention the exclusion of certain disputes (such as concerning maritime delimitation, territorial disputes or military use of the ocean) with other countries from the jurisdiction of international judiciary or arbitration.[49] It is therefore unlikely that China will be subjected to the jurisdiction of this tribunal.

China voted against the adoption of the Rome Statute of the International Criminal Court (ICC) despite its involvement in the negotiations of the statute. China has given several reasons to justify its refusal: (1) It cannot accept the universal jurisdiction of the ICC, (2) it has serious reservation on the inclusion of the crime of war in the ICC universal jurisdiction, (3) it has reservation on the provisions of the role of the UN Security Council, (4) it has serious reservation on the investigation power of the prosecutor and (5) it has reservation on the definition of crime against humanity. Therefore, some Chinese legal scholars criticised the passive attitude of the Chinese government by stating that the reasons China gave are not sufficient and convincing.[50] On the other hand, studies on the ICC and its operations have been undertaken in China. For example, the People's University of China established a research institute for the study of international criminal law.[51] Law books on this subject have also been published.[52] It is perceived that China may possibly join the ICC in the near future.[53] The current Chinese position is that China supports the establishment of an ICC 'characterized by its independence, impartiality, effectiveness and universality, capable of punishing the gravest international crimes' and it hopes that 'the Court will win the confidence of non-Contracting Parties and wide acceptance of the international community through its work'.[54] Since 2003, China has been attending the Conference of Parties of the Rome Statute as an observer. The attitudes of the ASEAN countries towards the ICC vary, but most of them seem to hold the same position as China, with only Cambodia having joined the ICC Statute.

India takes a different stand on international judiciary by accepting the compulsory jurisdiction of the ICJ. Table 2.1 lists the Asian countries which accept such jurisdiction. But the percentage within all the Asian countries is still quite low. Likewise, Table 2.2 shows the cases submitted to the ICJ. Out of these, only three cases relating to East Asia have

Table 2.1 **Asian countries accepting the ICJ compulsory jurisdiction[a]**

Cambodia
India
Japan
Pakistan
Philippines

[a]compiled by the author.

Table 2.2 **Cases submitted by Asian countries to the ICJ[a]**

States	Cases
Cambodia	Temple of Preah Vihear (with Thailand) (1959–62)
India	Right of Passage over Its Territory (with Portugal) (1955–60) Appeal Relating to the Jurisdiction of the ICAO Council (with Pakistan) (1971–2) Trial of Pakistani Prisoners of War (with Pakistan) (1973) Aerial Incident of 10 August 1999 (with Pakistan) (1999–2000)
Indonesia	Sovereignty over Pulau Litigan and Pulau Sipadan (with Malaysia) (1998–2002)
Iran	Anglo-Ianai Oil Co. (with the United Kingdom) (1951–2) United States Diplomatic and Consular Staff in Tehran (with the United States) (1979–81) Aerial Incident of 3 July 1988 (with the United States) (1989–96) Oil Platforms (with the United States) (1992–2003)
Malaysia	Sovereignty over Pulau Litigan and Pulau Sipadan (with Indonesia) (1998–2002) Sovereignty over Pedra Blanca, Middle Rocks and South Ledge (with Singapore) (2003–8)
Pakistan	Appeal Relating to the Jurisdiction of the ICAO Council (with India) (1971–2) Trial of Pakistani Prisoners of War (with India) (1973) Aerial Incident of 10 August 1999 (with India) (1999–2000)
Singapore	Sovereignty over Pedra Blanca, Middle Rocks and South Ledge (with Malaysia) (2003–8)
Thailand	Temple of Preah Vihear (with Cambodia) (1959–62)

[a]compiled by the author.

been dealt with before the ICJ: the case of *Temple of Preah Vihear (Cambodia/Thailand)* (1959–62), the case of *Sovereignty over Pulau Litigan and Pulau Sipadan (Malaysia/Indonesia)* (1998–2002) and the case of *Sovereignty over Pedra Branca/Pulau Batu Puteh, Middle Rocks and South Ledge* (Malaysia/Singapore) (2003–8). In July 2003 Malaysia and Singapore submitted their territorial dispute over tiny islets including the Pedra Blanca, Middle Rocks and South Ledge to the ICJ for settlement, based on the special agreement that they signed in February 2003 and entered into force in May 2003.[55] In 2003 Malaysia and Singapore also became the first East Asian countries to resort to the dispute mechanism of the ITLOS by submitting their *case concerning land reclamation by Singapore in and around the Straits of Johor (Malaysia v. Singapore)* for provisional measures.[56] In conclusion, the use of international judicial organs to resolve disputes is rare but beneficial for Asian countries. However, as shown in these cases, in comparison with China, some ASEAN member states are more willing to resort to the international judiciary for settling their disputes. Besides, the scenario of resorting infrequently to the international judiciary may change in the future with the coming true of the proposed 'ASEAN Court of Justice, comprising designated judges nominated by each member-state'.[57]

As more such international tribunals are to be established in the future, the question arises as to whether the world community needs them. Proliferation of international courts/tribunals has triggered a doubt as to the necessity and efficiency of their establishment. For example, the International Criminal Tribunal for Rwanda (ICTR) could complete only eight trials in its first eight years of operation. Second, such proliferation may also bring inconsistency in international jurisprudence as well as overlapping jurisdiction. Judge Gilbert Guillaume, the ex-president of the ICJ, once criticised such proliferation and brought his concerns to the United Nations.[58] Therefore, the most efficient way to solve the problem is to maximise the use of the existing international courts, instead of establishing more such courts.

Future prospects

The rise of Asia may not bring about an era of the rise of Asia's legal authority and power which can determine the direction of the development of international law. It is reasonably perceived, at least at the time of writing this book, that Asian states including the two biggest global players, China and India, to a large extent, will still follow and respond to, rather than initiate and proactively push forward, the development of international law. In other words, although China and India have become key players in global economic development, they may not be so in the formulation of the future global legal order. In some fields of international law, it is even doubtful whether Asian countries will be able to react to the development of international law timely and adequately. As I once commented, 'China faces a dilemma in the study of international law: on the one hand, it realizes that international law is developing with the globalization of the world community and new branches have emerged, such as law relating to human rights and environmental protection. On the other hand, it seems that China is not ready fully to respond to such new developments, particularly in the field of human rights law'.[59] At the time of writing this book, China had not ratified the International Covenant on Civil and Political Rights, though it had signed it in 1998. Even if China's ratification were inked, effective implementation of the covenant at the national level would still be a problem. Despite China's ratification of the UN Convention Against Torture and Other Cruel, Inhuman or Degrading Treatment or Punishment in as early as 1988, torture in China remains common and has become a topic of international criticism. This passivity towards human rights law may reflect in the practice of other Asian countries as well. As is commented, '[t]he development of a regional human rights approach in Asia has been slow, reflecting the preference of Asian nations not to interfere in each other's domestic affairs'.[60]

On the other hand, however, the rise of Asia may significantly impact on the future development of international law. For instance, although China has reiterated on many occasions that its rise will be peaceful, Europeans might worry about a rising China in the sense that China would 'learn wrong lessons from US unilateralism, selective application of multilateralism and the use of force, including the use of preemptive force'.[61] But the most significant contributions of Asian countries to the development of international law are the regional legal arrangements.

The emergence and expansion of regional organisations are noteworthy in the development of international law. The European Union (EU) has contributed a lot in this respect. Regional organisations, including those in Asia, follow suit. ASEAN is the most remarkable organisation in the Asian region in terms of its memberships and partnerships as well as its pivotal role in Asian integration.[62] In addition to political and economic cooperation, security and environment have gradually become its main agenda over the years. Within ASEAN, a number of legal documents have been concluded to facilitate the development of the organisation and of the cooperation among member states and/or between member states and other states, and to tackle regional issues such as the notorious Indonesian haze. ASEAN has become the centre of Asian integration. It establishes the regular mechanisms of 10+1 with China; 10+3 with China, Japan and South Korea; ASEAN + India; and ASEAN + Australia and New Zealand for the purpose of establishing regional free trade areas (FTA) and for further regional integration. Under the 10+1 mechanism, there is a China–ASEAN FTA Legal Affairs Forum. The second meeting of this forum was held in Guangxi, China, in October 2005. One of the purposes of the forum 'was principally to advance the construction of CAFTA legal system so as to be able to bridge the existing gaps between national legislation and internal regulations on the one hand and international customs and practices on the other'.[63] The ASEAN Regional Forum (ARF) is a consultative body encompassing countries in Asia Pacific for the purpose of promoting open dialogue on political and security cooperation in the Asia Pacific region.

With the endeavours of ASEAN, a so-called East Asian Community embracing ASEAN members – China, Japan, Korea, India, Australia, New Zealand and possibly other countries as well – has begun to emerge. ASEAN has adopted the ASEAN Charter, which could be a counterpart of the legal arrangement of the founding of the EU. In that sense, the increasing role of ASEAN in developing international law twenty-first century onwards cannot be ignored. It is even suggested that ASEAN, as one of the 'regional groupings', may play an important role in the United Nations including the UN Security Council after the restructuring of the international system.[64]

On the other hand, some difficulties still exist in the formulation of Asian regionalism. It is widely known that there are three flashpoints of potential conflict in East Asia: the Korean Peninsular, the Taiwan Strait and the South China Sea. These are all regional problems with the global concern. The disharmony between China and Japan also contributes to obstacles in the smooth process of Asian regionalism.

Besides ASEAN, other regional organisations also facilitate the development of international law, including the notable Shanghai Cooperation Organization (SCO), which was formed among China, Russia and some Central Asian countries with the aim to prevent and crack down on terrorism. It is the first organisation in the world which was designed specifically for this purpose. As a further development, the SCO now embraces economic topics on its agenda.

There is a debate on whether the booming of regional organisations and legal arrangements would bring about the fragmentation of international law, thus weakening its unity and integrity. In 2002 this issue caught the attention of the International Law Commission, which established a study group to examine the issue. The study group worked out some drafted conclusions in 2006.[65] Although debatable, the general view is that regional arrangements can facilitate rather than disintegrate international law. International organisations may not be 'a source of increased chaos in the international normative puzzle'.[66]

To some extent the development of international law needs the help of domestic legal catalysts in individual nation states. The 2005 World Summit called for universal adherence to and implementation of the rule of law at both national and international levels.[67] According to China, for the rule of law at the international level, several undertakings need to be fulfilled: (1) maintaining the authority of the UN Charter, (2) enhancing the democratisation of international relations, (3) strictly abiding by international treaties and international customary rules, and by the UN Security Council decisions with binding force, (4) ensuring the consistent application of international law and (5) further improving 'international legislation'.[68] China's positive attitude towards the rule of law at the international level has domestic background. Since 1978, China has been carrying out legal reforms and has adopted the concept of the rule of law in its constitution. Legal awareness among ordinary citizens in China has increased significantly. One figure tells us that China is a party to 273 multilateral international treaties, of which 239 became applicable to China only after 1979.[69] Inevitably, achievements of legal reform at the domestic level influence a nation state's practice in international law. In this sense, the realisation of the rule of law at the international level depends on the rule of law at the national level.

Finally, it must be pointed out that the development of international law depends on the efforts made by all the members of the world community. This, in turn, benefits all human beings. In this sense, it becomes meaningless to divide international law into Western international law, Eastern international law, capitalist international law and socialist international law by using old-fashioned ideologies. As international law is a common property of mankind, there should be no 'clash of civilisations' in the course of its development, not only in the twenty-first century but also in the far future.

Notes

1. 'China's GDP grows 10.7% in 2006', 25 January 2007, available at *http://www.chinadaily.com.cn/china/2007-01/25/content_792311_2.htm* (accessed 25 January 2007).
2. National Intelligence Council, *Mapping the Global Future*, Report of the National Intelligence Council's 2020 Project, December 2004, p. 47.
3. 'India on the Fire', *The Economist*, 3 February 2007, p. 73.
4. National Intelligence Council, supra note 2, p. 28.
5. 'Sino-India Joint Declaration', 21 November 2006, New Delhi, available at *http://www.peacehall.com/news/gb/intl/2006/11/200611220052.shtml* (accessed 22 November 2006).
6. Wang Tieya (ed.), *International Law* (Beijing: Law Press, 1995) (in Chinese), pp. 39–41.
7. Ram P. Anand, *International Law and the Developing Countries*, reprinted in Barry E. Carter, Phillip R. Trimble and Curtis A. Bradley, *International Law*, 4th edition (New York: Aspen Publishers, 2003), p. 24.
8. B. Larschan and B.C. Brennan, 'The Common Heritage of Mankind Principles in International Law', *Columbia Journal of Transnational Law*, vol. 21 (45), 1983, p. 318.
9. UN Doc. A/6695, reprinted in H.G. Knight, *The Law of the Sea: Documents and Notes* (Louisiana State University, 1969), pp. 461–2.
10. This means the international seabed area.
11. A. Pardo and C.Q. Christol, 'The Common Interest: Tension between Whole and Parts', in R.St.J. Macdonald and D.M. Johnston (eds.), *The Structure and Process of International Law: Essays in Legal Philosophy Doctrine and Theory* (The Hague: Martinus Nijhoff, 1983), p. 654.
12. Moragodage C.W. Pinto, 'Common Heritage of Mankind': From Metaphor to Myth, and the Consequences of Constructive Ambiguity', in Jerzy Makarczyk (ed.), *Theory of International Law at the Threshold of the 21st Century: Essays in Honour of Krzysztof Skubiszewski* (The Hague: Kluwer Law International, 1996), pp. 249–68.
13. Cui Bian, 'Mining in the Pacific', *Beijing Review*, May 3–9, 1999, p. 23.
14. Text is available at *http://www.recaap.org/about/pdf/ReCAAP%20Agreement.pdf* (accessed 22 July 2008).
15. A relevant meeting took place from 14 to 18 April 2008 in Dares Salaam. See UN Division for Ocean Affairs and the Law of the Sea, 'Advance and unedited material on "maritime security and safety" which will later be integrated into the Secretary-General's report on oceans and the law of the sea for the sixth-third session of the General Assembly and for the ninth meeting of the consultative process', 22 February 2008, p. 6, available at *http://www.un.org/Depts/los/consultative_process/documents/maritime_security_and_safety.pdf* (accessed 6 March 2008).
16. Text in UNTS 299:59 (1958).
17. Wang, supra note 6, p. 60.
18. Lazar Focsaneanu, 'Les cinq principes de coexistence et le droit international', *Annuaire français de droit international*, 1956, pp. 177–8.
19. Wang, supra note 6, p. 62.

20. In 2004, China commemorated the 50th anniversary of the Five Principles of Peaceful Coexistence, and some speeches made on that occasion including the speech by Wen Jiabao, the prime minister of China, were published in the *Chinese Journal of International Law*, vol. 3 (2), 2004, pp. 363–77.
21. Than Shwe, chairman of the Myanmar State Peace and Development Council, reiterated in January 2007, on the occasion of the independence day of Myanmar, that 'Myanmar always attaches great importance to developing friendly relations with all the countries in the world based on the Five Principles of Peaceful Coexistence', see 'Myanmar Emphasises the Adherence to the Principles of Peaceful Coexistence', *People's Daily* (in Chinese), 5 January 2007, p. 3.
22. For example, the Joint Statement of ASEAN–China Commemorative Summit: Towards an Enhanced ASEAN–China Strategic Partnership, done on 30 October 2006, available at *http://www.aseansec.org/China-Com-Summit.Doc* (accessed 20 May 2008).
23. Antony Anghie and B.S. Chimni, 'Third World Approaches to International Law and Individual Responsibility in Internal Conflicts', *Chinese Journal of International Law*, vol. 2 (1), 2003, pp. 80–2.
24. Makau Mutua, 'What is Twail?' 94 *ASIL Proceedings*, 2000, p. 31.
25. *Collected Works of Mao Zedong on Diplomacy* (Beijing: World Knowledge Press, 1994) (in Chinese), pp. 600–1. For related reference, see Wang Jisi, 'International Relations Theory and the Study of Chinese Foreign Policy: A Chinese Perspective', in Thomas W. Robinson and David Shambaugh (eds.), *Chinese Foreign Policy: Theory and Practice* (Oxford: Clarendon Press, 1994), pp. 481–505.
26. A number of Chinese legal scholars advocated that anti-hegemony was a principle of international law. For example, Sheng Yu, 'On the Principle of Anti-Hegemonism and International Law', in China Society of Law (ed.), *Theses of Law of China (I)* (Beijing: Law Press, 1984) (in Chinese), pp. 451–65. However, such an approach was not prevailing in China's international law circle.
27. *Black's Law Dictionary*, 6th edition (St. Paul: West Publishing, 1990), p. 1396.
28. Bai Guimei, 'Basic Rights and Obligations of the State', in Wang (ed.), supra note 6, 107–108.
29. J.A. Cohen, 'Attitudes toward International Law', in J.A. Cohen (ed.), *Contemporary Chinese Law: Research Problems and Perspectives* (Cambridge: Harvard University Press, 1970), p. 287.
30. Bai, supra note 28, p. 113.
31. Lihai Zhao, 'The Main Legal Problems in the Bilateral Relations between China and the United States', *New York University Journal of International Law & Politics*, vol. 16, 1984, p. 547.
32. Li Bian, 'NATO Challenges International Laws', *Beijing Review*, April 26–May 2, 1999, p. 7.
33. 'A Warning to the Portuguese Authorities in Macao', *People's Daily*, 26 October 1956; in J.A. Cohen and Hungdah Chiu, *People's China and International Law*, vol. 1 (Princeton, NJ: Princeton University Press, 1974), p. 376.

34. Commentator, 'Hong Kong Is Chinese Territory', *People's Daily*, 20 August 1967; in Cohen and Chiu, supra note 33, pp. 382–3.
35. Zhao Lihai, *Contemporary International Law Problems* (Beijing: China Legal System Publisher, 1993) (in Chinese), pp. 67–73 and 89–96.
36. Wang Tieya, 'International Law in China: Historical and Contemporary Perspectives', *Recueil des cours*, vol. II, 1990, p. 292.
37. Remarks of Liu Nanlai, in 'Human Rights Superior to Sovereignty: The Banner of the New Gunboat Policy', *People's Daily* (in Chinese), 14 May 1999.
38. Jia Qingguo, 'China', in Watanabe Koji (ed.), *Humanitarian Intervention: The Evolving Asian Debate* (Tokyo: Japan Center for International Change, 2003), pp. 22–3.
39. Mu Yaping and Wang Yue, 'Crisis of International Humanitarian Law', *Journal of Political Science and Law* (in Chinese), vol. 22 (2), 2005, pp. 61–3.
40. Jia Qingguo, supra note 38, p. 31.
41. Jasjit Singh, 'India', in Watanabe Koji (ed.), supra note 38, p. 87.
42. Singh, ibid., p. 94.
43. Singh, ibid., p. 106.
44. Simon Tay and Rizal Sukma, 'ASEAN', in Watanabe Koji (ed.), supra note 38, p. 121.
45. International Commission on Intervention and State Sovereignty, *The Responsibility to Protect*, Report, December 2001, p. xi.
46. Gao Yanping, 'International Dispute Settlement', in Wang (ed.), supra note 6, pp. 611–2.
47. Article 287 (3) of the LOS Convention provides that 'A State Party, which is a party to a dispute not covered by a declaration in force, shall be deemed to have accepted arbitration in accordance with Annex VII'.
48. Gao, supra note 46, p. 612.
49. 'China's Declaration in Accordance with Article 298 of the United Nations Convention on the Law of the Sea', 7 September 2006, available at *http://www.fmprc.gov.cn/chn/wjb/zzjg/tyfls/wjzdtyflgz/zgzhyflydgz/t270754.htm* (accessed 6 February 2007).
50. Huang Fang, 'Comments on China's Five Reasons to Vote against the ICC Statute', available at *http://www.iolaw.org.cn/showarticle.asp?id=1694* (accessed 2 February 2007).
51. Valeriane Toon, 'International Criminal Court: Reservations of Non-State Parties in Southeast Asia', *Contemporary Southeast Asia*, vol. 26 (2), 2004, pp. 218–32.
52. Gao Mingxuan and Zhao Bingzhi (eds.), *The International Criminal Court: Choice of China* (Bejing: People's Public Security University of China Press, 2005) (in Chinese).
53. Bing Bing Jia, 'China and the International Criminal Court: Current Situation', *Singapore Year Book of International Law*, vol. 10, 2006, available at *http://law.nus.edu.sg/sybil/downloads/coming/Jia_SYBIL_2006.pdf* (accessed 7 February 2007).
54. 'Position Paper of the People's Republic of China on the United Nations Reforms', 7 June 2005, available at *http://www.fmprc.gov.cn/eng/zxxx/t199318.htm* (accessed 7 February 2007).

55. 'Malaysia and Singapore jointly submit a dispute concerning sovereignty over Pedra Branca/Pulau Batu Puteh, Middle Rocks and South Ledge to the International Court of Justice', Press Release 2003/22, 24 July 2003, available at *http://www.icj-cij.org/icjwww/ipresscom/ipress2003/ipresscom2003-22_ms_20030724.htm* (accessed 26 July 2003).
56. For details, see *http://www.itlos.org/start2_en.html* (accessed 8 February 2007). For related reference, see C.L. Lim, 'The Use of Pacific Settlement Techniques in Malaysia–Singapore Relations', *Melbourne Journal of International Law*, vol. 6, 2005, pp. 313–41.
57. Jusuf Wanandi, 'ASEAN Future Challenges and the Importance of an ASEAN Charter', *Asien: Deutsche Zeitschrift für Politik, Wirtschaft und Kultur*, no. 100, 2006, p. 87.
58. Address by H.E. Judge Gilbert Guillaume, President of the International Court of Justice, to the United Nations General Assembly, 26 October 2000, available at *http://www.icj-cij.org/icjwww/ipresscom/SPEECHES/iSpeechPresident_Guillaume_GA55_20001026.htm* (accessed 19 December 2003). (He gave an example of jurisprudential inconsistency made by the ICTY in ruling on the merits in the Tadic case that 'the International Criminal Tribunal for the former Yugoslavia recently disregarded case-law formulated by the International Court of Justice in the dispute between Nicaragua and the United States of America. The court had found that the United States could not be held responsible for acts committed by the contras in Nicaragua unless it had had "effective control" over them. After criticising the view taken by the court, the tribunal adopted a less strict standard for Yugoslavia's actions in Bosnia and Herzegovina and replaced the notion of "effective control" with that of "overall control," thereby broadening the range of circumstances in which a state's responsibility may be engaged on account of its actions on foreign territory'.)
59. Zou Keyuan, *China's Legal Reform: Towards the Rule of Law* (Leiden/Boston: Martinus Nijhoff Publishers, 2006), p. 248.
60. David P. Fidler, 'The Asian Century: Implications for International Law', *Singapore Year Book of International Law*, vol. 9, 2005, pp. 34–5.
61. Reinhard Drifte, 'Leadership Issues for Asia in the 21st Century', *Asien: Deutsche Zeitschrift für Politik, Wirtschaft und Kultur*, no. 100, 2006, p. 35.
62. According to the ASEAN website, 'the ASEAN region has a population of about 500 million, a total area of 4.5 million square kilometers, a combined gross domestic product of almost US$ 700 billion, and a total trade of about US$ 850 billion', available at *http://www.aseansec.org/64.htm* (accessed 29 January 2007).
63. Sompong Sucharitkul, 'Report on the Second China–ASEAN Expo: 18–21 October 2005, Nanning, Guangxi, China', *Chinese Journal of International Law*, vol. 5 (2), 2006, p. 414.
64. Hans Köchler, 'The United Nations Organization and Global Power Politics: The Antagonism between Power and Law and the Future Legal Order', *Chinese Journal of International Law*, vol. 5 (2), 2006, p. 339.
65. 'Fragmentation of International Law: Difficulties Arising from the Diversification and Expansion of International Law', Report of the Study

Group of the International Law Commission, UN Doc A/CN.4/L.682/ Add.1, 2 May 2006.

66. Mario Prost and Paul Kingsley Clark, 'Unity, Diversity and the Fragmentation of International Law: How Much Does the Multiplication of International Organizations Really Matter?', *Chinese Journal of International Law*, vol. 5 (2), 2006, p. 341.
67. '2005 World Summit Outcome', UN Doc. A/RES/60/1, 24 October 2005, *http://daccessdds.un.org/doc/UNDOC/GEN/N05/487/60/PDF/N0548760 .pdf?OpenElement* (accessed 9 February 2007).
68. 'Speech of the Chinese Delegate Duan Jielong at the Sixth Committee of the 61st UN General Assembly on "the Rule of Law at the National and International Levels"', 17 October 2006, available at *http://www.fmprc .gov.cn/chn/wjb/zzjg/tyfls/lcybt/t283190.htm* (accessed 6 February 2007).
69. Hanqin Xue, 'China's Open Policy and International Law', *Chinese Journal of International Law*, vol. 4, 2005, p. 136.

Part II
Compliance with and implementation of international law

3

Legal framework for the development of China–ASEAN relations

Legal principles guiding the development of China–ASEAN relations

Generally speaking, all legal principles in international law can guide the relationship between China and ASEAN. The principles enshrined in the United Nations (UN) Charter, the Treaty of Amity and Cooperation in Southeast Asia (the TAC) and the Five Principles of Peaceful Coexistence initiated by Asian countries are particularly applicable to the development of China–ASEAN relations. As the *Joint Statement of ASEAN–China Commemorative Summit: Towards an Enhanced ASEAN–China Strategic Partnership* issued in October 2006 reaffirms, the two sides 'believe that the achievements made in the past 15 years in ASEAN-China dialogue relations have been the result of adherence by both sides to the principles enshrined in the TAC, the Five Principles of Peaceful Coexistence, the Ten Principles of the Bandung Asian-African Conference, the purposes and principles of the UN Charter and other relevant international laws, treaties, and conventions. ASEAN and China relations will continue to be fully guided by these principles'.[1]

It is generally recognised that the most important international organisation in the world today is the United Nations which was established in 1946 after the Second World War with the fundamental purpose of maintaining world peace and security and promoting the development of friendly relations and cooperation among nations. As of June 2008, there were 192 members of the United Nations including all the 10 ASEAN member states and China. Being UN members, they are bound by the

Charter of the United Nations including the legal principles contained in the Charter so as to carry out their corresponding obligations under the Charter.[2] There are seven fundamental principles in the UN Charter including (1) sovereign equality of all its members; (2) commitment of all members to fulfil in good faith the obligations assumed by them in accordance with the Charter; (3) settlement of international disputes by peaceful means; (4) refrain in international relations from the threat or use of force against the territorial integrity or political independence of any state, or in any other manner inconsistent with the purposes of the United Nations; (5) provision of assistance to the United Nations in any action it takes in accordance with the Charter; (6) surety that non-UN members act in accordance with the UN principles so far as may be necessary for the maintenance of international peace and security; and (7) non-intervention in matters which are essentially within the domestic jurisdiction of any state.[3] The above principles, except for Principles 5 and 6 which are specifically designed for the United Nations itself, are basic principles of international law. For UN members, these principles are regarded as superior to others as the UN Charter clearly provides that 'in the event of a conflict between the obligations of the Members of the United Nations under the present Charter and their obligations under any other international agreement, their obligations under the present Charter shall prevail'.[4] That means, in case there is such a conflict between UN obligations and obligations under any ASEAN agreement and/or any China–ASEAN agreement, both China and ASEAN members should fulfil the UN obligations first.

In December 2006, ASEAN was granted observer status to the UN General Assembly by the UNGA Resolution A61/44. In the following year, ASEAN and the UN signed the Memorandum of Understanding on ASEAN–UN Cooperation (the ASEAN–UN MOU) to officially establish the partnership between the two organisations for their full range of cooperation based on mutual benefits.[5] The partnership between ASEAN and the United Nations can promote the better fulfilment of the ASEAN members' obligations to maintain peace and security in the Asian region as well as in the world.

In pursuance of the principles enshrined in the UN Charter, the ASEAN member states adopted the following fundamental principles in their relations with one another, as contained in the 1976 Treaty of Amity and Cooperation in Southeast Asia: (1) mutual respect for the independence, sovereignty, equality, territorial integrity and national identity of all nations; (2) the right of every state to lead its national existence free from external interference, subversion or coercion; (3) non-interference in the internal affairs of one another; (4) settlement of differences or disputes in a peaceful manner; (5) renunciation of the threat or use of force; and (6) effective cooperation among themselves.[6] In 2003, as China acceded to the TAC, it was also bound by the above principles of that treaty. In fact, the TAC was mentioned in the documents signed by ASEAN and China even before China's accession. For example, the 1997 ASEAN–China Joint Statement affirms that 'the Charter of the United Nations, *the Treaty of Amity and Cooperation in Southeast Asia*, the Five Principles of Peaceful Coexistence and universally recognised international law should serve as basic norms governing their relations' (italics added).[7] This indicates that China had agreed to these principles as early as the establishment of its relationship with ASEAN.

The ASEAN Charter adopted in 2007, being the most important legal document in ASEAN, reaffirms and elaborates the above principles contained in the UN Charter as well as in the TAC. Accordingly, ASEAN and its member states reaffirm and adhere to the fundamental principles contained in the declarations, agreements, conventions, concords, treaties and other instruments of ASEAN. In addition, the ASEAN Charter contains the following 14 principles:

(a) respect for the independence, sovereignty, equality, territorial integrity and national identity of all ASEAN member states;

(b) shared commitment and collective responsibility in enhancing regional peace, security and prosperity;

(c) renunciation of aggression and of the threat or use of force or other actions in any manner inconsistent with international law;

(d) reliance on peaceful settlement of disputes;

(e) non-interference in the internal affairs of ASEAN member states;

(f) respect for the right of every member state to lead its national existence free from external interference, subversion and coercion;

(g) enhanced consultations on matters seriously affecting the common interest of ASEAN;

(h) adherence to the rule of law, good governance, the principles of democracy and constitutional government;

(i) respect for fundamental freedoms, the promotion and protection of human rights and the promotion of social justice;

(j) upholding the UN Charter and international law, including international humanitarian law, subscribed to by ASEAN member states;

(k) abstention from participation in any policy or activity, including the use of its territory, pursued by any ASEAN member state or non-ASEAN state or any non-state actor, which threatens the sovereignty, territorial integrity or political and economic stability of ASEAN member states;

(l) respect for the different cultures, languages and religions of the peoples of ASEAN, while emphasising their common values in the spirit of unity in diversity;

(m) the centrality of ASEAN in external political, economic, social and cultural relations while remaining actively engaged, outward-looking, inclusive and non-discriminatory; and

(n) adherence to multilateral trade rules and ASEAN's rules-based regimes for effective implementation of economic commitments and progressive reduction towards elimination of all barriers to regional economic integration, in a market-driven economy.[8]

In comparison, it can be seen that while the ASEAN Charter has incorporated the principles reflected in the UN Charter and the TAC, it also contains some new principles applicable to ASEAN and its members.

The Five Principles of Peaceful Coexistence, as discussed in Chapter 2, were initiated by China and India in the 1950s and contain the following principles: (1) mutual respect for sovereignty and territorial integrity, (2) mutual non-aggression, (3) non-interference in each other's internal affairs, (4) equality and mutual benefit and (5) peaceful coexistence. As China claims, the Five Principles constituted the basis for China establishing and developing diplomatic relations with 165 countries; carrying out trade, economic, scientific, technological and cultural exchanges and cooperation with over 200 countries and regions; resolving the boundary issues with neighbours and maintaining peace and stability in its surrounding areas.[9] Related are the ten principles of peaceful coexistence and friendly cooperation contained in the 1955 Final Communiqué of the Asian-African Bandung Conference in which China participated despite the blockade by the Western powers at that time.[10]

Of the above principles, two are particularly important in the context of the China–ASEAN relationship: the principle of good neighbourliness and cooperation and the principle of peaceful settlement of international disputes.

As for the first one, Article 74 of the UN Charter embodies this general principle and requires member states to apply it to the consideration of 'the interests and well-being of the rest of the world, in social, economic, and commercial matters'.[11] On the other hand, cooperation between/among states is a general duty under international law. Interdependence exists everywhere. There are common interests and common concerns over political and security matters, economic sustainable development, shared resources and the natural environment in the world community. Cooperation implies taking into account the interests of others and a share of certain authority, competence or power.[12] Cooperation can be reflected in international relations in various ways and forms. All the treaties in and related to East Asia, whether bilateral, multilateral, regional or global, are concluded on the basis of this principle. What is more important are the institutional arrangements for cooperation under these treaties which can help promote the development of the China–ASEAN relations through the creation of negotiation-centred mechanism, and/or the adoption of monitoring and reporting, information exchange mechanisms, and/or third-party dispute settlement mechanisms.

The second is the principle of peaceful resolution of disputes. As provided in the UN Charter, the parties to any dispute should seek a solution through means such as negotiation, enquiry, mediation, conciliation, arbitration, judicial settlement, resort to regional agencies or arrangements or other peaceful means of their own choice.[13] The principle reflects the very reality in dispute settlement: that no state is forced to accept a specific settlement procedure without its consent, whether *a priori* or *a posteriori*, and disputing parties should pursue in good faith one of the peaceful means available to settle their dispute in question. Most, if not all, of such peaceful means are stipulated in the treaties and agreements in the context of China–ASEAN relations. Although the East Asian countries are not active in their recourse to legal means for dispute settlement, they frequently and usually use political forms, particularly direct negotiation and consultation, or regional arrangements, as reflected in the agreements reached among the ASEAN members as well as those between the ASEAN/its members and China.

Through the operations of ASEAN, the unique 'ASEAN Way' has been created which refers to a loose arrangement including 'informal processes, weak regional institutions, and decisions by consensus'.[14] It contains three core values: (1) consultation – due to various diversities and contradictions between/among the states in Southeast Asia, regional integration must rely on consultation rather than on coercive forces; (2) harmony – ASEAN regards itself as a harmonious entity of states, like an orchestra consisting of its member states, without interfering in their domestic affairs and resort to peaceful dispute settlement; and (3) cooperation – unlike the 'hard way' of law used by the European Union (EU), ASEAN adopts the 'soft way' for cooperation.[15] It is commented that the ASEAN Way has played an active role in establishing the regional order, constructing a platform for states from outside the region to be involved in participation and dialogue, maintaining regional stability and balancing big powers' influences.[16] Frankly speaking, the ASEAN Way has been working successfully since the founding of ASEAN. Without it, it is hard to imagine that the ASEAN member states could reach agreements governing various areas of cooperation and regional integration. However, it is doubtful whether the ASEAN Way has become a legal principle, although there is no doubt that it is a political principle within ASEAN. In fact, the ASEAN member states realised the weaknesses inherent in the soft ASEAN Way over time and desired to find a harder way to undertake cooperation and integration through a legally binding document, that is the ASEAN Charter, which will be discussed below.

Legal status of ASEAN

As we know, ASEAN was formally established in August 1967 with only five member states: Indonesia, Malaysia, the Philippines, Singapore and Thailand, and witnessed a divided Southeast Asia.[17] However, ASEAN has made remarkable progress over the past 41 years. As the former ASEAN secretary-general summarises, the major achievements of ASEAN since 1967 have been '[p]lacing inter-state relations among ASEAN member-countries on a peaceful, stable and friendly basis; laying the foundations for regional economic integration; providing a framework for cooperation on common problems; slowly developing a regional consciousness; and, through creative diplomacy, engaging the Major Powers with a view to enhancing political stability and economic growth throughout the Asia-Pacific region'.[18] It has now embraced 10 members including Brunei (joined in 1984), Cambodia (1999), Laos (1997), Myanmar (1997) and Vietnam (1995), in addition to the 5 original members.

In terms of its legal status under international law, ASEAN is well defined as an inter-state/governmental international organisation. The founding document – the ASEAN Declaration (also known as the Bangkok Declaration) – expressly declared the establishment of ASEAN for promoting regional peace and stability, rule of law, economic growth and social and cultural development to build 'a prosperous and peaceful community of South-East Asian Nations'.[19] It created four mechanisms for the operation of the organisation: (a) annual meeting of foreign ministers, which should be by rotation and is referred to as ASEAN ministerial meeting; (b) a standing committee, under the chairmanship of the foreign minister of the host country or his representative, to carry on the work of the association in between meetings of foreign ministers; (c) ad hoc committees and permanent committees of specialists and officials on specific subjects; and (d) a national secretariat in each member country to carry out the work of the association on behalf of that country.[20] Being an international organisation, ASEAN wishes to 'maintain close and beneficial cooperation with existing international and regional organizations with similar aims and purposes'.[21] It is to be noted that ASEAN had no secretariat of its own until 1976, when the Agreement on the Establishment of the ASEAN Secretariat was signed. Accordingly, a permanent secretariat with the mission to 'provide for greater efficiency in the coordination of ASEAN organs and for more effective implementation of ASEAN projects and activities' was established with its headquarters located in Jakarta, Indonesia.[22] Representatives from the Investment and Enterprise Unit of the ASEAN Secretariat, together with representatives from 10 ASEAN states, have been involved in the negotiation of the ASEAN–China investment agreement under the ACFTA Framework Agreement.[23]

However, there has been a debate on whether ASEAN possesses legal personality under international law. As the former ASEAN secretary-general opines, 'ASEAN does not have juridical personality or legal standing under international law'.[24] This viewpoint has been supported by others including the following statement that 'ASEAN currently does not appear to have legal personality as it is not explicitly established as an international organization with such personality'.[25] Some scholars have doubts about the legal personality of ASEAN since the founding document – the Bangkok Declaration – and the subsequent instruments adopted within ASEAN do not give explicit legal personality to ASEAN or confer treaty-making power to the organisation.[26] Some scholars recognise the legal personality of ASEAN, but do not regard it as being 'meaningful'.[27]

Generally speaking, there are two theories about legal personality: the will theory ('if the founders of an international organization intend to endow their creation with personality then that is what it will receive') and the objective theory ('legal personality can be deduced not from the will of the founders but from the possession of certain attributes by the body itself').[28] According to Ian Brownlie, to enjoy legal personality an organisation must possess the following three attributes: (1) a permanent association of states, with lawful objects, equipped with organs; (2) a distinction, in terms of legal powers and purposes, between the organisation and its member states; and (3) the existence of legal powers exercisable on the international plane and not solely within the national systems of one or more states.[29]

It is recalled that the International Court of Justice (ICJ) rendered its advisory opinion on the case of *Reparation for Injuries Suffered in the Service of the United Nations* in 1948 and answered the question on whether the United Nations possessed international personality since the UN Charter does not expressly stipulate this but only the United Nation's 'legal capacity' necessary for the exercise of its functions within the territory of its member states.[30] According to the Court, the United Nations 'was intended to exercise and enjoy, and is in fact exercising and enjoying functions and rights which can be only explained on the basis of the possession of a large measure of international personality and the capacity to operate upon an international plane'.[31] The Court then concluded that the United Nations, though different from a state, was an international person, a subject of international law, capable of possessing international rights and duties.[32] While addressing the question on whether the United Nations could bring an international claim, the ICJ further emphasised that 'fifty States, representing the vast majority of the members of the international community, had the power, in conformity with international law, to bring into being an entity possessing objective international personality, and not merely personality recognised by them alone, together with the capacity to bring international claims'.[33] Thus, it can be concluded that the court tended to combine the will theory and the objective theory while emphasising more on the former.

Relevant international treaties also touch upon the issue of international legal personality of international organisations. For example, the Vienna Convention on the Law of Treaties between States and International Organizations or between International Organizations adopted in 1986 stated in its preamble that 'international organizations possess the capacity to conclude treaties, which is necessary for the exercise of their functions and the fulfillment of their purposes'.[34] The International Law Commission (ILC) has been discussing the 'responsibility of international organizations' since 2002 and trying to formulate an international treaty on this subject matter in near future.

Hence, judging from its past activities and existing founding documents, it seems that ASEAN possesses certain degree of international legal personality. As an international organisation, its existence in the international community is evidently objective. According to general international law, ASEAN, like other inter-governmental organisations, no doubt can be recognised as a subject of international law, enjoying and exercising corresponding functions and rights at the international plane. It has the power of making and implementing treaties under the authorisation of its member states. As demonstrated by the Memorandum of Understanding on Agricultural Cooperation signed between the ASEAN Secretariat and China in 2002, the executing agencies for the implementation of this MOU are the ASEAN Secretariat for the ASEAN member states and the Ministry of Agriculture of the People's Republic of China for China.[35]

However, being a regional organisation, its legal status under international law is incomparable to that of the United Nations. In terms of the effectiveness of its functions too, it is incomparable to a similar regional organisation – the European Union. There are a number of limits and ambiguity in its international legal personality. As pointed out, ASEAN has no compliance or enforcement mechanisms, such as those in the European Union. Its agreements carry no sanctions for failures to implement them.[36] Its founding instrument does not express the intention of the founding member states to grant it such personality. This is one of the main reasons for the advocacy of the need of the ASEAN Charter which would remedy this deficiency by expressly providing legal personality for ASEAN.

The ASEAN Charter

Having realised the weaknesses in enforcement and institutional arrangements, the ASEAN members started to consider adopting a more teeth-contained document. The initiative began with the adoption of the Vientiane Action Program in 2004 which recognised the need to strengthen ASEAN and to work towards the development of an ASEAN Charter.[37] The ASEAN member states expressed their determination to establish an ASEAN Charter through the Kuala Lumpur Declaration on the Establishment of the ASEAN Charter on 12 December 2005.[38] In January 2007 they finally reached the consensus to adopt this charter, as reflected in the Cebu Declaration on the Blueprint of the ASEAN Charter that 'we are committed to establish an ASEAN Charter as a crowning achievement of 40 years of ASEAN to enable ASEAN to meet future challenges and opportunities', and 'we reiterate our conviction that an ASEAN Charter will serve as a firm foundation in achieving one ASEAN Community by providing an enhanced institutional framework as well as conferring a legal personality to ASEAN'.[39]

The 13th ASEAN Summit held in November 2007 in Singapore formally adopted the ASEAN Charter. According to the Singapore Declaration on the ASEAN Charter, it will serve as 'a legal and institutional framework' of ASEAN.[40] The Charter contains 13 chapters, 55 clauses and 4 annexes. It is a legal document similar to the UN Charter. Some wordings in the ASEAN Charter are borrowed from the UN Charter, such as 'We, the Peoples' in the preamble. It sets forth 15 objectives and 14 principles[41] for the building of the ASEAN community – a caring and sharing community with one vision and one identity. The ASEAN members enjoy the equal rights and obligations under the Charter and are obliged to 'take all necessary measures, including the enactment of appropriate domestic legislation, to effectively implement the provisions of this Charter and to comply with all obligations of membership'.[42] The ASEAN Charter reaffirms the establishment of the existing relevant institutions of ASEAN, including (1) the ASEAN summit, which is the supreme policy-making body of ASEAN, deliberating and providing policy guidance and taking decisions on key issues pertaining to the realisation of the objectives of ASEAN (Article 7); (2) the ASEAN Coordinating Council, which, comprised of ASEAN foreign ministers, prepares for the ASEAN Summit meetings and coordinates the implementation of agreements and decisions of the ASEAN summit, besides other tasks provided for in the ASEAN Charter (Article 8); (3) ASEAN community councils, including the ASEAN Political-Security Community Council, ASEAN Economic Community Council and ASEAN Socio-Cultural Community Council, which should work to ensure the implementation of the relevant decisions of the ASEAN Summit, and coordinate the work of the different sectors under its purview, and on issues which cut across the other community councils (Article 9); (4) ASEAN Sectoral Ministerial Bodies, which function in accordance with their respective established mandates and implement the agreements and decisions of the ASEAN Summit under their respective purview (Article 10); (5) ASEAN Secretariat and the secretary-general who is appointed by the ASEAN Summit and acts as the chief administrative officer of ASEAN, carrying out the duties and responsibilities in accordance with the ASEAN Charter and relevant ASEAN instruments, protocols and established practices (Article 11); (6) Committee of Permanent Representatives to ASEAN, which supports the work of the ASEAN community councils and ASEAN sectoral ministerial bodies;[43] (7) ASEAN National Secretariats, which serve as national focal points; (8) ASEAN Human Rights Body; and (9) ASEAN Foundation. Consultation and consensus still remain as the basic principle for decision-making in ASEAN.[44]

Although the ASEAN Charter reconfirms the functions and activities of the existing ASEAN institutions, it is significant that it embodies them into a legal instrument, which could grant more formal legal status to these organs with clear-cut stipulated mandates. What is more significant is the creation of a new body on human rights protection, which is a milestone in the ASEAN history. Tracing back to history, as early as 1993, ASEAN foreign ministers agreed that ASEAN should consider the establishment of a regional human rights mechanism. Accordingly the Working Group for an ASEAN Human Rights Mechanism was established, which in 1998 made recommendations on how to formulate such a mechanism.[45] It is reported that the ASEAN members had differences regarding the human rights mechanism. While some states such as Indonesia, Malaysia, the Philippines and Thailand were supportive, other states like Cambodia, Laos, Myanmar and Vietnam were reluctant; they failed to reach consensus on whether the human rights body would have the right to monitor and investigate domestic human rights issues of individual ASEAN member states.[46] Nevertheless, the 41st ASEAN Foreign Ministers' Meeting held in Singapore from 17 to 24 July 2008 decided to establish a high-level panel (HLP) to draft the terms of reference of the ASEAN human rights body to be submitted at the 14th ASEAN Summit in December 2008.[47] We have to wait to see whether the human rights body to be established is toothless or contains enough teeth, penetrating the long-established practice of the so-called 'ASEAN Way' – utter non-interference in domestic affairs.

The Charter reconfirms that ASEAN is an inter-governmental organisation and for the first time, among all the ASEAN documents, mentions that this organisation possesses 'legal personality'.[48] ASEAN, its secretary-general, staff working at the secretariat and permanent representatives and officials on ASEAN duties should enjoy immunities and privileges in the territory of the member states as agreed between ASEAN and relevant member states.[49] According to the Charter, ASEAN has the capacity to conduct external relations and may conclude agreements with countries or subregional, regional and international organisations and institutions. The procedures for concluding such agreements shall be prescribed by the ASEAN Coordinating Council in consultation with the ASEAN community councils.[50] Non-ASEAN member states and relevant inter-governmental organisations may appoint and accredit ambassadors to ASEAN.[51]

As for dispute settlement between member states, the ASEAN Charter follows the traditional ASEAN Way of preferring dialogue, consultation and negotiation while allowing third-party involvement including good offices, conciliation and mediation provided by the ASEAN chairman or secretary-general. On the other hand, the ASEAN members agree to establish and maintain dispute settlement mechanisms in all fields of ASEAN cooperation including arbitration. However, there are two additional provisions for dispute settlement beyond the ASEAN Charter: (1) disputes relating to specific ASEAN instruments should be settled through the mechanisms and procedures provided for in such instruments (Article 24), and (2) member states have the right of recourse to the modes of peaceful settlement contained in Article 33(1) of the UN Charter or any other international legal instruments to which the disputing member states are parties (Article 28). Finally, it is to be noted that while all member states are required to comply with any findings, recommendations or reports for dispute settlement, there is no enforcement organ within ASEAN and any non-compliance issue is to be referred to the ASEAN Summit for a decision. In this context, the stipulations concerning dispute settlement and compliance can be regarded as a weak and toothless part in the ASEAN Charter.

According to the ASEAN Charter, it should prevail in case of any inconsistency between the rights and obligations of ASEAN member states under the Charter and any other ASEAN valid instruments such as treaties, conventions, agreements, concords, declarations and protocols.[52] It is understood through the wording of the relevant provision that the ASEAN Charter prevails over not only all the legal instruments but also all the political instruments formulated under ASEAN.

As for the membership, the ASEAN Charter, while specifying the existing 10 member states, leaves room to admit new member(s) geographically located in Southeast Asia.[53] ASEAN may thus intend to include Timor-Leste in future. Unlike the TAC which is open to non-Southeast Asian states for accession, the ASEAN Charter is more exclusive, confining itself only to Southeast Asian nations.

The ASEAN Charter will enter into force on the 30th day following the date of deposit of the 10th instrument of ratification with the secretary-general of ASEAN (Article 47). That means it requires the ratification of all the ASEAN member states. The Singapore Declaration on the ASEAN Charter urges the ASEAN members to complete ratification as soon as possible in order to bring the ASEAN Charter into force.[54] As of July 2008, seven countries (Brunei, Cambodia, Laos, Malaysia, Myanmar, Singapore and Vietnam) had ratified the ASEAN Charter.

The creation of the ASEAN Charter has several significant implications for ASEAN itself, its member states, the East Asian region and even the world. Firstly, the Charter has consolidated the legal status of ASEAN as an inter-governmental international organisation with legal personality under international law. Unlike its predecessor documents such as the Bangkok Declaration or the TAC, the Charter for the first time expressly stipulated that ASEAN possesses legal personality and the capacity to conduct external relations. It is acknowledged that in the past ASEAN 'has managed its affairs with a minimum of formality, with few legally binding arrangements, and with relatively weak regional institutions'.[55] But now, the Charter is actually the constitution of ASEAN, based on which ASEAN has been reconstructed to be a 'new' organisation with legally binding principles, institutions and procedures. Secondly, with the legal document like the ASEAN Charter in place, all political arrangements either regarding principles and objectives or institutions and mechanisms have been legalised; thus, principles and objectives contained in political documents such as the Declaration of ASEAN Concord (1976), the ASEAN Vision 2020 (1997) and the Declaration of ASEAN Concord II (2003) have been converted into legal principles and objectives. Existing institutions of ASEAN have become more permanent and carry out legal duties under the Charter constantly. They are given clear-cut functions and roles and act in accordance with the Charter. The traditional loose and informal ASEAN Way will give way to collective responsibility of the member states under the legal principles and norms of the ASEAN Charter, thus enhancing the effectiveness of ASEAN functions and activities. Thirdly, ASEAN is granted the power to conduct external relations with neighbouring states in East Asia, like China, and states in the rest of the world, international organisations like the United Nations and other legal entities under international law. Therefore, its legal authority in this respect has been established, which can promote its international prestige and status and facilitate the development of its external relations and cooperation.

Legal nature of the China–ASEAN relationship

In international law, the relationship between China and ASEAN is the relationship between a state and an international organisation. They are both subjects of international law, but their legal statuses under international law are different and the execution of some bilateral matters requires the necessary involvement of the member states of ASEAN.

There are three levels to define such a relationship vis-à-vis China: global (in terms of international treaties), regional (concerning ASEAN itself) and bilateral (in the context of individual ASEAN member states). However, the most important one is the second, that is at the regional level between ASEAN and China.

In terms of the bilateral relations between ASEAN together with its members and China, they both uphold the principles and objectives enshrined in the UN Charter. China and individual ASEAN member states are members of the United Nations, and also signatories to various important international treaties such as WTO treaties, the UN Law of the Sea Convention and the UN Framework Convention on Climate Change. In this context China and ASEAN member states have the shared international responsibility under these treaties as well as rights arising from these shared treaties. Furthermore, the objectives and concrete duties stipulated in such international treaties are embodied in the relevant documents including the legal ones signed by China and ASEAN for the purpose of their implementation and realisation. However, there are constraints to the development of the China–ASEAN relations within the legal frameworks provided by international treaties. The salient obstacle lies in the fact that ASEAN has not yet obtained such legal status at the global level as the European Union, that is the independent power to join global treaties. While the EU can sign international treaties and become members of international organisations, ASEAN does not have a corresponding authorisation from its member states, though it may sign agreements with other international organisations such as the United Nations. Things may change after the entry into force of the ASEAN Charter.

At the regional level, there are many legal and political documents signed between China and ASEAN including the TAC, the ACFTA Framework Agreement, etc. Several important documents including the 1994 Exchange of Letters, the 1997 Joint Statement, the 2002 Framework Agreement on Comprehensive Economic Cooperation, the 2002 Joint Declaration on Cooperation in the Field of Non-Traditional Security Issues, the 2002 Declaration on the Conduct of the Parties in the South China Sea and the 2003 Joint Declaration of Strategic Partnership serve as a legal basis for the development of their bilateral relationship. Assisted by these documents, China and ASEAN are able to develop their cooperative relations smoothly and rapidly. What is most important is that China acceded to the TAC in October 2003, the first non-ASEAN country to join the treaty. China became the ASEAN's Consultative Partner in 1995 and ASEAN accorded to China the full Dialogue Partner status in July 1996. In October 2003 at the ASEAN–China Summit, the two sides adopted the Joint Declaration of the Heads of State/Government of the Association of the Southeast Asian Nations and the People's Republic of China on Strategic Partnership for Peace and Prosperity, which has elevated the China–ASEAN relationship to new heights. Relevant mechanisms for dialogue and cooperation have been established: the ASEAN–China Summit, 10 at the ministerial level and 5 at the working level. According to a Chinese scholar, the establishment of the China–ASEAN cooperative relationship was 'legally formalised' by the Exchange of Letters between the ASEAN secretary-general and the Chinese foreign minister on 23 July 1994, agreeing to create the Joint Committee on Economic and Trade Cooperation and the Joint Committee on Cooperation in Science and Technology.[56]

As for the legal nature of the bilateral agreements signed between ASEAN and China, there are different views. Take the ACFTA Framework Agreement as an example; some regard it as a bilateral treaty between the two parties, that is China and ASEAN, as a whole,[57] while others regard it as a multilateral one with 11 contracting parties.[58] As the former scholar states, the ambiguous legal personality and the division of ASEAN members into two groups do not refute the bilateral nature of the agreement. As the treaty deals with comprehensive economic cooperation between ASEAN and China, it is clear that one contracting party is China, while the other parties are the 10 ASEAN members taken as a whole.[59] The latter author regards the ACFTA Framework Agreement as a multilateral agreement signed by 11 nation-states rather than a 'bilateral agreement' between China and ASEAN. In its nature, it mainly contains bilateral obligations between China and individual ASEAN countries. This legal reality will have a profound impact on the enforcement of treaty obligations as well as on the resort to the dispute settlement mechanism in the implementation of the ACFTA Framework Agreement.[60]

The different views are accounted for by the peculiar form of the agreement in that it takes the form of the two parties (China and ASEAN) but with 11 signatures (China and 10 ASEAN member states). For the ACFTA Framework Agreement, it uses the wording 'WE, the Heads of Government/State of Brunei Darussalam, the Kingdom of Cambodia, the Republic of Indonesia, the Lao People's Democratic Republic ("Lao PDR"), Malaysia, the Union of Myanmar, the Republic of the Philippines, the Republic of Singapore, the Kingdom of Thailand and the Socialist Republic of Viet Nam, Member States of the Association of South East Asian Nations (collectively, "ASEAN" or "ASEAN Member States", or individually, "ASEAN Member State"), and the People's Republic of China ("China")' and was signed respectively by them. It is not like a treaty concluded between China and an international organisation (e.g. the Shanghai Cooperation Organisation) or a multilateral treaty to which China accedes (e.g. the UN Convention on the Law of the Sea). In that sense, the ACFTA Framework Agreement can be regarded as a new form of international treaties. Ten ASEAN countries agreed to sign the Framework Agreement under the name of ASEAN, which indicated that they were determined to fulfil their treaty obligation collectively. Otherwise, there is no point to sign such an agreement and respective bilateral agreements between China and individual ASEAN states would suffice. Similar formality is used for other agreements (such as the China–ASEAN Agreement on Trade in Goods) signed by respective governments at the ministerial level. It is interesting to note that protocols which amend existing agreements even signed at the state level are concluded at the ministerial level, but the amendments can overtake the relevant existing provisions of the agreements. For example, the Protocol to Amend the Framework Agreement on Comprehensive Economic Cooperation between the Association of Southeast Asia and the People's Republic of China,[61] signed at the vice-ministerial level in 2003, revised several key articles of the ACFTA Framework Agreement regarding the Early Harvest Program as well as rules of origin.

Nevertheless, this new form seems to be endorsed only for important and general agreements between ASEAN and China. For agreements on very specific matters, the ASEAN member states allow the secretary-general of ASEAN to ink the agreement on their behalf. For example, the MOU on Strengthening Sanitary and Phytosanitary Cooperation signed in November 2007 uses the wording 'the Governments of the Member Countries of the Association of Southeast Asian Nations (ASEAN) and the Government of the People's Republic of China' at the beginning of the document and it is signed by the secretary-general of ASEAN and the Chinese Minister of the General Administration of Quality Supervision, Inspection and Quarantine.[62]

While some agreements between ASEAN and China use non-legal titles such as 'plan of action', they are in legal language and implementable in the legal sense. This can be seen through the Plan of Action to Implement the Beijing Declaration on ASEAN–China ICT Cooperative Partnership for Common Development signed by the Chinese Foreign Minister and the secretary-general of ASEAN in January 2007.[63]

It is to be noted that the implementation of all agreements, whether signed between China and respective ASEAN members under the name of ASEAN or between China and the ASEAN secretary-general, relies largely on individual ASEAN member states in addition to their collective commitment. Only in this sense, these agreements can be seen as bilateral agreements between China and any of these states, though signed collectively through ASEAN. In other aspects, they are clearly different from bilateral agreements signed between China and a particular ASEAN member state. However, China may get into some potential trouble in the implementation of the economic agreements signed between China and ASEAN since it has 'to pursue every ASEAN member to enforce the trade privileges accorded to it' while ASEAN gives no 'legal assistance by commanding the individual country concerned to perform its obligations'.[64]

Conclusion

There is no doubt that international law plays an indispensable part in the China–ASEAN relations.[65] The legal framework provides the guarantee for the smooth and proactive development of these relations.

There is still room for improvement in the legal framework of the China–ASEAN relations. For example, many documents adopted between China and ASEAN are political ones belonging to the category of 'soft law'[66] such as the 2002 Declaration on the Conduct of the Parties in the South China Sea. Soft-law documents without legal binding force are more difficult to be enforced and that is why there are frequent incidents in the South China Sea after the adoption of the 2002 Declaration. Clearly there is a need to increase the number of hard-law documents so as to effectively govern the China–ASEAN relations. Fortunately in the latest developments between the two sides, more hard-law documents have come into being. In 2007 alone, the two sides signed the Agreement on Trade in Services, the MOU on Agricultural Cooperation, the Second Protocol to Amend the ACFTA, the Protocol to Amend the Agreement on Trade in Goods and the MOU on Strengthening Sanitary and Phytosanitary Cooperation. However, one piece argues that China uses international agreements with ASEAN to break barriers to the fulfilment of its aspiration as a leader.[67] If this were the case, the ASEAN member states would be wary of China's insincere intention to sign international agreements since they do not like China to dominantly direct the course of the bilateral relationship of the two sides and play the leading role. This can be seen in the ASEAN Charter which provides that ASEAN should be the primary driving force for any regional arrangements that it initiates and maintain its centrality in regional cooperation and community building.[68] In fact, being small countries as compared to China, ASEAN states find it much easier to cooperate with China under legally binding agreements which can guarantee their rights and interests more than any pure political promise.

The effectiveness of the legal documents signed between China and ASEAN rely on the one hand on the efforts exerted by both sides and on the other on the effectiveness of the operations of ASEAN itself. Since ASEAN is still a weak organisation without enforcement mechanisms, despite the existence of the ASEAN Charter, such weakness would adversely affect the smooth implementation of the ASEAN–China agreements. Doubts still remain on whether ASEAN will become a 'rules-based organization' based on the ASEAN Charter because 'there is no assurance that ASEAN compliance with its rules will be any better than its practice during the preceding 40 years when only 30 per cent of ASEAN agreements were implemented'.[69] Furthermore, the division of the ASEAN members based on their economic conditions and different treatments provided by relevant documents also affects the effective implementation of these agreements.

In a word, it is to be noted that while more political documents are turned into legal documents so as to consolidate the legal framework of the China–ASEAN relations, ASEAN itself has to build up its own legal capacity with necessary implementation and enforcement measures.

Notes

1. 'Joint Statement of ASEAN–China Commemorative Summit: Towards an Enhanced ASEAN–China Strategic Partnership', 30 October 2006, available at *http://www.aseansec.org/China-Com-Summit.Doc* (accessed 20 May 2008).
2. As Article 4 of the UN Charter provides, UN membership is open to those nations which accept the obligations contained in the Charter and are able and willing to carry out these obligations.
3. Article 2 of the UN Charter. Text is available at *http://www.un.org/aboutun/charter/index.html* (accessed 17 June 2008).
4. Article 103 of the UN Charter.
5. See Article 1 of the ASEAN–UN MOU, done on 27 September 2007. Text is available at *http://www.aseansec.org/4984.htm* (accessed 17 June 2008).
6. See Article 2 of the TAC. Text is available at *http://www.aseansec.org/1217.htm* (accessed 17 June 2008).
7. See 'Joint Statement of the Meeting of Heads of State/Government of the Member States of ASEAN and the President of the People's Republic of China', Kuala Lumpur, Malaysia, 16 December 1997. Text is available at *http://www.aseansec.org/5225.htm* (accessed 4 July 2008).
8. Article 2 of the ASEAN Charter. Text is available at *http://www.aseansec.org/21054.htm* (accessed 13 June 2008).
9. Wen Jiabao, 'Carrying Forward the Five Principles of Peaceful Coexistence in the Promotion of Peace and Development', Speech at the Rally Commemorating the 50th Anniversary of the Five Principles of Peaceful Coexistence, 28 June 2004, available at *http://www.fmprc.gov.cn/eng/topics/seminaronfiveprinciples/t140777.htm* (accessed 17 June 2008).

10. Amitav Acharya, 'Bandung's 1955 Asia-Africa Conference and Indonesia', *Jakarta Post*, 18 April 2005, available at *http://www.indonesia-ottawa.org/information/details.php?type=news_copy&id=820* (accessed 4 July 2008).
11. See Article 74 of the UN Charter.
12. Franz Xaver Perrez, *Cooperative Sovereignty: From Independence to Interdependence in the Structure of International Environmental Law* (The Hague: Kluwer Law International, 2000), p. 260.
13. See Article 33 (1) of the UN Charter.
14. Rodolfo C. Severino, 'Framing the ASEAN Charter: An ISEAS Perspective', in Rodolfo C. Severino (comp.), *Framing the ASEAN Charter: An ISEAS Perspective* (Singapore: Institute of Southeast Asian Studies, 2005), p. 4.
15. Zhang Yunlin, 'The Valuable ASEAN Way', *People's Daily* (in Chinese), 8 August 2007, p. 3.
16. Zhang Yunlin, ibid.
17. At that time, Brunei was still a British colony. Burma and Cambodia turned down the invitation from the ASEAN's founders to join it in the making. See Rodolfo C. Severino, 'ASEAN Beyond Forty: Towards Political and Economic Integration', *Contemporary Southeast Asia*, vol. 29 (3), 2007, p. 408.
18. Severino, ibid., 413–14.
19. See the ASEAN Declaration, adopted on 8 August 1976, available at *http://www.aseansec.org/1212.htm* (accessed 11 June 2008).
20. See the ASEAN Declaration, ibid.
21. See the ASEAN Declaration, ibid.
22. See Articles 1–2 of the Agreement. Text is available at *http://www.aseansec.org/1265.htm* (accessed 11 June 2008).
23. See Chen Huiping, 'China-ASEAN FTA: An Investment Perspective', in John Wong, Zou Keyuan and Zeng Huaqun (eds.), *China–ASEAN Relations: Economic and Legal Dimensions* (Singapore: World Scientific, 2006), p. 144.
24. Rodolfo C. Severino, supra note 14, p. 6.
25. Locknie Hsu, 'Towards an ASEAN Charter: Some Thoughts from the Legal Perspective', in Rodolfo C. Severino (comp.), ibid., p. 47.
26. Jiangyu Wang, 'The International Legal Personality of ASEAN and the Legal Nature of the China-ASEAN FTA', in John Wong, Zou Keyuan and Zeng Huaqun (eds.), supra note 23, pp. 123–24.
27. Simon Chesterman, 'Does ASEAN Exist? The Association of Southeast Asian Nations as an International Legal Person', p. 4, available at *http://papers.ssrn.com/sol3/papers.cfm?abstract_id=1113612* (accessed 11 June 2008).
28. Chesterman, ibid., pp. 6–10.
29. Ian Brownlie, *Principles of Public International Law*, 5th ed. (Oxford: Clarendon Press, 1998), pp. 679–80.
30. See Article 104 of the UN Charter.
31. International Court of Justice, *Reports of Judgments, Advisory Opinions and Orders: Reparation for Injuries Suffered in the Service of the United Nations. Advisory Opinion of April 11th, 1949*, p. 179, available at *http://www.icj-cij.org/docket/files/4/1835.pdf* (accessed 24 June 2008).

32. ICJ, ibid.
33. ICJ, ibid., p. 185.
34. Vienna Convention on the Law of Treaties between States and International Organizations or between International Organizations, done at Vienna, 21 March 1986, available at *http://untreaty.un.org/ilc/texts/instruments/english/conventions/1_2_1986.pdf* (accessed 11 June 2008).
35. Article 3 of the MOU on Agricultural Cooperation, done on 2 November 2002; text is available at *http://www.aseansec.org/13214.htm* (accessed 5 July 2008).
36. Rodolfo C. Severino, *Southeast Asia in Search of an ASEAN Community: Insights from the Former ASEAN Secretary-General* (Singapore: Institute of Southeast Asian Studies, 2006), p. 249.
37. See the Vientiane Action Programme, p. 4. The document is available at *http://www.aseansec.org/16474.htm* (accessed 24 June 2008).
38. Text is available at *http://www.aseansec.org/18030.htm* (accessed 24 June 2008).
39. See Cebu Declaration on the Blueprint of the ASEAN Charter, 13 January 2007, available at *http://www.aseansec.org/19257.htm* (accessed 11 June 2008).
40. See Singapore Declaration on the ASEAN Charter, 20 November 2007, available at *http://www.aseansec.org/21233.htm* (accessed 13 June 2008).
41. See Articles 1 and 2 of the ASEAN Charter.
42. See Article 5 of the ASEAN Charter.
43. According to the Statement on the ASEAN Charter, done on 21 July 2008, it is scheduled to be established by 1 January 2009. The text of the Statement is available at *http://www.aseansec.org/21796.htm* (accessed 22 July 2008).
44. See Article 20 of the ASEAN Charter.
45. Working Group for an ASEAN Human Rights Mechanism, 'Synopsis of a Policy Initiative for the Establishment of an ASEAN Human Rights Mechanism', 17 April 1998, Bangkok, annexed to Miriam Defensor Santiago, *International Law: With Philippine Cases and Materials and ASEAN Instruments* (Quezon, Philippines: Central Professional Books, Inc., 1999), pp. 387–89.
46. 'Representatives from ASEAN members discuss on the item of a human rights body', *Lianhe Zaobao* (in Chinese) (Singapore), 13 June 2008, available at *http://www.zaobao.com.sg/sp/sp080613_512.shtml* (accessed 13 June 2008).
47. See Statement on the ASEAN Charter, available at *http://www.aseansec.org/21796.htm* (accessed 22 July 2008).
48. See Article 3 of the ASEAN Charter.
49. See Articles 17–19 of the ASEAN Charter. It is noted that immunities and privileges granted to permanent representatives and officials on ASEAN duties should be governed by the 1961 Vienna Convention on Diplomatic Relations or in accordance with national laws of ASEAN member States concerned.
50. Article 41(7) of the ASEAN Charter.
51. Article 46 of the ASEAN Charter.
52. See Article 52 of the ASEAN Charter.

53. See Article 6 of the ASEAN Charter.
54. See Singapore Declaration on the ASEAN Charter, 20 November 2007, available at *http://www.aseansec.org/21233.htm* (accessed 13 June 2008).
55. Rodolfo C. Severino, supra note 14, p. 3.
56. Zeng Lingliang, 'ASEAN-China Relations: An International Law Perspective', in John Wong, Zou Keyuan and Zeng Huaqun (eds.), supra note 23, p. 35.
57. Zeng Huaqun, 'WTO Rules and China-ASEAN FTA Agreement', in John Wong, Zou Keyuan and Zeng Huaqun (eds.), supra note 23, p. 96.
58. Jiangyu Wang, supra note 26, pp. 126–27.
59. Zeng Huaqun, supra note 55, p. 96.
60. Jiangyu Wang, supra note 26, pp. 126–27.
61. Text is available at *http://www.aseansec.org/15157.htm* (accessed 4 July 2008).
62. Text is available at *http://www.aseansec.org/21054.htm* (accessed 24 June 2008).
63. Text is available at *http://www.aseansec.org/19283.htm* (accessed 24 June 2008).
64. Jiangyu Wang, supra note 26, p. 131.
65. Zeng Lingliang, supra note 56, p. 33.
66. Soft law refers to those documents without legally binding force, such as UN General Assembly resolutions, codes of conducts, etc. However, sometimes non-treaty agreements are more flexible and easier to reach between the parties concerned. For reference, see Hartmut Hillgenburg, 'A Fresh Look at Soft Law', *European Journal of International Law*, vol. 10 (3), 1999, pp. 499–515.
67. Juliana W. Chen, 'Achieving Supreme Excellence: How China is Using Agreements with ASEAN to Overcome Obstacles to Its Leadership in Asian Regional Economic Integration', *Chicago Journal of International Law*, vol. 7 (2), 2006–2007, pp. 655–74.
68. Article 41 (3) of the ASEAN Charter.
69. Barry Desker, 'Is the ASEAN Charter Necessary'? *RSIS Commentaries 77/2008* (S. Rajaratnam School of International Studies, Nanyang Technological University, Singapore), 17 July 2008, p. 2.

4

Law and economic integration

Globalisation has fostered the need for regional integration across the world, particularly in the economic sector. Regional integration in Europe was initiated with the establishment of the European Coal and Steel Community in the 1950s. Gradually, the European Economic Community has evolved into a European Union (officially established in 1993, based on the Maastricht Treaty), consisting of 27 member states (as of 2007), which aims to achieve cooperation in various fields among its member states. On the other side of the Atlantic, the North American Free Trade Area (NAFTA) has been functioning well since its inception in 1994. Regional mechanisms for economic integration are also emerging in other parts of the world including Latin American and African regions.

Regional economic integration in East Asia comparatively lags behind. Although a regional mechanism called the Asian Pacific Economic Cooperation (APEC)[1] was established in 1989 to work towards building closer economic ties among its members, its functioning has been restricted to that of an economic forum. It has therefore become imperative that Asian countries follow the practices successfully adopted by other regions in terms of regional economic integration.

The Association of Southeast Asian Nations (ASEAN) took the first step in this direction in the East Asian region. One of the original purposes of establishing ASEAN was to 'accelerate economic growth . . . through joint endeavours in the spirit of equality and partnership' for the ASEAN region.[2] In order to realise this purpose, the ASEAN members have been exerting efforts in working towards the integration of regional economy. On 28 January 1992, six original ASEAN members (i.e. Brunei, Indonesia, Malaysia, the Philippines, Singapore and Thailand, also known as ASEAN 6) signed the Framework Agreement on Enhancing ASEAN Economic Cooperation (ASEAN Framework Agreement) in Singapore.[3] In the agreement, the members agreed to establish and participate in the ASEAN Free Trade Area (AFTA) within 15 years (Article 2.A.1). Simultaneously, the Agreement on the Common Effective Preferential Tariff (CEPT) Scheme for the AFTA was also signed.[4] According to the ASEAN Framework Agreement, the CEPT scheme should be the main mechanism for AFTA (Article 2.A.2). Just after the agreement was signed, the ASEAN Meeting of Economic Ministers was held in September 1994 wherein it was decided to move up the schedule for the establishment of AFTA: the period of 15 years provided for in the ASEAN Framework Agreement was shortened to 10 years, that is, AFTA was to be formed in 2003. The Sixth ASEAN Summit held in December 1998 further moved up the schedule so as to establish AFTA in 2002 for the original ASEAN 6; the schedule was different for newer members: for Vietnam in 2003, Laos and Myanmar in 2005 and Cambodia in 2007. It was also decided that the tariff rates levied on traded products in the ASEAN region would be reduced to 5 per cent or less. The Vientiane Action Programme adopted in 2004 further commits to remove barriers to the free flow of goods, services and skilled labour, allow freer flow of capital by 2010 and eliminate tariffs on products by 2010 for ASEAN 6 and by 2015 for four newer members.[5] In addition, the ASEAN Framework Agreement lists other economic areas of cooperation such as food and agriculture, banking and finance, industry and energy, transportation and communications.

Economic integration centred on the ASEAN Framework Agreement can be seen as an economic and legal basis for the establishment of the China–ASEAN FTA. In fact, the ASEAN Framework Agreement was later used for the negotiation of the agreement on the ASEAN–China comprehensive economic cooperation and other related agreements signed between ASEAN and China. In 2001, the two sides decided to establish such an FTA within 10 years and formulated a bilateral trade negotiation committee in the following year to work out ways to achieve cooperation.

The development of trade relations between ASEAN countries and China has been fast and steady. As of the end of 2006, China–ASEAN bilateral trade and investment volume reached US$160.8 billion, 1.9 times of that in 2002.[6] The ASEAN has become the fifth-largest trading partner of China.[7] Gao Hucheng, the Chinese vice-minister of commerce, expressed in September 2007 that the China–ASEAN bilateral trade and investment volumes increased rapidly and exceeded US$200 billion, two years prior to the schedule.[8]

The Framework Agreement on Comprehensive Economic Cooperation between ASEAN and the People's Republic of China (the ACFTA Framework Agreement) in Phnom Penh on 5 November 2002 stands as a culmination of the China–ASEAN economic cooperation. It has laid the legal foundation for the two sides to launch comprehensive cooperative activities towards regional economic integration in East Asia.

Legal framework

In addition to the East Asian response to the economic regionalisation throughout the world, the ACFTA Framework Agreement was concluded in line with relevant international laws, in particular, laws deriving from the practices of the World Trade Organisation (WTO) and other international economic organisations which have most ASEAN states and China as their members (see Table 4.1). As recommended by the

Table 4.1 **East Asian Accession to the WTO (as of July 2008).**

Territory	Date
Brunei Darussalam	1 January 1995
Cambodia	13 October 2004
China	11 December 2001
Hong Kong, China	1 January 1995
Indonesia	1 January 1995
Japan	1 January 1995
Laos	in progress
Macao, China	1 January 1995
Malaysia	1 January 1995
Mongolia	29 January 1997
Myanmar	1 January 1995
Philippines	1 January 1995
Republic of Korea	1 January 1995
Singapore	1 January 1995
Chinese Taipei	1 January 2002
Thailand	1 January 1995
Vietnam	11 January 2007

Source: Compiled by the author based on *http://www.wto.org/english/thewto_e/whatis_e/tif_e/org6_e.htm* (accessed 19 July 2008).

ASEAN–China Expert Group on ASEAN–China economic relations, 'ASEAN and China should adopt a comprehensive and forward-looking framework of economic cooperation to build upon the momentum of China's accession to the WTO, reduce and eliminate existing barriers to trade and investments, and move towards greater economic integration in the long-run.'[9]

The WTO is a global trade organisation that has a set of detailed rules and regulations governing world trade, activities related to trade and settlement of trade disputes. As of the end of June 2008, it had 152 members.[10] The WTO law embodies a number of legal principles relating to world trade activities that have legal implications for regional economic arrangements, such as the principle of non-discrimination (with two key elements: (1) providing the trading partners with the most-favoured nation (MFN) status and (2) providing equal and national treatment in terms of their products, services and nationals); free trade through negotiations by lowering trade barriers; predictability through binding and transparency; promoting fair competition and encouraging economic development and reform.[11] Moreover, as long as the WTO principles and norms are followed, the WTO allows its members to conclude regional free trade agreements. Accordingly, the purpose of an FTA is that 'a customs union or a free-trade area should be to facilitate trade between the constituent territories and not to raise barriers to the trade of other contracting parties with such territories.'[12] As one Chinese paper describing the background of the ACFTA asserts, China needed a regional economic organisation to exert its influence over the formulation of international economic rules after its entry into the WTO.[13]

Based on the WTO norms and rules, China and the ASEAN member states concluded the ACFTA Framework Agreement as mentioned above,[14] which provides a comprehensive legal framework for the economic integration between China and the ASEAN members. The ACFTA Framework Agreement lists four main objectives: (a) to strengthen and enhance economic, trade and investment co-operation between the parties; (b) to liberalise progressively and promote trade in goods and services as well as create a transparent, liberal and facilitative investment regime; (c) to explore new areas and develop appropriate measures for closer economic cooperation between the parties and (d) to facilitate the more effective economic integration of the newer ASEAN member states and bridge the development gap among the parties.[15] Both sides agreed to establish an ACFTA within 10 years, and to progressively eliminate tariffs and non-tariff barriers to trade in goods, to progressively liberalise trade in services with substantial sectoral coverage, and to establish an open and competitive investment regime (Article 2). Besides the above objectives, the agreement designs a programme of early harvest for products designated by the agreement to enjoy zero per cent tariff rates before the establishment of the ACFTA.[16] This scheme is actually a concession made by China to ASEAN members. In addition, the two sides also agreed to strengthen their cooperation in priority areas such as agriculture, information and communications technology, human resources development, investment, and Mekong River basin development, and explore other areas including banking, finance, tourism, industrial cooperation, transport, telecommunications, intellectual property rights, small and medium enterprises (SMEs), environment, bio-technology, fishery, forestry and forestry products, mining, energy and sub-regional development.[17] The agreement came into force on 1 July 2003 and, as agreed, China rendered MFN status to all ASEAN member states.

The ACFTA Framework Agreement is the cornerstone of China–ASEAN relations on the basis of which later developments will follow. One of the weaknesses of the international laws of China–ASEAN relations is the lack of sufficient 'hard law' components in the form of treaties.[18] The conclusion of the Framework Agreement has significantly changed the situation of 'soft law' dominance in the China–ASEAN relations. From an international law perspective, the signing of this agreement was an epic-making event in the history of China–ASEAN relations since it is 'the first formal treaty that regulates the mutual relations of the two parties.'[19] Some scholars tend to study the Framework Agreement under the legal context of the regional trade agreements (RTAs).[20] However, the Framework Agreement covers contents not only relating to RTAs, but also relating to other matters in the economic domain such as investment, agriculture, etc. Its coverage is thus much wider than RTAs, and limiting it only to the context of RTAs for examination would narrow its significance as an agreement of comprehensive economic cooperation. In the interest of ASEAN, ACFTA 'offers an effective means for smaller ASEAN states to overcome their disadvantage of smallness by pooling resources and combining markets'.[21] It is to be noted that at the time of signing of the ACFTA Framework Agreement, only seven of the ASEAN member states were WTO members, but China's concessions were rendered to all ASEAN member states regardless of their WTO status. However, the Framework Agreement treats ASEAN states differently in accordance with their level of economic development. That is why there are specific wordings in the agreement such as 'ASEAN 6', 'non-WTO members' and 'newer ASEAN member states'. For the linkage of the Framework Agreement to the WTO regulations, it is commented that it is unique in the history of RTAs.[22]

Since the signing of the Framework Agreement, the two sides have held regular meetings and negotiations to reach the goals set forth in the agreement. The agreement has also been amended with the passage of time. The first protocol was signed in 2003 that amended the provisions of the Framework Agreement regarding the Early Harvest Programme.[23] On 8 December 2006, the Second Protocol to amend the Framework Agreement on Comprehensive Economic Co-operation between the Association of Southeast Asian Nations and the People's Republic of China was adopted[24] to amend Annex 2 of the Framework Agreement regarding products lists.

Economic dispute settlement mechanism

In pursuance of the requirement set forth in the ACFTA Framework Agreement regarding the establishment of a dispute settlement mechanism for comprehensive economic cooperation between the two sides,[25] China and ASEAN member states signed the Agreement on Dispute Settlement Mechanism of the Framework Agreement on Comprehensive Economic Co-Operation between the Association of Southeast Asian Nations and the People's Republic of China (the Dispute Settlement Mechanism Agreement) on 29 November 2004.[26] It is a very important step to ensure the effectiveness of the implementation of the Framework Agreement as well as other agreements within the framework of China–ASEAN comprehensive economic cooperation. As provided for in the Dispute Settlement Mechanism Agreement and other agreements such as the Trade in Goods Agreement and the Trade in Service Agreement (to be discussed in the following sections), any dispute arising from the application and implementation of these agreements and their annexes and amended protocols should go through any of the mechanisms provided for in the agreement, which designates three means of dispute settlement in international law as its working mechanisms: consultation, conciliation or mediation, and arbitration. The first two means are political while the third is legal. The difference between them lies in that the ruling from arbitration carries a legal binding force.

The complaining party and the party complained against should make every effort to reach a mutually satisfactory resolution of their dispute through consultation. When a request for consultation is made, the party complained against should reply to the request within seven days after the date of its receipt and should enter into consultations in good faith within a period of not more than 30 days after the date of receipt of the request. If the party complained against does not respond within the aforesaid seven days, or does not enter into consultation within the aforesaid 30 days, then the complaining party may directly proceed to request for the appointment of an arbitral tribunal (Article 4.3). In cases of urgency (e.g. perishable goods), the time limit for consultation can be shortened to 10 days, and if there is no response from the party complained against within a period of 20 days, the complaining party can institute the arbitral procedure (Article 4.7). In addition, the parties to a dispute can choose conciliation or mediation provided by a third party for dispute resolution.[27]

The most important part of the agreement is the establishment of the arbitral procedures. If the consultations do not solve the dispute within the prescribed time limit, the complaining party may make a written request to the party complained against to appoint an arbitral tribunal. The parties to the dispute can appoint one single arbitral tribunal which 'shall organise its examination and present its findings to all the parties to the dispute in such manner that the rights which they would have enjoyed had separate arbitral tribunals examined the same matter are in no way impaired'.[28] If more than one arbitral tribunal is appointed to examine the same matter, the parties concerned should appoint, to the greatest extent possible, the same arbitrators to serve on each of the separate arbitral tribunals (Article 6.5). As for the composition of the arbitral tribunal, it should generally have three members (one appointed by the complaining party, another by the party complained against and the third jointly agreed upon by both parties and who should serve as chair and not become a national of either of the disputant parties).[29] If any party to the dispute fails to appoint an arbitrator within the prescribed time limit, 'the arbitrator appointed by the other party to the dispute shall act as the sole arbitrator of the tribunal'.[30] According to the agreement, the arbitral tribunal is required to 'make an objective assessment of the dispute before it, including an examination of the facts of the case and applicability of and conformity with the Framework Agreement'. 'Where the arbitral tribunal concludes that a measure is inconsistent with a provision of the Framework Agreement, it shall recommend that the party complained against bring the measure into conformity with that provision' (Article 8.1). As for its other functions, the arbitral tribunal should (1) consult regularly with the parties to the dispute and provide adequate opportunities for the development of a mutually satisfactory resolution; (2) take its decision in accordance with the Framework Agreement and the rules of international law applicable between the parties to the dispute and (3) set out, in its decision, its findings of law and facts, together with the reasons thereof.[31] The decision of the arbitral tribunal is final and binding on the parties to the dispute.

The arbitral tribunal, after consulting the parties to the dispute, should, 'as soon as practical and possible within 15 days after the composition of the arbitral tribunal, fix the timetable for the arbitral process' (Article 9.1). The arbitral tribunal should release its final report within 120 days from the date of its composition, and in no case should the period from the composition of an arbitral tribunal to the release of the report to parties to the dispute exceed 180 days (Article 9.8). When the parties to a dispute find a solution to their dispute, they can agree to terminate the proceedings of the arbitral tribunal.[32] The party complained against should implement the recommendations and rulings of the arbitral tribunal within 30 days of the release of the final report. The complaining party can take temporary measures such as compensation and suspension of concessions or benefits if the recommendations and rulings of the arbitral tribunal are not implemented within a reasonable period of time.[33] Such measures should be repealed when they are found to be inconsistent with the Framework Agreement or the recommendations and rulings of the arbitral tribunal have been implemented (Article 13.6).

As agreed by the signing parties, the Dispute Settlement Mechanism Agreement came into force on 1 January 2005. The signing of this agreement is hailed as having 'far-reaching significance' even beyond the China–ASEAN relations as it is 'a sign of the changing attitude of the Chinese government towards international dispute settlement methods', and it is the first time that China 'had signed such a special and detailed agreement with other states or international organisations'.[34]

Although the Dispute Settlement Mechanism Agreement was significant in the development of the China-ASEAN relations given the fact that China has always been reluctant to invoke judicial means for dispute settlement, it has its limitations. First, it is limited to economic disputes within the realm of the Framework Agreement. Moreover, as is expressly mentioned in Annex 1 to the Dispute Settlement Mechanism Agreement, non-violation disputes are not permitted under it, even if they are economic in nature. Second, though there is a stipulation on transparency regarding the flow of information between the disputant parties, the arbitral tribunal keeps all the sessions and documents confidential, thus making it vulnerable to pressures from the disputant parties and raising the doubts about the impartiality of the tribunal. Third, though the decision of the tribunal is final, the implementation provisions are not strong enough to force the failing party to implement the recommendations and rulings of the tribunal. The retaliation measures taken by the complaining party are only temporary and should be discontinued when found inconsistent with the Framework Agreement. In case such temporary measures are not discontinued, it is likely that a new dispute arises among the parties to the ACFTA Framework Agreement. It is obvious that the relevant provisions regarding the implementation of the arbitral awards need to be improved in future. It remains to be seen whether the dispute settlement mechanisms established in the agreement can function well in practice, and by judging the attitudes and policies of China and most of the ASEAN countries towards dispute settlement, it is reasonably assumed that most, if not all, of the potential disputes will be solved through consultations.

Trade

Trade is the main part of the overall FTA arrangement. According to the ACFTA Framework Agreement, trade contains two separate but associated parts: trade in goods and trade in services. So far as of 2008, ASEAN and China have reached on two agreements governing their bilateral trades: the Agreement on Trade in Services of the Framework Agreement on Comprehensive Economic Co-operation between the Association of Southeast Asian Nations and the People's Republic of China (Trade in Service Agreement)[35] that was signed on 14 January 2007 and the Agreement on Trade in Goods of the Framework Agreement on Comprehensive Economic Co-operation between the Association of Southeast Asian Nations and the People's Republic of China (the Trade in Goods Agreement)[36] that was signed on 29 November 2004.

The Trade in Goods Agreement

The Trade in Goods Agreement follows the general provisions stipulated in the Framework Agreement by further detailing them.[37] It clearly links itself to the WTO regulations: it provides that Article III regarding national treatment on internal taxation and regulation (see Article 2) and Article X governing transparency (see Article 4) of the 1994 General Agreement on Tariffs and Trade (GATT 1994), form an integral part of the agreement. Furthermore, Article 7 prescribes WTO disciplines on 'among others, non-tariff measures, technical barriers to trade, sanitary and phytosanitary measures, subsidies and countervailing measures, anti-dumping measures and intellectual property rights', and provides that '[t]he provisions of the WTO Multilateral Agreements on Trade in Goods, which are not specifically mentioned in or modified by this

Agreement, shall apply, *mutatis mutandis,* to this Agreement unless the context otherwise requires'. Qualitative restrictions should not be imposed unless otherwise permitted under the WTO disciplines.[38] The Understanding on Balance-of-Payments provisions of the GATT 1994 are also mentioned regarding the adoption of measures to safeguard the balance of payments (Article 11). Due to the fact that at the time of signing the agreement, not all ASEAN member states were WTO members, the agreement set forth different treatments for WTO and non-WTO members regarding the MFN tariff rates applicable as of 1 July 2003.

The most important legal arrangement of the agreement is the tariff reduction and elimination as is stipulated in Article 3:

> 1. The tariff reduction or elimination programme of the Parties shall require the applied MFN tariff rates on listed tariff lines to be gradually reduced and where applicable, eliminated, in accordance with this Article.
>
> 2. The tariff lines which are subject to the tariff reduction or elimination programme under this Agreement shall include all tariff lines not covered by the Early Harvest Programme under Article 6 of the Framework Agreement, and such tariff lines shall be categorised for tariff reduction and elimination as follows:
>
> (a) *Normal Track*: Tariff lines placed in the Normal Track by each Party on its own accord shall have their respective applied MFN tariff rates gradually reduced and eliminated in accordance with the modalities set out in Annex 1 of this Agreement with the objective of achieving the targets prescribed in the thresholds therein.
>
> (b) *Sensitive Track*: Tariff lines placed in the Sensitive Track by each Party on its own accord shall have their respective applied MFN tariff rates reduced or eliminated in accordance with the modalities set out in **Annex 2** of this Agreement.
>
> 3. Subject to **Annex 1** and **Annex 2** of this Agreement, all commitments undertaken by each Party under this Article shall be applied to all the other Parties.

It is to be noted that these provisions were first stipulated in the Framework Agreement and then reaffirmed in the Trade in Goods Agreement with minor changes.

The agreement contains a complicated set of safeguard measures in Article 9 so as to allow its contracting parities to retain some corresponding rights and obligations either under Article XIX of GATT 1994 or the WTO Agreement on Safeguards or ACFTA safeguard measures. Accordingly, a party has the right to initiate an ACFTA measure on a product within the transition period for that product.[39] The agreement provides 'If an ACFTA safeguard measure is taken, a Party taking such a measure may increase the tariff rate applicable to the product concerned to the WTO MFN tariff rate applied to such product at the time when the measure is taken.'[40] The provision establishes a link between an ACFTA measure and safeguard measures under the WTO Agreement on Safeguards as it provides that 'in applying ACFTA safeguard measures, the Parties shall adopt the rules for the application of safeguard measures as provided under the WTO Agreement on Safeguards, with the exception of the quantitative restriction measures set out in Article 5, and Articles 9, 13 and 14 of the WTO Agreement on Safeguards',[41] and 'when applying ACFTA safeguard measures, a Party shall not have simultaneous recourse to the WTO safeguard measures.'[42] However, an ACFTA safeguard measure has its limitation as it cannot 'be applied against a product originating in a Party, so long as its share of imports of the product concerned in the importing Party does not exceed 3% of the total imports from the Parties',[43] and parties which feel they have been unfairly treated can seek compensation through special offices of the body established under the agreement.[44] In addition, the agreement set forth 'general exceptions' and 'security exceptions' for the contracting parties.[45]

Apart from main stipulations relating to trade in goods, the agreement also deals with other matters such as the recognition of China's market economy status (Article 14), institutional arrangements (Article 16) and dispute settlement (Article 21). As prescribed in the agreement, the Trade in Goods Agreement came into force on 1 January 2005.[46]

Like the Framework Agreement, the Trade in Goods Agreement is also subject to amendment when needed. On 8 December 2006, the Protocol to Amend the Agreement on Trade in Goods of the Framework Agreement on Comprehensive Economic Co-operation between the Association of Southeast Asian Nations and the People's Republic of China was adopted,[47] and it revised Annexes 1 and 2 to the Trade in Goods Agreement.

It seems that the Trade in Goods Agreement has been implemented well. According to recent statistics, in late 2007, the tariffs for the ASEAN products imported to China had been reduced to 5.8 per cent, which is 4.1 per cent lower than the existing MFN rates, and by 2010 zero tariff will have been placed on more than 7000 ASEAN products, accounting for 93 per cent of the total ASEAN exports to China.[48]

The Trade in Service Agreement

The Trade in Service Agreement is the sister agreement of the Trade in Goods Agreement, but was concluded more than two years later in 2007. The structures of the two agreements are quite similar but govern different subject matters. Compared to trade in goods, trade in services is more complicated. This is one of the reasons that the Trade in Services Agreement was reached between China and ASEAN after the Trade in Goods Agreement.

Following the Framework Agreement,[49] this agreement defines 'trade in services' as 'the supply of a service (1) from the territory of a Party into the territory of any other Party ("cross-border"); (2) in the territory of a Party to the service consumer of any other Party ("consumption abroad"); (3) by a service supplier of a Party, through commercial presence in the territory of any other Party ("commercial presence"); (4) by a service supplier of a Party, through presence of natural persons of a Party in the territory of any other Party ("presence of natural persons").'[50] The agreement allies to measures by the parties effecting trade in services but excluding its application from 'services supplied in the exercise of governmental authority', and 'regulations or requirements governing the procurement by governmental agencies of services purchased for governmental purposes' (Article 2).

The important provisions on contracting parties' obligation are Articles 5 and 6 concerning 'domestic regulation' and 'recognition' respectively. According to Article 5, each contracting party has to ensure 'that all measures of general application affecting trade in services are administered in a reasonable, objective and impartial manner', and 'maintain or institute as soon as practicable judicial, arbitral or administrative tribunals or procedures which provide, at the request of an affected service supplier, for the prompt review of, and where justified, appropriate remedies for, administrative decisions affecting trade in services'. It further provides that:

> [w]here authorization is required for the supply of a service on which a specific commitment under this Agreement has been made, the competent authorities of each Party shall: a. in the case of an incomplete application, at the request of the applicant, identify all the additional information that is required to complete the application and provide the opportunity to remedy deficiencies within a reasonable timeframe; b. at the request of the applicant, provide without undue delay, information concerning the status of the application;

and c. if an application is terminated or denied, to the maximum extent possible, inform the applicant in writing and without delay the reasons for such action. The applicant will have the possibility of resubmitting, at its discretion, a new application.

Article 6 provides in detail that:

1. For the purposes of fulfilment of their respective standards or criteria for the authorisation, licensing or certification of service suppliers, each party may recognise the education or experience obtained, requirements met, or licenses or certifications granted in another party. Such recognition, which may be achieved through harmonisation or otherwise, may be based upon an agreement or arrangement between the parties or the relevant competent bodies or may be accorded autonomously.
2. Two or more parties may enter into, or encourage their relevant competent bodies to enter into, negotiations on recognition of qualification requirements, qualification procedures, licensing and/or registration procedures for the purposes of fulfilment of their respective standards or criteria for the authorisation, licensing or certification of service suppliers.
3. A party that is a party to an agreement or arrangement of the type referred to in paragraph 1 of this Article, whether existing or future, shall afford adequate opportunity for other interested parties to negotiate their accession to such an agreement or arrangement or to negotiate comparable ones with it. Where a party accords recognition autonomously, it shall afford adequate opportunity for any other party to demonstrate that education, experience, licenses or certifications obtained or requirements met in that other party's territory should be recognised.
4. A party shall not accord recognition in a manner which would constitute a means of discrimination between countries in the application of its standards or criteria for the authorisation, licensing or certification of services suppliers, or a disguised restriction on trade in services.

The agreement obliges contracting parties to ensure that 'any monopoly supplier of a service in its territory does not, in the supply of the monopoly service in the relevant market, act in a manner inconsistent with that Party's obligations under specific commitments' (Article 7.1). 'If any Party has reason to believe that a monopoly supplier of a service of any other Party is acting in a manner inconsistent with paragraph 1 or 2 of this Article, that Party may request the Party establishing, maintaining or authorising such supplier to provide specific information concerning the relevant operations' (Article 7.3). Related to this is the curbing of unfair business practices which may restrain competition and restrict trade in services.[51] Thus, safeguarding provisions are set forth in Article 9, requiring contracting parties to comply with Article X of the General Agreement on Trade in Services (GATS) based on the principle of non-discrimination when they conduct multilateral negotiations.

As for specific commitments, the agreement takes the approach of progressive liberalisation by determining packages of specific commitments step by step.[52] However, market access for the first package has been provided for in the agreement. According to Articles 18 and 19, equal treatment and national treatment should be given to service suppliers of the contracting parties, and the contracting parties should not maintain or adopt measures which would restrict the number of service suppliers and value of service transactions and assets.[53] In this respect, China has promised to make a single schedule of its specific commitments applicable to all the ASEAN members, while ASEAN member states can make their own individual schedules.[54]

Like the Trade in Goods Agreement, this agreement also links itself to relevant WTO agreements such as the GATS[55] and WTO norms and regulations regarding transparency (Article 3), disclosure of confidential information (Article 4), safeguards (Article 9), subsidies (Article 14) and WTO disciplines (Article 15). Likewise, the agreement also set the date of its entry into force, i.e. 1 July 2007.

Investment

Investment is one of the important and crucial matters in the development of the China-ASEAN FTA. Article 5 of the ACFTA Framework Agreement provides that:

> To promote investments and to create a liberal, facilitative, transparent and competitive investment regime, the Parties agree to: enter into negotiations in order to progressively liberalise the investment regime; strengthen co-operation in investment, facilitate investment and improve transparency of investment rules and regulations; and provide for the protection of investments.

As is commented, despite its generality and simplicity, 'it covers almost all issues an international investment agreement should cover'.[56]

Following the ACFTA Framework Agreement, the two sides commenced the negotiation on investment agreement in June 2003, and for that purpose the China–ASEAN Trade Negotiation Committee Working Group on Investment was established in pursuance of the relevant provision in the Framework Agreement. It was agreed that the Framework Agreement on ASEAN Investment Area[57] be used as a model for the negotiation of the ACFTA investment agreement.[58] The following principles and elements should be included: (1) definitions on terms such as 'investment' and 'investor'; (2) liberalisation; (3) protection, facilitation and promotion; (4) dispute settlement mechanism and (5) general provisions including safeguarding measures.[59] In comparison with other areas of economic cooperation listed in the Framework Agreement including trade in goods, trade in services, agriculture and transport, the investment issue has become the toughest one in the China–ASEAN negotiation. Though China has signed numerous bilateral investment agreements with other countries, this was the first time that China was engaged in negotiating a multilateral investment agreement with 10 countries in the name of ASEAN.[60] As reported, the negotiation on investment was originally scheduled for completion by the end of 2004, but due to the differences between the two sides, the negotiation is still going on. While ASEAN insisted on a deadline for the negotiation, China did not agree to it.[61] There are a number of difficulties to be tackled before the negotiation is complete. For China, the main obstacle lies in its current prematurity to accept a liberalised investment agreement with ASEAN. China expects the agreement to cover only investment protection and facilitation with broad principles; on the other hand, ASEAN expects to make a comprehensive agreement covering not only investment promotion and facilitation but also liberalisation so as to protect the ASEAN investment in China as well as to further open up the Chinese market for the ASEAN investors.[62] Despite difficulties and obstacles, the two sides will eventually reach the expected agreement by compromising their differences and interests. Gradual liberalisation may be accepted by China. As is rightly pointed out, 'the signing of the China–ASEAN investment agreement will help to form a unified position and perspective in the investment legal systems for developing countries and benefit them in future international investment agreements.'[63]

As reported, during 2002–7, foreign direct investment (FDI) to China remained on the rise: over US$50 billion in 2002 and US$63 billion in 2006; as of the end of 2006, Chinese enterprises had invested in more than 160 countries.[64] There is therefore a concern whether China would compete with the ASEAN countries for FDI. Some research findings demonstrate that this may not be the case since there is no clear evidence to show that China has squeezed the FDI inflow to ASEAN though some competition for FDI between China and ASEAN does exist.[65] Evidences presented by another paper showed that 'at least some of the pessimism regarding economic competition between ASEAN and China is misplaced.'[66] On the other hand, 'as Chinese enterprises emerge more competitive as a result of domestic restructuring, they could spearhead Chinese overseas investment in Southeast Asia, rather than diverting foreign investment from their ASEAN neighbors.'[67] For example, China has been the largest investor in Laos since 2007. In this sense, the investment agreement, once concluded, will produce a win-win result, benefiting both sides.

Agriculture

In the ACFTA Framework Agreement, the contracting parties have identified five priority sectors, including agriculture, as other areas of cooperation. For the purpose of realising what they pledged to commit in the agreement, ASEAN and China signed the Memorandum of Understanding on Agricultural Cooperation (Agriculture MOU) on 14 January 2007 in Cebu, the Philippines, to renew the old similar MOU signed in November 2002.[68] Accordingly, they have pledged to cooperate in agriculture and forestry, but subject to the compliance with laws and regulations of their respective countries (Article 1). The cooperative areas mainly include training courses in the fields of agriculture, fisheries and aquaculture, bio-technology application in agriculture, farm machinery, agro-industry, agricultural extension and livestock provided by China for the ASEAN member countries.[69] The two sides identified the possibility of cooperation in other areas 'such as advanced technology in agriculture, forestry, post-harvest technology, and food security' (Article 2). The MOU will remain for a period of 5 years from 2007 to 2011 and may be extended for additional periods as agreed by participants (Article 10). It is to be noted that cooperation in the field of agriculture between the two sides is still in the preliminary stage.

Pan-Beibu Gulf economic cooperation

The efforts of the ASEAN member states and China have resulted in the launch of the pan-Beibu Gulf (Gulf of Tonkin) economic cooperation. The first Beibu Gulf Rim Economic Cooperation Forum was held in

Nanning in July 2006, has been held annually since then. After several meetings and discussions on economic cooperation around the Gulf of Tonkin Rim under the auspice of the Guangxi Zhuang Autonomous Region, the Development Plan for Guangxi Beibu Gulf Economic Zone (2006–20) was officially approved by China's State Council in January 2008. The Beibu Gulf Economic Zone is defined for the China–ASEAN cooperation in areas of commodities interflow, commerce and trade, manufacturing and processing, and information communications. Geographically, the economic zone includes three coastal cities of the Beibu Gulf, that is, Beihai, Qingzhou and Fangchenggang, as well as Nanning, the capital city of Guangxi, with an area of 42,500 km^2 and a population of more than 12 million, becoming the largest multiparty cooperative zone in China.[70] Guangxi established the Beibu Gulf Economic Zone with the support of the annual China-ASEAN Expo (CAEXPO) convened in Nanning since 2004, which is a pragmatic endeavour to promote the construction of the ACFTA,[71] and also with the encouragement of the China–ASEAN Comprehensive Economic Cooperation Framework, which supports sub-regional cooperation between ASEAN and China. The Fourth CAEXPO held during 28–31 October 2007 attracted 182 international economic cooperative projects valued at US$6.15 billion and 138 domestic cooperative projects valued at RMB58.2 billion, 5 per cent up over the last CAEXPO.[72] Prominent government leaders who attended this event included Zeng Peiyan, vice premier of the State Council of China; Al-Muhtadee Billah, the prince of Brunei; Samdech Hun Sen, prime minister of Cambodia; Bouasone Buouphavanh, prime minister of Laos; Nguyen Tan Dung, prime minister of Vietnam and Ong Keng Yong, secretary general of ASEAN.[73]

The Beibu Gulf economic cooperation is basically a maritime economy including three layers: China–Vietnam cooperation centred in the Gulf of Tonkin, China–ASEAN sub-regional cooperation centred in the whole South China Sea and China–ASEAN cooperation under the 10+1 Framework. In addition, domestic cooperation within China centred in Guangxi can be well envisaged, and Guangxi can use this platform to attract funds from other places in China. For that reason, cooperation in the maritime sectors is most important. In October 2007, in Nanning, ASEAN and China adopted the Joint Statement on Port Development in which both sides agreed to 'consider and adopt the Strategic Plan for ASEAN–China Transport Cooperation as soon as possible, and sign the ASEAN–China Maritime Transport Agreement at the Sixth ASEAN–China Transport Ministers' Meeting, so as to develop the port cooperation plan of ASEAN and China and identify the top priority cooperation projects.'[74] Port development in the Beibu Gulf Economic Zone is a priority for which it has maintained business contacts with over 220 ports around the world.[75] The zone, when well established, can contribute a great deal in promoting China–ASEAN economic cooperation at the sub-regional level, parallel to the Greater Mekong Sub-regional Economic Cooperation (GMS), which is discussed in Chapter 5.

Conclusion

As predicted in 2001, 'the establishment of an FTA between ASEAN and China will create an economic region with 1.7 billion consumers, regional GDP of about US$2 trillion and total trade estimated at US$1.23 trillion. It will be the biggest FTA in the world in terms of population size. It will also be the largest FTA, made up of developing countries, in terms of population, GDP and trade.'[76] Against the background that both the ASEAN states and China are developing countries, the comprehensive economic cooperation based on the above agreements is 'an arrangement of South-South cooperation with win-win results'.[77] With time, the China–ASEAN economic cooperation will strengthen, bringing in new areas of cooperation within its ambit. The latest example is the Beibu Gulf economic cooperation.

However, in the short run, both the ASEAN and China will face challenges, particularly increased competition in their similar labor-intensive and low-value-added sectors, but, in the long run, the ACFTA will help the ASEAN states and China restructure their economies and increase their economic efficiency and competitiveness.[78]

The ACFTA can start off a process of the 'New-Age economic integration in East Asia'.[79] The proactive move of China towards ASEAN stimulated Japan and South Korea – two more important economies in East Asia – to negotiate and conclude FTAs with ASEAN,[80] thus furthering economic integration in the region. The 10+1 mechanisms including ASEAN–China, ASEAN–Japan and ASEAN–South Korea economic cooperation, together with cooperation under the 10+3 mechanism among the 10 ASEAN countries and China, Japan and South Korea, will inevitably lead to the establishment of an East Asian FTA in the future.

Notes

1. Its members include 21 Pacific Rim countries and regions including China, Chinese Hong Kong and Chinese Taipei, and seven ASEAN countries, i.e. Brunei, Indonesia, Malaysia, the Philippines, Singapore, Thailand and Vietnam.
2. 'The Bangkok Declaration, 8 August 1976', available at *http://www.aseansec.org/1212.htm* (accessed 21 February 2008).
3. Text is available at *http://www.aseansec.org/12374.htm* (accessed 21 February 2008).
4. Text is available at *http://www.aseansec.org/12375.htm* (accessed 29 January 2008).
5. It was adopted on 29 November 2004 for the period between 2004 and 2010. Text is available at *http://www.aseansec.org/VAP-10th%20ASEAN%20Summit.pdf* (accessed 25 February 2008).
6. 'More than Half of the China–ASEAN Bilateral Trade are Made via Sea Ports', *People's Daily* (in Chinese), 1 November 2007, p. 6.
7. 'Getting on New Steps for Our Opening up to the Outside', *People's Daily* (in Chinese), 20 September 2007, p. 1.
8. 'China–ASEAN Bilateral Trade Volume Exceeds US$200 Billion', *People's Daily* (in Chinese), 15 September 2007, p. 5.
9. 'Forging Closer ASEAN–China Economic Relations in the Twenty-First Century', Report submitted by the ASEAN–China Expert Group on Economic Cooperation, October 2001, p. 27. Text is available at *http://www.aseansec.org/asean_chi.pdf* (accessed 27 June 2008).
10. 'What is the WTO?', available at *http://www.wto.org/english/thewto_e/whatis_e/whatis_e.htm* (accessed 28 June 2008). Unlike the United Nations, the WTO allows non-state independent economies as 'customs territories' to join. The examples include Macau, Hong Kong and Taiwan.
11. 'Principles of the Trade System', available at *http://www.wto.org/english/thewto_e/whatis_e/tif_e/fact2_e.htm* (accessed 4 July 2008).
12. Article 24 (4) of the General Agreement on Tariffs and Trade (GATT). Text is available at *http://www.wto.org/english/docs_e/legal_e/gatt47_02_e.htm* (accessed 4 July 2008).
13. Qingjiang Kong, 'China's WTO Accession and the ASEAN–China Free Trade Area: The Perspective of a Chinese Lawyer', *Journal of International Economic Law*, vol. 7 (4), 2004, p. 845.
14. Text is available at *http://www.aseansec.org/13196.htm* (accessed 18 April 2008).
15. Article 1 of the Framework Agreement.
16. For details, see Article 6 of the Framework Agreement and Annex 2 to it.
17. Article 7 of the Framework Agreement.
18. Zeng Lingliang, 'ASEAN–China Relations: An International Law Perspective', in John Wong, Zou Keyuan and Zeng Huaqun (eds.), *China–ASEAN Relations: Economic and Legal Dimensions* (Singapore: World Scientific, 2006), pp. 50–1.
19. Zeng Lingliang, supra note 18, p. 37.

20. For relevant literature, see Zeng Huaqun, 'WTO Rules and China–ASEAN FTA Agreement', in Wong, Zou and Zeng (eds.), supra note 18, pp. 98–104. As defined, an FTA is an arrangement among countries whereby tariffs and non-tariff barriers are abolished among members. Compared to customs unions and common markets, an FTA is the least institutionalized form of economic integration. See John Wong and Sarah Chan, 'China–ASEAN Free Trade Agreement: Shaping Future Economic Relations', *Asian Survey*, vol. 43 (3), 2003, p. 509.
21. John Wong, 'China–ASEAN Relations: An Economic Perspective', in Wong, Zou and Zeng (eds.), supra note 18, p. 29.
22. Zeng Huaqun, supra note 20, p. 105.
23. Text is available at *http://www.aseansec.org/15157.htm* (accessed 4 July 2008).
24. Text is available at *http://www.aseansec.org/19214.htm* (accessed 29 January 2008).
25. Article 11 (1) of the Framework Agreement.
26. Text is available at *http://www.aseansec.org/16636.htm* (accessed 21 April 2008).
27. Article 5 of the Dispute Settlement Mechanism Agreement.
28. Article 6 (4) of the Dispute Settlement Mechanism Agreement.
29. Article 7 of the Dispute Settlement Mechanism Agreement. The Agreement has a detailed provision on how the arbitral tribunal chair is appointed if the two parties to the dispute are not able to reach an agreement on appointment.
30. Article 7 (2) of the Dispute Settlement Mechanism Agreement.
31. Article 8 (3) of the Dispute Settlement Mechanism Agreement.
32. Article 11 (2) of the Dispute Settlement Mechanism Agreement.
33. Article 13 (1) of the Dispute Settlement Mechanism Agreement.
34. Zeng Lingliang, supra note 18, pp. 54–5.
35. Text is available at *http://www.aseansec.org/19346.htm* (accessed 29 January 2008).
36. Text is available at *http://www.aseansec.org/16646.htm* (accessed 29 January 2008).
37. Article 3 of the Framework Agreement.
38. Article 8 of the Trade in Goods Agreement.
39. According to this Article, the transition period for a product means the period which begins from the date of entry into force of the agreement and ends five years from the date of completion of tariff elimination/reduction for that product.
40. Article 9 (4) of the Trade in Goods Agreement.
41. Article 9 (6) of the Trade in Goods Agreement.
42. Article 9 (11) of the Trade in Goods Agreement.
43. Article 9 (7) of the Trade in Goods Agreement.
44. Article 9 (8) of the Trade in Goods Agreement.
45. For details, see Articles 12 and 13 of the Trade in Goods Agreement.
46. This stipulation to set forth a date of entry into force of an international treaty is unusual.
47. Text is available at *http://www.aseansec.org/19218.htm* (accessed 29 January 2008).

48. *People's Daily*, supra note 8.
49. Article 4 of the ACFTA Framework Agreement deals generally with trade in services.
50. Article 1 (t) of the Trade in Services Agreement.
51. Article 8 of the Trade in Services Agreement.
52. Article 23 of the Trade in Services Agreement.
53. Article 18 of the Trade in Services Agreement.
54. Article 22 of the Trade in Services Agreement.
55. For example, Article 28 of the Agreement provides that 'the GATS Annexes, namely: Annex on Movement of Natural Persons Supplying Services, Annex on Air Transport Services, Annex on Financial Services, and Annex on Telecommunications shall apply to this Agreement, mutatis mutandis.'
56. Chen Huiping, 'China–ASEAN Investment Agreement Negotiations: The Substantive Issues', *The Journal of World Investment and Trade*, vol. 7 (1), 2006, p. 144.
57. Text is available at *http://www.aseansec.org/7994.pdf* (accessed 30 January 2008).
58. Chen, supra note 56, p. 146.
59. Chen Huiping, 'China–ASEAN FTA: An Investment Perspective', in Wong, Zou and Zeng (eds.), supra note 18, p. 141.
60. It is to be noted that nine ASEAN states (except Brunei) signed bilateral investment treaties with China.
61. Chen Huiping, supra note 59, p. 140.
62. Chen Huiping, supra note 59, p. 145.
63. Chen Huiping, supra note 59, p. 156–7.
64. *People's Daily*, supra note 7.
65. Chen Wen, 'Are China and ASEAN Competing for FDI?', in Wong, Zou and Zeng (eds.), supra note 18, 199–215.
66. John Ravenhill, 'Is China an Economic Threat to Southeast Asia?', *Asian Survey*, vol. 46 (5), 2006, p. 674.
67. John Wong and Sarah Chan, supra note 20, p. 526.
68. Text is available at *http://www.aseansec.org/19286.htm* (accessed 29 January 2008). It is to be noted that the ASEAN secretariat and the ministry of agriculture of China signed the MOU under the authorisation of the respective governments concerned.
69. Article 2 of the Agriculture MOU.
70. 'Guangxi Got the Approval to Establish the Beibu Gulf Economic Zone', 23 January 2008, available at *http://news.chinatimes.com/2007Cti/2007Cti-News/2007Cti-News-Content/0,4521,130505+132008012301084,00.html* (accessed 23 January 2008).
71. 'The China–ASEAN Expo', available at *http://eng.caexpo.org/ab_caexpo/t20080324_78351.html* (accessed 5 July 2008).
72. 'Closure of the China–ASEAN Expo', *People's Daily* (in Chinese), 1 November 2007, p. 6.
73. 'The China–ASEAN Expo', supra note 71.
74. 'Joint Statement on ASEAN–China Port Development', available at *http://www.aseansec.org/21000.htm* (accessed 5 July 2008).

75. 'Guangxi Beibu Gulf Economic Zone', available at *http://www.nanning.china.com.cn/english/nanning_zhuan/3941.htm* (accessed 5 July 2008).
76. 'Forging Closer ASEAN–China Economic Relations in the Twenty-First Century', report submitted by the ASEAN–China Expert Group on Economic Cooperation, October 2001, p. 30. Text is available at *http://www.aseansec.org/asean_chi.pdf* (accessed 27 June 2008).
77. Zeng Huaqun, supra note 20, p. 109.
78. Kevin G. Cai, 'The ASEAN–China Free Trade Agreement and East Asian Regional Grouping', *Contemporary Southeast Asia*, vol. 25 (3), 2003, p. 401.
79. John Wong, supra note 19, p. 17.
80. Japan and South Korea signed framework agreements on comprehensive economic cooperation with the ASEAN in 2003 and 2005 respectively. While the ASEAN–Korea framework agreement is similar to that of ASEAN–China, the ASEAN–Japan agreement only created the framework of cooperation (in lieu of a legal document). The ruling Liberal Democratic Party in Japan would have been most reluctant to forge FTAs with the Southeast Asian countries if not for the perceived competition from China. See Lam Peng Er, 'China's Ties with Southeast Asia in the Post-Cold War Era: Japan's Response', in Wong, Zou and Zeng (eds.), supra note 18, p. 310. According to a Korean scholar, the China–ASEAN FTA will significantly affect the Korean economy. See Moon-Soo Chung, 'China–ASEAN FTA and Korean FTA Policies', in Wong, Zou and Zeng (eds.), supra note 18, p. 294.

5

Law and cooperation for the Greater Mekong River sub-region

The 4800-km-long Mekong River runs from its headwaters on the Tibetan Plateau through the Yunnan Province of China, Burma, Thailand, Cambodia, Laos and Vietnam.[1] In China, the upper stream of the river is named Lancang Jiang. It is the 12th longest river in the world[2] and is the heart and soul of mainland Southeast Asia. Over 60 million people depend on the Mekong and its tributaries for food, water, transport and many other aspects of their daily lives.[3] Legally it is an international river.

A new economic sub-region has emerged in the surroundings of the Mekong River, between China and Southeast Asian Mekong River riparian countries, namely Cambodia, Laos, Myanmar, Thailand and Vietnam. This sub-region is known as the Greater Mekong River sub-region (GMS) and covers an area of 2.3 million km^2, with a total population of 225 million.

This chapter addresses two interlinked and interdependent, but slightly different, subject matters: the discussion on Mekong River per se, which will be centred around the international law of rivers as well as around the 1995 Agreement on the Cooperation for the Sustainable Development of the Mekong River Basin and the Mekong River Commission it has established, and the discussion on Mekong basin development, which focuses on programmes under the GMS framework.

Legal status of international rivers

Under international law, an international river passes through more than two countries.[4] Therefore, the riparian states along an international river usually reach some kind of agreement for sharing the river water and natural resources. Some rivers are fully internationalised; in such case, ships of all countries enjoy the freedom of navigation through the river: the Danube under the 1856 Treaty of Paris and the Rhine under the 1868 Manheim Convention have got the status of fully internationalised rivers. On 20 April 1921, more than 40 countries, including China, concluded the Convention and Statute on the Régime of Navigable Waterways of International Concerns in Barcelona (commonly known as the Barcelona Convention).[5] The contracting parties agreed to 'accord free exercise of navigation to the vessels flying the flag of any one of the other Contracting States on those parts of navigable waterways specified above which may be situated under its sovereignty or authority' (Article 3 of the statute) and to treat 'the nations, property and flags of all Contracting States [. . .] in all respects on a footing of perfect equality' (Article 4 of the statute). According to Article 10 of the statute, each riparian state is obliged 'to refrain from all measures likely to prejudice the navigability of the waterway, or to reduce the facilities for navigation, and, on the other hand, to take as rapidly as possible all necessary steps for removing any obstacles and dangers which may occur to navigation'. However, 'a riparian State has the right of reserving for its own flag the transport of passengers and goods loaded at one port situated under its sovereignty or authority and unloaded at another port also situated under its sovereignty or authority' (Article 5 of the statute). Thus, the Barcelona Convention provides some preferential rights to the riparian states.

Early legal documents limit this sharing to only navigation, without considering resource use, much less with an approach to sustainable development. Recent trend shows that focus on environment and ecology protection has been strengthened and economic development for a whole river basin has been carried out.[6] For this, the United Nations International Law Commission prepared the Convention on the Law of the Non-Navigational Uses of International Watercourses, which was adopted by the UN General Assembly on 21 May 1997.[7]

Rights and obligations of riparian states

The 1997 Convention is basically a treaty of environment protection, which encourages watercourse states to reach agreements based on the principles contained in the convention. It has established several legal principles governing non-navigational uses of international rivers/watercourses in terms of sustainable development and environmental protection. In fact, some of these principles already exist in international environmental law.

The principle of equitable and reasonable utilisation and participation requires watercourse states to 'utilize an international watercourse in an equitable and reasonable manner', with a view to attaining optimal and sustainable utilisation (Article 5.1) and to 'participate in the use, development and protection of an international watercourse in an equitable and reasonable manner'; such participation includes both the right to utilise the watercourse and the duty to cooperate in its protection and development (Article 5.2). The convention lists seven factors and circumstances which should be considered by a state for using its watercourse judiciously. These factors include: '(a) geographic, hydrographic, hydrological, climatic, ecological and other factors of a natural character; (b) the social and economic needs of the watercourse States concerned; (c) the population dependent on the watercourse in each watercourse State; (d) the effects of the use or uses of the watercourses in one watercourse State on other watercourse States; (e) existing and potential uses of the watercourse; (f) conservation, protection, development and economy of use of the water resources of the watercourse and the costs of measures taken to that effect; (g) the availability of alternatives, of comparable value, to a particular planned or existing use'.[8] These factors are elaborate and innovative, but may be difficult to implement in practice. This is because of the 'uncertainty in application [which] is the main difficulty affecting the principle of reasonable and equitable use'.[9] During the UN General Assembly 99th Plenary Meeting of the 51st Session, the Indian delegation criticised the convention for having 'superimposed the concept of sustainable utilization on the principle of optimal utilization, without defining what sustainable utilization is in the present context'.[10]

The second legal principle mandates a watercourse state to take all appropriate measures to prevent any significant harm to another watercourse state (Article 7). This reflects the rule of customary international law that 'one should exercise one's right so as not to injure another' (*sic utero tuo ut alienum non laedas*) as it is noted that 'a state, in spite of its territorial authority, may not alter the natural conditions of its own territory to the disadvantage of the natural conditions of the territory of a neighbouring state – for instance, to stop or divert or to pollute the flow of a river which runs from its own into neighbouring territory'.[11]

The third principle is the principle of international cooperation, which requires watercourse states to cooperate 'on the basis of sovereign equality, territorial integrity, mutual benefit and good faith' (Article 8). For the purpose of cooperation, watercourse states may establish joint institutions to facilitate cooperation, and exchange relevant data and information regularly.

The convention imposes that watercourse states must notify any planned measures which might affect the environment of the international watercourse. In case of disagreement with the notified state, consultation and negotiation should be conducted. This obligation is, in fact, related to environment protection and pollution control. Watercourse states are also required to take individual or collective measures to prevent or mitigate conditions related to an international watercourse that may be harmful to other watercourse states (Article 27).

The convention not only contains some innovative stipulations concerning the use of international watercourses, but also absorbs some existing elements in international customary law. In 1929 the Permanent Court of International Justice (PCIJ) held that riparian states shared a 'natural community of interest' and therefore a 'common legal right' to equally use both contiguous and successive rivers.[12] Its ruling is now reflected in the principle of equitable and reasonable utilisation and participation. Advocates of the 'community of interests' approach, which 'requires that decision-making be undertaken collectively and in consideration of the best use of the entire basin', view equitable and reasonable use as a middle course between the approach of 'limited territorial sovereignty' and that of 'community of interest'.[13]

On the other hand, the emergence of the 1997 Convention signals the formal death of the obsolete legal doctrines on the use of international waters. The most notorious one was the Harmon Doctrine which claimed absolute territorial sovereignty over a river.[14] Another was the theory of absolute territorial integrity which gave exclusive right to the lower riparians for natural, uninterrupted flow of the river from the territory of upstream riparians. It also implied that the natural flow of river in the upstream state needs the consent of the lower riparian.[15]

During the voting on the 1997 Convention, China, together with Turkey and Burundi, cast its vote against the convention. The Chinese representative gave several reasons for China's opposing position. One was that the convention did not affirm the principle of territorial sovereignty, which in China's view is 'a basic principle of international law' that confers 'a watercourse State ... indisputable territorial sovereignty over those parts of international watercourses that flow through its territory'.[16] Furthermore, China perceives that in the 1997 Convention, there is an 'obvious imbalance' between the rights and obligations 'of States on the upper reaches of an international watercourse and those of States on the lower reaches'.[17] Thus, China still sticks very tightly to the principle of territorial sovereignty.

Although China refused to sign the convention, it stated that it reserved 'the right to address the question of the non-navigational uses of international watercourses with its neighbors in a fair and reasonable manner and in accordance with relevant international practice and with bilateral watercourse agreements'.[18]

On the contrary, a majority of states in Southeast Asia, including Brunei, Cambodia, Indonesia, Laos, Malaysia, the Philippines, Singapore, Thailand and Vietnam, adopted the 1997 Convention. This difference of opinions will undoubtedly be reflected in the use of regional international rivers such as the Mekong River and the distribution of river resources among the interested states.

Although the concept of basin drainage was not accepted during the deliberations of the 1997 Convention on international watercourse, for the purpose of water/resources management, the concept has been adopted by Mekong riparians for, at least, economic development. Therefore, the scope of Mekong development is limited not only to the river per se, but covers the whole river basin.

Sustainable economic cooperation

The Mekong basin is an underdeveloped area, some parts of which are least developed as per the UN standards. On the other hand, it is abundant in natural resources, which can be used for human welfare and sustainability. In terms of living resources, the Mekong River is the richest, next only to the Amazon River.[19] In terms of water resources, 'each year an average of more than 475,000 million m^3 of water flows through the Mekong Delta into the South China Sea, almost completely not utilized'.[20] As for hydropower resources, its estimated potential is 44,000 MW, but less than 10 per cent of this potential has been harnessed.[21] In addition, non-living resources with a potential for facilitating economic development are also abundant in the basin.

Any regional economic development requires an institution that can implement regulations. In the Mekong River basin, the two main regional institutions which dominate the process of sustainable development are the Mekong River Commission (MRC) and the Greater Mekong Sub-Region Economic Cooperation Program.

Mekong River Commission

The first cooperation for the management of the Mekong River can be traced back to 1957 when the three downstream states, Cambodia, Laos and Vietnam (South), formulated the MRC. It was made dysfunctional in 1975 when Cambodia withdrew itself from the group. The current cooperation framework was created under the 1995 Agreement on the Cooperation for the Sustainable Development of the Mekong River Basin.[22] Thus, the new MRC was established on 5 April 1995 and consists of four member states: Cambodia, Laos, Thailand and Vietnam. It has three permanent bodies – the Council (composed of one member from each participating riparian state at the ministerial and the cabinet level), the Joint Committee (composed of one member from each participating riparian state at no less than the head of department level) and the Secretariat (composed of a chief executive officer [CEO] who is appointed by the Council and around 120 professional and general support staff, and located in Vientiane). The Council is the decision-making body and convenes annually, while the Joint Committee is the policy-implementing organ which functions 'as a board of management'.[23]

The 1995 Agreement requires the contracting states 'to cooperate in all fields of sustainable development, utilization, management and conservation of the water and related resources of the Mekong River Basin including, but not limited to irrigation, hydro-power, navigation, flood control, fisheries, timber floating, recreation and tourism, in a manner to optimize the multiple-use and mutual benefits of all riparians and to minimize the harmful effects that might result from natural occurrences and man-made activities'.[24] Specifically, the riparian states are obliged 'to protect the environment, natural resources, aquatic life and conditions, and ecological balance of the Mekong River Basin from pollution or other harmful effects resulting from any development plans and uses of water and related resources in the Basin'.[25] Although the 1995 Agreement emphasises on the protection of the environment, sustainable development is the other important mission that it demands from the MRC. In order to comply with the treaty, the Mekong Programme – a regional cooperation programme for the sustainable development of water and related resources in the Mekong basin – was formulated by the four member states. According to the latest information source, four main goals have been set out for 2006–10:

Goal 1: To promote and support coordinated, sustainable, and pro-poor development;

Goal 2: To enhance effective regional cooperation;

Goal 3: To strengthen basin-wide environmental monitoring and impact assessment;

> *Goal 4:* To strengthen the Integrated Water Resources Management capacity and knowledge base of the MRC bodies, National Mekong Committees, Line Agencies and other stakeholders.[26]

The programme covers various sustainable developmental activities, including those related to irrigation and drought management, navigation, hydropower, flood management, fisheries, watershed management, environment and tourism.

What is more significant in the context of the development of international law at the regional level is the incorporation of the principle of equitable utilisation into the 1995 Agreement. Now, the agreement reads as follows:

> To utilise the waters of the Mekong River system in a reasonable and equitable manner in their respective territories, pursuant to all relevant factors and circumstances, the Rules for Water Utilization and Inter-Basin Diversion provided for under Article 26 and the provisions of A and B below:
>
> A. On tributaries of the Mekong River, including Tonle Sap, intra-basin uses and inter-basin diversions shall be subject to notification to the Joint Committee.
>
> B. On the mainstream of the Mekong River:
>
> 1. During the wet season:
>   a) Intra-basin use shall be subject to notification to the Joint Committee.
>   b) Inter-basin diversion shall be subject to prior consultation which aims at arriving at an agreement by the Joint Committee.
> 2. During the dry season:
>   a) Intra-basin use shall be subject to prior consultation which aims at arriving at an agreement by the Joint Committee.
>   b) Any inter-basin diversion project shall be agreed upon by the Joint Committee through a specific agreement for each project prior to any proposed diversion. However, should there be a surplus quantity of water available in excess of the proposed uses of all parties in any dry season, verified and unanimously confirmed as such by the Joint Committee, an inter basin diversion of the surplus could be made subject to prior consultation.[27]

In order to avoid any disputes on the use of the river resources, the agreement set forth the rules for water utilisation and inter-basin diversions.[28] The agreement mentions notification and prior consultation as the two processes to avoid environmental disputes. Should substantial environmental damages occur, 'the party(ies) concerned shall determine all relative factors, the cause, extent of damage and responsibility for damages caused by that State in conformity with the principles of international law relating to state responsibility, and to address and resolve all issues, differences and disputes in an amicable and timely manner by peaceful means as provided in Articles 34 and 35 of this Agreement, and in conformity with the Charter of the United Nations'.[29] According to Articles 34 and 35, any dispute can be resolved by (a) the MRC[30] and (b) governments.[31] Therefore, the dispute settlement mechanisms provided in the agreement include negotiation and consultation, mediation and involvement of the organisation established under the agreement. While all of these elements are within the political and diplomatic domain, one is remarkable and more ambitious than all others, that is mediation, which allows the intervention of a third party in dispute settlement.

After the 1995 Agreement, the member countries have signed sub-agreements on Data and Information Sharing and Exchange, a Flood Management and Mitigation Strategy and a formal agreement with China on the exchange of data on hydropower and other data (April 2002).

Although the MRC maintains regular dialogue with the two upstream states of the Mekong River basin, namely China and Myanmar,[32] these two countries remain outside this mechanism and have only participated as observers since 1996. This is definitely one of the shortcomings of the MRC. It has been rightly commented, '[w]ithout China and Burma as members, the MRC's representation is incomplete and its authority curtailed'.[33] What is worse is that with the emergence and development of the Greater Mekong Sub-Region Economic Cooperation Program, the role of the MRC in Mekong River management has been gradually marginalised or 'sidelined', 'not because the tasks for which it was created have become any less important (much to the contrary), but because changes in the broader political and economic context have shifted the incentives for states to cooperate'.[34] This might be another reason that prevents China and Myanmar to enthusiastically participate in the functioning of the committee. However, despite these drawbacks, the MRC is still an indispensable institution for the overall cooperation in the Mekong River basin. Recent trends indicate that the MRC has shifted its functional strategy by cooperating more closely with the GMS programme in dealing with matters concerning the Mekong River basin.[35]

Greater Mekong Sub-Region Economic Cooperation Program

In addition to the MRC, another regional institution which dominates the process of sustainable development is the Greater Mekong Sub-Region Economic Cooperation Program sponsored by the Asian Development Bank (ADB) in 1992. Unlike in the case of the MRC, all six Mekong riparian states participated in this program. Three years later, in 1995, the GMS states established a two-level institutional mechanism to sustain cooperation and ensure effective project implementation: (1) At the policy level, a ministerial conference was set up to coordinate sub-regional cooperation and provide overall guidance and support, (2) while at the operational level, sector-specific forums and working groups were established to discuss and recommend approaches to issues affecting implementation.[36] In addition, the GMS Summit of Leaders is being held since 2002 every three years and is attended by primer ministers of the GMS countries. The GMS cooperation is based on the principle of equality and mutual respect and pragmatism. Any decision reached among the GMS countries is by consensus.

Unlike the MRC, the GMS mechanism has no permanent Secretariat. To remedy this, the original sponsor – the ADB – agreed to provide it with technical, administrative and logistical support. In fact, the ADB provides not only technical, administrative and logistical support, but also financial support for the development of GMS projects. As of the end of December 2006, 28 GMS projects cost an estimated US$6.8 billion, for which the ADB has offered loans amounting to US$1.9 billion, co-financed US$2.7 billion and mobilised a total of US$155 million grant resources. Of these, US$73 million have been provided by the ADB, to finance 133 technical assistance focusing on development of human resource, tourism, environment, trade and investment.[37]

The first GMS Summit held in November 2002 endorsed a 10-year strategic framework which focuses on five development thrusts to achieve the goal of sustainable development:

- to strengthen infrastructure linkages through a multisectoral approach;
- to facilitate cross-border trade and investment;
- to enhance private sector participation in development and improve its competitiveness;
- to develop human resources and skill competencies;
- to protect the environment and promote sustainable use of the sub-region's shared natural resources.[38]

Based on the strategic framework, the Indicative Rolling Regional Cooperation Operations Business Plan (RCOBP) was adopted for the GMS for 2008–10, which includes four strategic pillars: 'strengthening connectivity and facilitating cross-border movement and tourism; integrating national markets to promote economic efficiency and private sector development; addressing health and other social, economic and capacity building issues associated with subregional linkages; and managing the environment and shared natural resources to help ensure sustainable development and conservation of natural resources'.[39] Accordingly, a plan of action has been designed for the GMS cooperation, which contains details of the strategic pillars implemented through concrete projects starting from 2004. It can be reviewed, revised and expanded with new items of GMS activities in a rolling manner. As of May 2007, the *Status Report of the GSM Plan of Action* contains 37 projects in eight sectors: transport, energy, telecommunications, agriculture, environment, tourism, human resources development and trade facilitation.[40] The progress of some of these projects will be discussed in the following sections.

As revealed by the Chinese Premier Wen Jiabao at the second GMS Summit in 2005, China has been participating in all cooperative activities with other Mekong riparian states since the launch of the GSM mechanism. China provided financial support to projects such as the ones related to Kunming–Bangkok road, upper Mekong waterway navigation and trainings for more than 500 people in the areas of agriculture, customs or telecommunication. In 2004, China provided a special fund of US$20 million for human resource development and poverty reduction in Asian developing countries.[41] In order to coordinate its domestic cooperation for its participation in the GMS, China established a national coordinating task force in 1994. It has regarded the GMS as one of the five important cooperative areas between China and ASEAN. In 2002, China issued its *National Report on Participation in GSM* for the first time. During the second GMS Summit, China issued its second report. Table 5.1 shows bilateral agreements signed between China and other Mekong riparian states, covering various matters of common interest.

The use of the Mekong River waterway is one of the areas of cooperation that interests China. On 20 April 2000, ministers of transport of China, Laos, Myanmar and Thailand signed the Agreement on the Navigation of Merchant Vessels in the Lancang-Mekong River;[42] in March 2001, a memorandum of understanding (MOU) was signed for the implementation of the agreement. Based on this, a joint coordinating committee was established. On 26 June 2001, a navigable waterway was

Table 5.1 **Economic cooperation agreements signed between China and other GMS countries**

Country	Agreement
Cambodia	Trade (1996); investment promotion and protection (1996); establishment of economic, trade and technology cooperation committee (2000); tourism (1999); and agricultural cooperation (2000).
Laos	Trade (1988); investment promotion and protection (1993); establishment of economic, trade and technology cooperation committee (1997); double taxation avoidance (1999); border trade (1988); banking or currency (2002); tourism (1996); agricultural cooperation (2000); Aviation (1991); and vehicle transport (1993).
Myanmar	Trade (1971); investment promotion and protection (2001); establishment of economic, trade and technology cooperation committee (1997); double taxation avoidance; border trade (1994); tourism (2000); agricultural cooperation; Aviation; science and technology (2000); and fauna and flora quarantine (2000).
Thailand	Trade; investment promotion and protection (1985); establishment of economic, trade and technology cooperation committee; double taxation avoidance (1986); banking or currency (2001); tourism (1993); agricultural cooperation; Aviation (1980); science and technology (1978); and medicine (1997).
Vietnam	Trade (1991); investment promotion and protection (1992); establishment of economic, trade and technology cooperation committee (1994); double taxation avoidance (1995); border trade (1995); banking or currency (1993); tourism; agricultural cooperation; Aviation (1992); vehicle transport (1994); science and technology; and medicine (1996).

Source: National Report on China's Participation in GMS, March 2004, available at *http://www.lmsec.org/main/china/sitemap/default.asp?classid=32&class=*中国参与湄公河次区域合作国家报告 (accessed 29 October 2007).

opened between Simao in China and Luang Prabang in Laos (886.1 km), thus making navigation possible along the Lancang-Mekong River.[43] With the consent by all parties and based on the environmental impact report prepared by experts from states parties, China funded the project of waterway improvement (US$5 million) in the upper Mekong for safe navigation. In 2003 alone, the volume of transported goods along the river exceeded 235,000 tons.[44] Politically, this quadrilateral accord on navigation is 'the first instance in which Chinese (as well as Burmese) authorities are party to an agreement on the use of the Mekong River with downstream countries'.[45]

In addition, China signed bilateral Lancang-Mekong transport agreements with Laos (1994) and Myanmar (1997).[46] Accordingly, the contracting parties agreed to open the Lancang-Mekong for commercial shipping from both countries, and consented to sailing of vessels from either party between the ports open to foreign vessels, transporting goods and/or passengers. However, vessels of one party can sail or anchor at the port of the other party complying with relevant laws and regulations, including those on environmental protection and ecological balance (Article 4 of both agreements). The agreements also contain provisions on jurisdictional matters, rescue and refuge, and taxation, among others. While these agreements are important components of the legal arrangements of the GMS cooperation, they have limited functions and are applicable only to some of the GMS countries. In this context, the following two agreements are more significant.

Agreement on the Cross-Border Transport of Goods and People in the Greater Mekong Sub-Region

So far the most significant multilateral legal document resulting from the GMS cooperation is the Agreement on the Cross-Border Transport of Goods and People in the Greater Mekong Sub-Region originally concluded between Laos, Thailand and Vietnam on 26 November 1999,[47] and later ratified by Cambodia (29 November 2001), China (3 November 2002) and Myanmar (19 September 2003). The agreement aims 'to facilitate the cross-border transport of goods and people between and among the Contracting Parties; to simplify and harmonize legislation, regulations, procedures, and requirements relating to the cross-border transport of goods and people; and to promote multimodal transport' (Article 1). For facilitating and simplifying border formalities, the agreement requires the contracting parties to take necessary measures for single-window inspection, single-stop inspection, coordination of hours of operation and advance exchange of information and clearance.[48] The contracting parties agree to improve the road/bridge infrastructure and, gradually, to unify road signs and signals. While the agreement is designed to facilitate the movement of goods and people in the GMS, it does not directly deal with trade and/or immigration matters, nor does it supersede relevant national laws and regulations of the contracting parties. As for institutional arrangement, each contracting party is required to establish a permanent National Transport Facilitation Committee. Representatives of the respective committee form the Joint Committee, which monitors and assesses the functioning of the agreement, serves as a platform for discussion and a forum for amicable settlement of disputes, and may advise the contracting parties and formulate proposals for making amendments to the agreement (Article 29).

One of the characteristics of the agreement is its mechanism of producing subsequent protocols and annexes, which, according to the agreement, are its integral part. As of 2007, 17 annexes and three protocols covered the following issues: 'carriage of dangerous goods', 'registration of vehicles for international traffic', 'carriage of perishable goods', 'cross-border movement of people', 'facilitation of frontier crossing formalities', 'transit and inland clearance customs regime', 'road regulation and signage', 'temporary importation of motor vehicles', 'criteria for licensing of transport operators for cross-border transport operations', 'conditions of transport', 'road and bridge design and construction standards and specifications', 'border crossing and transit facilities and services', 'multimodal carrier liability regime', 'criteria for licensing of multimodal transport operators for cross-border transport operations', 'container customs regime', 'commodity classification system', 'criteria for driving licences', 'designation of corridors, routes and points of entry and exit (border crossings)' and 'charges concerning transit traffic'. The latest protocol adopted in March 2007 deals with 'frequency and capacity of services (quotas) and issuance of permits'.[49] These annexes and protocols make the agreement more smooth to be implemented. In fact, it has already been implemented. At the eighth meeting of the GMS Transport Forum held in Phnom Penh (3–4 August 2004), the contracting parties agreed to preempt the ratification of annexes and protocols by implementing the agreement for the first time at some key border-crossing points such as Lao Bao-Dansavanh, Poipet-Aranyaprathet, Mukdahan-Savannakhet, Bavet-Moc Bai, Mae Sot-Myawaddy, Mae Sai-Tachilek and Hekou-Lao Cai.[50] As a supplement to this, China, Laos and Thailand signed an agreement in June 2007 for building a bridge across the Mekong River (at Chiang Khong in northern Thailand and Houayxay in Laos), which can connect China's Yunnan Province directly to Bangkok by road.[51]

Inter-Governmental Agreement on Regional Power Trade in the Greater Mekong Sub-Region

Another important agreement from the GMS cooperation is the Inter-Governmental Agreement on Regional Power Trade in the Greater Mekong Sub-Region signed by all six Mekong riparian states on 3 November 2002.[52] The agreement requires states parties to 'coordinate and cooperate in the planning and operation of their systems to minimize costs while maintaining satisfactory reliability; fully recover their costs and share equitably in the resulting benefits; and promote reliable and economical electric service to the customers of each country'.[53] It led to the creation of an inter-governmental body – the Regional Power Trade Coordination Committee (RPTCC) – that coordinates the implementation of regional power trade, including drafting the Regional Power Trade Operating Agreement (PTOA), which includes rules for governing power trade. 'Subregional electricity trade based on interconnected electric power networks under the IGA will provide significant economic and environmental benefits for individual countries and the entire GMS. It will enable nations to reduce national investments in their power reserves maintained to meet peak demand'.[54] Following the agreement, the GMS states signed an MOU in July 2005, providing guidelines for the first-stage implementation of the agreement on regional power trade operation. When the agreement was signed, it was expected that the power-transmission line could become a reality by 2008,[55] but it seems there are obstacles still to be overcome. To eradicate this, the Chinese delegate called for 'member countries to make every effort to speed up the discussion and negotiation on PTOA'.[56]

It is well perceived that with the development of the GMS programme, more and more agreements concerning sustainable development and cooperation will be signed among the riparian states.

Although the GMS programme was designed mainly to promote economic development and alleviate poverty in the developing sub-region, it also places due emphasis on the importance of environment protection. A sub-programme called the 'Core Environment Program' was endorsed by the second GMS Summit in July 2005 and was officially launched in April 2006 after the implementing office – the Environment Operations Center, located in Bangkok – was established.[57] It is regarded as an integral part of the overall GMS Economic Development Program and aims at enhancing the development potential, performance and impact of the GMS Economic Cooperation Program and the integrated approach to managing shared resources. It consists of five components: strategic environmental assessments of GMS economic corridors and priority sectors, biodiversity conservation corridors initiative, environmental performance assessments (EPAs), capacity building for environmental management and programme development, delivery and sustainable financing.[58] In addition, some other environment-related programmes have also been implemented, such as the Subregional Environmental Training and Institutional Strengthening Project (SETIS) and the Subregional Environment Monitoring and Information System (SEMIS).

In May 2005, ministers of environment of the GMS countries gathered in Shanghai, China, to issue a Joint Ministerial Statement on Environment. The statement reaffirmed the three core elements of the GMS environment programmes – regional connectivity, competitiveness and sense of community.[59] The ministers endorsed the launch of the Core Environment Program and agreed to submit it to the second GMS Summit for endorsement.

ASEAN also considers the Mekong basin development cooperation as one of its activities. Fearing that it might lag behind or possibly be marginalised from the Mekong cooperation, ASEAN, together with China, held a meeting in June 1996 in Kuala Lumpur to initiate the basic framework of the ASEAN–Mekong Basin Development Cooperation (AMBDC).[60] According to this document, the objectives of the cooperation are to enhance economically sound and sustainable development of the Mekong basin, to encourage dialogue and common project identification which can result in firm economic partnerships for mutual benefit and to strengthen the interconnections and economic linkages between the ASEAN member countries and the Mekong riparian countries.[61] It covers the areas of cooperation similar to those contained in the GMS scheme. As of 10 August 2006, there were 47 projects, at various stages of implementation. Fifteen projects still require funding worth US$44 million.[62] A mechanism was established to conduct the annual meeting of ministers together with the secretary general of ASEAN and a steering committee. In the Eighth Ministerial Meeting on AMBDC, held in Kuala Lumpur on 26 August 2006, it was decided that the AMBDC Ministerial Meeting would be placed under the ASEAN Economic Ministers Meeting process. The significance of this mechanism lies in the efforts made by the ASEAN member states to bridge the gap between old but relatively advanced member states and new but relatively less developed ones.

Ecological concerns

Under the traditional international law, open access system is applicable to an international river such as the Mekong River. However, from the perspective of environment protection and sustainable development, such an open access may be detrimental to the natural environment and ecosystems of the river, on the one hand, and may subsequently result in environmental disputes, on the other. Thus, multilateral cooperation among the riparian states is required. Such a cooperation in the area of environment protection and sustainable development is reflected in the mechanisms of the MRC and the GMS. However, environmental issues remain a focal concern for the Mekong riparian states, and some of them may get aggravated with the ongoing economic development in the sub-region.

The most serious concern about environment and ecology protection is the construction of dams along the Mekong River, particularly those built at the upper reaches of the river within the Chinese border. Such constructions threaten the aqua ecosystem to various degrees and bring about negative impact on the normal lifeblood of the region. Over the past 10 years, construction of more than 100 large dams in the Mekong basin has been proposed by institutions like the ADB and the MRC. Some of these dams have already been built. There are cause–effect linkages between upstream dams and downstream fishery depletion and appreciable harm to production in the Mekong delta.[63] One of the greatest alleged threats is China's plans to construct eight dams on the upper Mekong/Lancang.[64] Construction of two of these dams has already been completed, and construction of the third dam, Xiaowan, which began in January 2002, will be fully completed by 2012. As reported, the 4.2-million-kW Xiaowan Hydroelectric Power Station is the second largest in China, next to the Three Gorges Power Station on the Yangtze River.[65] Once operational, the eight hydroelectric power stations will generate 74.1 billion kW-h of electricity annually.[66] As viewed by environmentalists, these dams will have widespread impacts on the livelihoods of Mekong communities and on the natural ecology of the river system.[67] One main problem identified is that 'Chinese discussions of the implications of their hydropower plans do not take a basin-wide view, concentrating only on the impacts within Chinese territory, when it is the downstream riparians who will suffer most disproportionately the ill effects of China's plans'.[68] While upstream riparians are concerned more about navigation and hydropower, downstream countries pay more attention to flood control, irrigation and fisheries.[69] For example, the greatest concern in Cambodia is 'how upstream projects could affect the sensitive Tonle Sap (Great Lake) ecosystem, the region's most productive freshwater fishery and a principal source of protein for the country's rural population'.[70] Since the Mekong River is a shared resource, '[a]ny substantial interference by one country on the waters of such basins or aquifers may have effects – beneficial or detrimental – on the territory of another upstream or downstream State'.[71]

Conflicts over shared rivers are not uncommon. Construction of dams is also a matter of disputation. The most famous case is the one concerning the Gabcikovo-Nagymaros Project between Hungary and Czechoslovakia (later Slovakia) brought to the International Court of Justice (ICJ). The two countries entered into a bilateral agreement in 1977 on the construction of the Gabcikovo-Nagymaros dam. Due to economic recessions and ecological considerations, Hungary was reluctant to proceed further in the joint venture. Finally in May 1992, the Hungarian government unilaterally declared its termination of the 1977 Agreement, thus resulting in a dispute with Slovakia.[72] On 7 April 1993, Hungary and Slovakia signed a *compromis* on the submission of the dispute to the ICJ, requesting the court to decide on (1) whether Hungary was entitled to suspend and subsequently abandon, in 1989, the works on the Nagymaros project and on its part of the Gabcikovo project, (2) whether Czechoslovakia was entitled, in November 1991, for the 'provisional solution' and for putting into operation from October 1992 the system which dams the Danube at river kilometer 1851.7 on its territory, resulting in adverse consequences on water navigation course and (3) what are the legal effects of the notification, on 19 May 1992, of the termination of the treaty by Hungary.[73] The court rendered its judgement in September 1997, ruling that Hungary was not entitled to terminate the 1977 Agreement and to suspend and subsequently abandon the dam project. While in November 1991 Czechoslovakia was entitled to proceed with its 'provisional solution', it was not entitled to put it into operation from October 1992. The court found that in order to resolve their dispute, 'Hungary and Slovakia must negotiate in good faith in the light of the prevailing situation, and must take all necessary measures to ensure the achievement of the objectives of the Treaty of 16 September 1977, in accordance with such modalities as they may agree upon'.[74] Despite the court's ruling, Hungary is still reluctant to reach any agreement with Slovakia as adjudged by the court. Slovakia requested the ICJ for an additional judgement in September 1998, to determine the modalities to execute the judgement. So far, the case remains pending before the ICJ.

While there are various reasons for Hungary to abandon the project, the main reason is environmental consideration. As Hungary stated in its 1992 Declaration, the Gabcikovo-Nagymaros Barrage System contains ecological-environmental risks. Hungary cannot accept the following scenarios: irreversible damage to the ecological and environmental resources of the region, threat of degradation and, in certain cases, extinction of the vegetation and fauna of the region, serious damage to unique landscapes and imminent catastrophic threat to the population 'due to barrages and dikes of insufficient stability'.[75] Although Hungary's arguments based on environmental considerations could not legalise its unilateral termination of a bilateral treaty, these arguments have in fact become effective obstacles to the execution of the court's judgement and subsequent construction and operation of the joint dam project with Slovakia.

The case concerning the Gabcikovo-Nagymaros Project has some implications for the management of dam construction along the Mekong-Lancang River. First, environmental consideration becomes a priority in the case of dam construction. It is hard to put into operation any proposed dam project without a thorough assessment of its impact on environment. The procedure for environmental impact assessment along the Mekong River needs improvement at both national and regional levels. Lesson can be learnt from the experiences of the Espoo Convention on Environmental Impact Assessment in a Transboundary Context containing detailed rules concerning environmental impact assessment and applicable to Europe.[76] Secondly, cooperation is essential for any joint project between two countries. Sometimes, even a project within the territory of a country, with transboundary impact, requires necessary cooperative measures between/among riparian states. Now it is more and more difficult for a riparian state to act as it wants within its territory without considering the rights and interests of other riparian counterparts. Thirdly, there is an irreversible trend that sustainable development requires all the members of the world community to take care of the natural environment not only for the present generation but also for future generations. Precautionary measures therefore need to be taken when dams are designed and constructed.

According to relevant international legal rules, a riparian state, which intends to utilise the river or its resources, has the obligation to inform and consult other riparian states. The reason why China has been widely criticised for its construction of dams in the upper stream of the Mekong River lies largely in the fact that it did not inform, much less consult, other Mekong countries before the commencement of the project. This has partially answered the question why China voted against the adoption of the 1997 Convention on the Law of the Non-Navigational Uses of International Watercourses which imposes obligations on contracting states for information and consultation. Some scholars in China even invoke the principle of 'common but differentiated responsibilities' to argue that China, as an upstream riparian state and a main developer of the Mekong River, has sufficient reasons to take greater responsibility for any adverse impacts on downstream ecology and environment, and to provide comparable compensation if necessary so as to balance the interests between the upstream and the downstream states.[77]

China has realised that the utilisation of river water resources, particularly in dry seasons, is a major concern of downstream states. Some Chinese scholars attempt to prove that the impact of dam construction within China may not be that serious so as to endanger the environment and normal flow of the lower Mekong River. Rather it is beneficial, as it has been stated, '[w]hen the Xiaowan and Nuozhadu reservoirs are completed, the regulating discharge into the lower Mekong River on average is 1869 m^3/s at very dry years, an increase of 1180 m^3/s against the dry weather natural average 689 m^3/s. When other cascaded reservoirs are put into operation on the Lancang River, regulated discharge will be further increased during the dry season. This can not only improve navigational condition on the lower Mekong River, but also provide sufficient water for irrigation in northeast Thailand and Vientiane plain of Laos'.[78] On the other hand, in order to mitigate lower Mekong riparians' concerns, China signed an agreement with the MRC in April 2002. According to this agreement, China agreed to provide annual hydrological information to the four downstream countries of Cambodia, Laos, Thailand and Vietnam during the flood season from 15 June to 15 October. Two hydrological stations located in Jinghong and Man'an in Yunnan Province are responsible for monitoring and sending the hydrological information to the MRC, which includes information on rainfall and water level.[79] The information is particularly relevant, given the concerns of the lower Mekong countries about fluctuations in river levels.[80] This agreement can be seen as China's fulfillment, though partially, of its international obligation for information and consultation.

The rapid construction of dams in China also caused problems for the localities where these dams were situated. China's environment protection record is very poor, and its environmental laws are poorly implemented. Although there is a Law on Environmental Impact Assessment,[81] any assessment procedure is usually ignored by dam developers and, if required, they do it in a very perfunctory way. As is commented, '[e]xisting Chinese studies largely do not take into account environmental costs downstream of the Lancang cascade'.[82] Thus, once dams are constructed, environmental problems follow one after another. Related to this is the relocation of residents from the area where a dam is built. As reported, the rights and interests of the residents are largely ignored by developers and local governments. Residents removed from the area where the Manwan Power Station was built have still not been resettled, and some of them earn their living by picking recyclable garbage.[83]

Nevertheless, while China is widely criticised for randomly constructing dams at the upstream reaches, it is also fair to consider the benefits that China might bring to the downstream states. The Columbia River Treaty concluded between Canada (upstream watercourse state) and the United States (downstream watercourse state) in the 1960s recognised that 'the construction and operation of three Treaty projects in Canada would increase both the useable energy and dependable capacity of power plants in the United States' and entitled Canada to 'a lump sum payment for various downstream (flood control benefits), as well as one half of the additional power generated by power plants in the United States that resulted from storage across the border in Canada'.[84] Another example is the Rhine Chlorides Agreement which provides that the Netherlands should pay to France a substantial share of the cost of disposing of waste salts from the Mines de Potasse d'Isace, in ways so as to avoid their discharge into the Rhine (freedom from pollution).[85] Downstream benefits are regarded as a reflection of the principle of equitable utilisation.[86] From this point of view, China argues that the dams built along the Lancang River can at least benefit the downstream states in respect of flood control.

By 2020, the Chinese government aims to increase hydropower generating capacity by nearly 200 GW compared with 2005.[87] This will definitely bring more pressure on the Mekong River environment as well as on the lower riparian users. In this context, it is perceived that China will receive more pressure from its neighbouring GMS members as well as from the international community questioning its global environmental responsibilities.

Conclusion

It is clear that an integrated management approach to treat the river as a whole should be adopted for sustainable development and environmental protection of the Mekong River. Even for China it is advocated that the experiences from the management of the Danube can be borrowed and used for the management of the Mekong.[88] In 1985 eight riparian states of the Danube signed the Declaration on the Cooperation of the Water Management of the Danube, establishing the unified monitoring network for the whole river basin; the Action Plan for the Danube Strategy was prepared at the Sofia Meeting in 1991; in 1994 the Convention on Cooperation in the Protection and Sustainable Use of the Danube was adopted, which established the International Commission for Protection of the Danube. As was put, agreements concluded for African rivers are also multi-purpose and basin-wide in character.[89] Although the MRC contains similar objectives and goals, it only covers part of the river, and not all riparian states are involved in its activities. China's reluctance in getting involved in the MRC also results from the historic legacy of this organisation: prior to 1975 when the United States exercised its dominant influence, cooperation based on the Mekong Committee was encouraged to deter Communist Chinese influence.[90] For this reason, a regional organisation including all riparian states of the Mekong River evolving from the existing GMS mechanism will be appreciated.[91]

Notes

1. Another figure is 4200 km (2610 miles); see *http://www.thewaterpage.com/mekong_river.htm* (accessed 27 May 2003).
2. In terms of water capacity and volume, it is the 10th largest river in the world and the third largest in Asia; see Ed Lee, 'The Mekong River Basin Agreement', *Asia Pacific Journal of Environmental Law*, vol. 1, 1996, pp. 134–9.
3. 'Mekong River – The Lifeblood of Southeast Asia', available at *http://www.irn.org/programs/mekong* (accessed 23 May 2003).
4. There are different terminologies for referring to an international river, such as international watercourse, international waterway, transboundary river, transfrontier river or transnational river. In this chapter, they all mean the same thing, though the term 'watercourse' under the UN Convention on the Law of the Non-Navigational Uses of International Watercourses includes not only surface waters but also groundwaters.
5. Text is available at *http://internationalwaterlaw.org/intldocs/barcelona_conv.html* (accessed 25 September 2007).
6. Zou Keyuan, 'Territory in International Law', in Wang Tieya (ed.), *International Law* (Beijing: Law Press, 1995) (in Chinese), p. 232.
7. Text is available at *http://untreaty.un.org/ilc/texts/instruments/english/conventions/8_3_1997.pdf* (accessed 26 September 2007).
8. Article 6 (1) of the 1997 Convention.
9. Patricia W. Birnie and Alan E. Boyle, *International Law and the Environment* (Oxford: Clarendon Press, 1992), p. 222.

10. UN Doc. A/51/PV.99, 21 May 1997, p. 9.
11. R. Jennings and A. Watts (eds.), *Oppenheim's International Law*, 9th edition, vol. 1, 1992, p. 391.
12. Case concerning the International Commission of the River Oder, PCIJ Series A., no. 23, 1929, p. 27.
13. Eric W. Sievers, 'Transboundary Jurisdiction and Watercourse Law: China, Kazakhstan, and the Irtysh', *Texas International Law Journal*, vol. 37 (1), 2002, p. 16.
14. This doctrine was made by the then–US Attorney General Judson Harmon, who stated in 1895 in response to Mexico's protest of the United States' diversion of water from the Rio Grande that 'the rules, principles, and precedents of international law impose no liability or obligation upon the United States', Treaty of Guadalupe Hidalgo – International Law, 21 Opinions of the Attorney General, 1895, p. 283.
15. Birnie and Boyle, supra note 9, p. 219.
16. UN Doc. A/51/PV.99, 21 May 1997, p. 6.
17. Ibid.
18. UN Doc. A/51/PV.99, 21 May 1997, p. 7.
19. Chen Li-hui, Zeng Zun-gu and He Da-ming, 'Coordinating the Relationships between Interest Parties in Development of the International River: A Case Study of Lancang-Mekong', *World Regional Studies* (in Chinese), vol. 12 (1), March 2003, p. 72.
20. Kathleen I. Matics, 'Development of the Mekong River and Law: Some Environmental Problems', in Gerald Blake, Chia Lin Sien et al. (eds.), *International Boundaries and Environment Security: Frameworks for Regional Cooperation* (London/The Hague: Kluwer Law International, 1997), p. 293.
21. Blake D. Ratner, 'The Politics of Regional Governance in the Mekong River Basin', *Global Change*, vol. 15 (1), 2003, p. 62.
22. Text is available at *http://www.mrcmekong.org/agreement_95/agreement_95.htm* (accessed 17 October 2007).
23. 'About the MRC', available at *http://www.mrcmekong.org/about_mrc.htm#nmc* (accessed 19 October 2007).
24. Article 1 of the 1995 Agreement.
25. Article 3 of the 1995 Agreement. Article 7 further obliges the state parties 'to make every effort to avoid, minimize and mitigate harmful effects that might occur to the environment, especially the water quantity and quality, the aquatic (eco-system) conditions, and ecological balance of the river system, from the development and use of the Mekong River Basin water resources or discharge of wastes and return flows. Where one or more States is notified with proper and valid evidence that it is causing substantial damage to one or more riparians from the use of and/or discharge to water of the Mekong River, that State or States shall cease immediately the alleged cause of harm'.
26. 'The Mekong River Commission', available at *http://www.mrcmekong.org/* (accessed 19 October 2007).
27. Article 5 of the 1995 Agreement.
28. Article 26 of the 1995 Agreement: 'The Joint Committee shall prepare and propose for approval of the Council, inter alia, Rules for Water Utilization

and Inter-Basin Diversions pursuant to Articles 5 and 6, including but not limited to; (1) establishing the time frame for the wet and dry seasons; (2) establishing the location of hydrological stations, and determining and maintaining the flow level requirements at each station; (3) setting out criteria for determining surplus quantities of water during the dry season on the mainstream; (4) improving upon the mechanism to monitor intra-basin use; and (5) setting up a mechanism to monitor inter-basin diversions from the mainstream'.

29. Article 8 of the 1995 Agreement.
30. Article 34 of the 1995 Agreement: 'Whenever any difference or dispute may arise between two or more parties to this Agreement regarding any matters covered by this Agreement and/or actions taken by the implementing organization through its various bodies, particularly as to the interpretations of the Agreement and the legal rights of the parties, the Commission shall first make every effort to resolve the issue as provided in Articles 18.C and 24.F'.
31. Article 35 of the 1995 Agreement: 'In the event the Commission is unable to resolve the difference or dispute within a timely manner, the issue shall be referred to the Governments to take cognizance of the matter for resolution by negotiation through diplomatic channels within a timely manner, and may communicate their decision to the Council for further proceedings as may be necessary to carry out such decision. Should the Governments find it necessary or beneficial to facilitate the resolution of the matter, they may, by mutual agreement, request the assistance of mediation through an entity or party mutually agreed upon, and thereafter to proceed according to the principles of international law'.
32. *http://www.mrcmekong.org/about_us/about_us.htm* (accessed 23 May 2003). Since 1996 China has been a regular dialogue partner at yearly meetings with the Mekong River Commission.
33. Ratner, supra note 21, p. 69.
34. Ratner, ibid., p. 62.
35. For example, the MRC is one of the partners for the GMS Core Environment Program. For details of the program, see *http://www.adb.org/Projects/core-environment-program/default.asp* (accessed 22 October 2007).
36. 'Institutional Arrangements', available at *http://www.adb.org/GMS/Program/institutional-arrangements.asp* (accessed 22 October 2007).
37. 'GMS Program', available at *http://www.adb.org/GMS/Program/default.asp* (accessed 22 October 2007).
38. 'The GMS Strategic Framework', available at *http://www.adb.org/GMS/strategic-framework.asp* (accessed 22 October 2007).
39. 'Greater Mekong Subregion', available at *http://www.adb.org/Documents/CPSs/GMS/2007/default.asp* (accessed 22 October 2007). Complete text is available at *http://www.adb.org/Documents/CPSs/GMS/2007/RCOBP-GMS-2008-2010.pdf* (accessed 22 October 2007).
40. *Status Report of the GSM Plan of Action*, available at *http://www.adb.org/Documents/Events/2007/14th-Ministerial-Conference/GMS-Plan-of-Action-17May.pdf* (accessed 23 October 2007).
41. Speech by Premier Wen Jiabao at the opening ceremony of the Second GMS Summit, 5 July 2005, Kunming, China, available at *http://www.fmprc*

.gov.cn/chn/wjb/zzjg/gjs/gjzzyhy/GMSCO/t311849.htm (accessed 2 October 2007).

42. The Chinese version of the agreement is reprinted in Mi Liang (ed.), *Selected Ecomonic and Trade Laws of the Lao People's Democratic Republic* (Beijing: China Legal System Press, 2006) (in Chinese), pp. 61–5. The authentic version of the agreement is written in English.
43. *National Report on China's Participation in GMS*, 2002, available at *http://www.yn.gov.cn/yunnan,china/76844876288753664/20050625/379242.html* (accessed 29 October 2007). Yunnan Province passed its provincial regulations on the Management of Shipping in the Lancang River in May 1995.
44. 'The Booming International Shipping in the Lancang-Mekong', 27 August 2004, available at *http://www.xsbnly.com/info/1952-1.htm* (accessed 29 October 2007).
45. Ratner, supra note 21, p. 68.
46. The texts of these two agreements are available at *http://www.lmsec.org/main/china/sitemap/default.asp?classid=21&class=国内法规* (accessed 30 October 2007).
47. Complete text is available at *http://www.adb.org/GMS/Cross-Border/agreement.asp* (accessed 11 October 2007). The agreement entered into force with its ratification by all six GMS member countries in December 2003.
48. Article 4 of the Cross-Border Transport Agreement.
49. All texts of annexes and protocols are available at *http://www.adb.org/GMS/Cross-Border/annex.asp* (accessed 11 October 2007).
50. 'Initial Implementation of the Cross-Border Transport Agreement', available at *http://www.adb.org/GMS/Cross-Border/implementation.asp* (accessed 11 October 2007).
51. 'Mekong Countries Agree on Bridge Linking PRC to Bangkok', 21 June 2007, available at *http://www.adb.org/media/printer.asp?articleID=11970* (accessed 2 October 2007).
52. The text of the agreement is available at *http://www.adb.org/Documents/Others/GMS/Sector-Activities/Regional-Power-Trade-IGAandMOU.pdf* (accessed 24 October 2007). China signed it on the same day. See 'Multilateral and international treaties China has joined', available at *http://www.fmprc.gov.cn/chn/premade/45115/duobian.htm* (accessed 4 July 2003).
53. Article 2 (3) of the 2002 Agreement; see also 'Agreement for Regional Power Trade will Greatly Expand Electricity Distribution', available at *http://www.adb.org/Documents/Events/Mekong/2002/bn-02.asp* (accessed 11 October 2007).
54. Ibid.
55. Ibid.
56. Address by Mr. Zhang Yesui, Vice Minister, Ministry of Foreign Affairs of the People's Republic of China at the opening ceremony of the First Task Force Meeting for the Preparation of the Second GMS Summit, 30 July 2004, available at *http://www.fmprc.gov.cn/eng/zxxx/t144328.htm* (accessed 11 October 2007).

57. The Working Group on Environment within the GMS Program was set up as early as 1995.
58. 'GMS Core Environment Program (CEP) 2006–2015', available at *http://www.gms-eoc.org/CEP/Component.aspx* (accessed 23 October 2007).
59. Text is available at *http://www.adb.org/Documents/Events/2005/GMS-Environment-Ministers-Meeting/joint-ministerial-statement.pdf* (accessed 24 October 2007).
60. Text is available at *http://www.aseansec.org/6353.htm* (accessed 30 October 2007).
61. Ibid.
62. 'Joint Media Statement of the Eighth Ministerial Meeting of the ASEAN-Mekong Basin Development Cooperation'. Text is available at *http://www.aseansec.org/18845.htm* (accessed 30 October 2007).
63. Prachoom Chomchai, 'Transboundary Environmental Issues in the Mekong Basin', in Gerald Blake, Chia Lin Sien et al. (eds.), supra note 20, p. 316.
64. As criticised, 'China's Lancang hydropower plans and Mekong navigation scheme will turn the Mekong into a biologically degraded, badly polluted, dying river like the Yangtze and other big rivers in China. . . . China will not be able to regulate the Mekong any more than she can regulate the Yangtze, Europe can regulate the Danube, or the USA can regulate the Mississippi. Damming the Lancang for hydropower and turning the Mekong into a navigation highway will force the downstream countries into exhausting and largely futile efforts to protect themselves from the environmental impacts and make up for the damage to their agriculture, fisheries, and way of life'. See Tyson Roberts, 'Downstream ecological implications of China's Lancang Hydropower and Mekong Navigation project', available at *http://www.irn.org/programs/lancang/index.asp?id=021112.ecoimplications.html* (accessed 27 May 2003).
65. 'Lancang River to Become Southeast Asian Energy Base: Economists', *Asia Pulse*, 1 February 2002; and 'Hydroelectric Development Targets Are Identified for the Lancing River', 2 December 2003, available at *http://www.hsm.com.cn/node2/node116/node275/node276/userobject6ai137432.html* (accessed 2 December 2003).
66. 'Lancang River to Become Southeast Asian Energy Base: Economists', ibid.
67. 'Mekong River – The Lifeblood of Southeast Asia', available at *http://www.irn.org/programs/mekong* (accessed 23 May 2003).
68. Evelyn Goh, 'China in the Mekong River Basin: The Regional Security Implications of Resource Development on the Lancang Jiang', IDSS Working Paper no. 69, July 2004, p. 11.
69. Chen Li-hui, Zeng Zun-gu and He Da-ming, 'Coordinating the Relationships between Interested Parties in Development of the International River – A Case Study of Lancang-Mekong', *World Regional Studies* (in Chinese), vol. 12 (1), March 2003, p. 73.
70. Ratner, supra note 21, p. 64.
71. Dante A. Caponera, 'Shared Waters and International Law', in Gerald H Blake et al. (eds.), *The Peaceful Management of Transboundary Resources* (London: Graham & Trotman/Martinus Nijhoff, 1995), p. 121.

72. For details on the background of the dispute, see Paul R. Williams, 'International Environmental Dispute Resolution: The Dispute Between Slovakia and Hungary Concerning Construction of the Gabcikovo and Nagymaros Dams', *Columbia Journal of Environmental Law*, vol. 19 (1), 1994, pp. 9–14. Also see Valerie J. Assetto and Hans Bruyninckx, 'Environment, Security and Social Conflict: Implications of the Gabcikovo-Nagymaros Controversy', in Gerald Blake, Chia Lin Sien et al. (eds.), supra note 20, pp. 349–70.
73. Article 2 of the Special Agreement. The text is available at *http://www.icj-cij.org/docket/files/92/10835.pdf* (accessed 20 November 2007).
74. Case concerning the Gabcikovo-Nagymaros Project (Hungary/Slovakia), Judgment of 25 September 1997, p. 83. Text of the judgment is available at *http://www.icj-cij.org/docket/files/92/7375.pdf* (accessed 4 December 2007).
75. Declaration of the Government of the Republic of Hungary on the Termination of the Treaty Concluded Between the People's Republic of Hungary and the Socialist Republic of Czechoslovakia on the Construction and Joint Operation of the Gabcikovo-Nagymaros Barrage System, signed in Budapest on 16 September 1977, annexed to Alexander Kiss, 'Legal Procedures Applicable to Interstate Conflicts on Water Scarcity: The Gabcikovo Case', in Edward HP Brans et al. (eds.), *The Scarcity of Water: Emerging Legal and Policy Responses* (London: Kluwer Law International, 1997), p. 76.
76. It was concluded on 13 March 1991. Text is reprinted in 30 ILM 800 (1991).
77. Zhang Xizheng, 'Progress of, Obstacles and Outlets to China's Participation in the Cooperation of the Greater Mekong Sub-region', *Southeast Asian Affairs* (bimonthly in Chinese), no. 3, 2007, p. 9.
78. He Da-ming and Hsiang-te Kung, 'Facilitating Regional Sustainable Development through Integrated Multi-Objective Utilization, Management of Water Resources in the Lancang-Mekong River Basin', *Journal of Chinese Geography*, vol. 7 (4), 1997, p. 19.
79. 'China and MRC Signed the Cooperative Agreement', *People's Daily* (in Chinese), 2 April 2002, p. 7.
80. 'China Signs Data-Sharing Agreement', *Mekong News*, April–June 2002/2, pp. 1–2.
81. The Law was adopted in October 2002 and entered into force on 1 September 2003. Text is available at *http://hbj.boz.gov.cn/readfl.asp?newsID=2* (accessed 17 December 2007).
82. Goh, supra note 67, p. 9.
83. Zhang Xizheng, supra note 74, p. 7.
84. Richard Kyle Paisley, 'International Water Law and Downstream Benefits', in Helen Lansdowne, Philip Dearden and William Neilson (eds.), *Communities in Southeast Asia: Challenges and Responses* (Centre for Asia Pacific Initiatives, University of Victoria, British Columbia, Canada, 2002), p. 72.
85. Paisley, ibid., note 29, p. 88. The agreement is reprinted in 16 ILM 265 (1977).
86. Paisley, ibid., pp. 72–3.

87. Rachel M. Wasser, 'Clean Ambitions: Can China Achieve a Sustainable Energy Future?' *World Conservation*, July 2007, p. 25.
88. Jing Shusheng, 'Endless Love for Each Other, Drink Water together from One River', *People's Daily* (in Chinese), 24 June 2005, p. 7.
89. C.O. Okidi, 'International Law and Water Scarcity in Africa', in Edward HP Brans et al. (eds.), supra note 75, p. 178.
90. Ratner, supra note 21, p. 69.
91. As Ratner puts it, 'With cross-border economic ties growing and prospects of significant future trade providing a strong rationale for continued political rapprochement in the subregion, the conditions now are better than ever before for a comprehensive accord that includes all six Mekong states'. Ratner, supra note 21, p. 74. Another suggestion advocates the conversion of the existing MRC into the 'Mekong Basin Authority' to embrace all riparian states based on the rationale that '[i]n the long run, the interdependencies between the upper and the lower Mekong would seem to require integrated basin-wide planning'. See Prachoom Chomchai, 'Management of Transboundary Water Resources: A Case of the Mekong', in Gerald H Blake et al. (eds.), supra note 71, pp. 258–9.

6

Law for the protection of the environment

Introduction

Rapid economic growth, together with industrialisation and urbanisation, has caused environmental problems throughout the world. Asia faces a so-called triad of environmental problems – regional, international and global. The big question is how to create a framework that suits the region[1] and whether it can prove to be an effective vehicle for environment protection so as to avoid economic development at the cost of environmental deterioration. Various environmental problems, encompassing soil erosion, water logging, industrial pollution, deforestation and loss of natural habitats, prevail in China and Southeast Asia. Some of these are very serious and extensive. For example, land degradation in Asia (20 per cent of all vegetated land) exceeds the world average (17 per cent); the suspended load per square kilometre of drainage basin, which is an indication of soil erosion, is three to eight times more prevalent in Asia than in the whole world.[2] Even the severe acute respiratory syndrome (SARS) outbreak, which originated in China in the spring of 2003, bears a strong connection to environmental problems.[3] Such problems boomerang against the environment as well as economic development. According to an estimation by the Asian Development Bank (ADB), the economic costs of environmental degradation in Asia are estimated to range from 1 to 9 per cent of national GNPs.[4] Thus, the principle of sustainable development should be strictly applied to Asian economic development, which requires countries to have their economic development without affecting the nature as well as the interests of future generations. The Report of the World Commission on Environment and Development – *Our Common Future* – defines sustainable development as 'development that meets the needs of the present without compromising the ability of future generations to meet their own needs'.[5] To reach this goal, protection of the environment is a necessity.

Cooperation between China and ASEAN in the area of environment protection has already begun, as is seen, for example, in the cooperative activities of the Greater Mekong Sub-Region (GMS) programme discussed in Chapter 5. Cooperation in public health sector or natural disaster management is also related to the environment.[6] Such activities are undertaken under the ASEAN Plus Three institutional arrangement, which defined a mechanism for environment protection in 2004. From 17 to 24 August 2004, the China–ASEAN Environment Policy Dialogue was held, which was particularly directed at environmental education and environmentally sound technologies.[7] However, in comparison with other areas, there is a lack of cooperation in the environmental field. It was not until 2007 that China and ASEAN agreed to include 'environment' as the 11th priority area of cooperation between the two sides.[8] At the 11th ASEAN–China Summit held in 2007, China proposed, and ASEAN agreed to consider, the formulation of 'an ASEAN–China Environmental Protection Cooperation Strategy' and the establishment of 'an ASEAN–China Environmental Protection Centre'.[9] It is perceived that the two sides will intensify their environmental cooperation in the near future.

In addition, China and ASEAN have exerted much effort in environment protection and conservation of natural resources. Apart from their individual efforts, they have joined hands in regional and global environmental programmes and regimes, as will be discussed in the following sections.

ASEAN treaties

As a regional organisation, ASEAN aims to accelerate economic growth, social progress and cultural development in the Southeast Asia region, and to promote regional peace and stability through joint efforts. It has expanded its original mission to cover the field of environment protection as well. For this the member states signed the ASEAN Agreement on the Conservation of Nature and Natural Resources in July 1985.[10] The agreement covers various areas of environment protection including species, vegetation and forest, soil, water, air, environmental degradation, pollution, land use, protected areas, impact assessment, scientific research, international cooperation, shared resources and transfrontier environmental effects. It has also set the principle that the contracting parties should adopt protective measures singly or through concerted action to reach the goal of sustainable development, including adopting national conservation strategies.[11] Although the agreement was concluded among the six old ASEAN members, it can be extended to newer ASEAN members through the procedure of accession provided for in the agreement.

Several plans of action have been adopted for environment protection. Regional initiatives on environment protection are guided by the ASEAN Vision 2020, which called for 'a clean and green ASEAN with fully established mechanisms for sustainable development to ensure the protection of the region's environment, the sustainability of its natural resources and the high quality of life of its peoples'[12] and by the Hanoi Plan of Action (HPA)(2000–4), which contains 15 objectives. The Strategic Plan of Action on the Environment (SPAE) sets out specific and measurable activities for each of the 15 objectives of the HPA. Major areas of cooperation include (a) transboundary haze, (b) nature conservation and biodiversity, (c) coastal and marine environment, (d) global environmental issues and (e) other environmental issues.[13] Working groups were established within the framework of the ASEAN cooperation, but in coordination with a member country for Seas and Marine Environment, Nature Conservation, Transboundary Pollution and Environmental Management.[14] As of May 2008 there were five working groups, one each for multilateral environmental agreements, coastal and marine environment, environmentally sustainable cities, water resources management and nature conservation and biodiversity.[15] Although these efforts are commendable, the 1985 Agreement remains ineffective due to insufficient ratifications. To justify this, it has been commented: 'the ASEAN environmental undertakings may be characterized as plans for cooperation between national institutions, rather than the creation or strengthening of any regional institutions as a central hub for policy-making or implementation'.[16] On the other hand, lack of ratification may reflect the inability to meet the obligations stipulated in the agreement[17] despite the fact that that the agreement 'contains many admirable and innovative features'.[18]

In comparison, the Treaty on the Southeast Asia Nuclear Weapon-Free Zone concluded in Bangkok on 15 December 1995[19] has more teeth. According to the treaty, the 'Southeast Asia Nuclear Weapon-Free Zone' is the 'the area comprising the territories of all States in Southeast Asia, namely, Brunei Darussalam, Cambodia, Indonesia, Laos, Malaysia, Myanmar, Philippines, Singapore, Thailand and Vietnam, and their respective continental shelves and Exclusive Economic Zones (EEZ)' (hereafter referred to as 'the Zone').[20] For protecting the environment, each state party should refrain from dumping into the sea or discharge into the atmosphere anywhere within the Zone any radioactive material or wastes, disposing radioactive material or wastes on land in the territory of or under the jurisdiction of other states, or allowing any other state within its territory to do so.[21]

The treaty established the Commission for the Southeast Asia Nuclear Weapon-free Zone, which oversees the implementation of the treaty and ensures compliance with its provisions.[22] In addition, the treaty has also set up a control system for verifying the compliance with the obligations of the state parties under the treaty. It contains four key elements: (a) the IAEA safeguard system, (b) report and exchange of information, (c) request for clarification and (d) request and procedures for a fact-finding mission.[23] Safeguard provisions are also reflected in the provisions on remedial measures.[24]

While the treaty guarantees a nuclear-weapon-free Southeast Asia, it does not bar the ASEAN member states from developing nuclear energy for civilian use. Due to excessive depletion of non-renewable natural energy resources and soaring oil prices, some ASEAN member states have found alternative energy resources such as nuclear energy. In 2007 Thailand expressed its mission to hire about 200 nuclear power experts to set up its first nuclear power station in 10–15 years; Malaysia planned to build such a station within 10 years; Indonesia,[25] Myanmar, the Philippines and Vietnam have also started working on projects and programmes for developing nuclear energy.[26] However, there are a number of environmental and safety concerns, for example earthquake-prone regions such as Indonesia, nuclear waste management and leakage disasters like the one that struck Chernobyl, which may deter the ASEAN nuclear motives. Environmental concerns due to development of nuclear energy can be addressed at the institutions established within the ASEAN, such as the ASEAN Centre for Energy established in 1999. Finally, it is notable that China supports the ASEAN commitment to maintain Southeast Asia as a nuclear weapon-free zone and has expressed its willingness to sign the Protocol to the Treaty on the Southeast Asia Nuclear Weapon-Free Zone.[27]

Although there are a number of legal documents on environment protection, ASEAN activities in this area are still mainly guided by 'soft law', thus qualifying its efforts in environmental management despite the applause from the United Nations Environmental Programme (UNEP) that its environmental management is 'thorough' and 'may provide a model for other regional organizations'.[28] Regional cooperation with China and other neighbouring countries can no doubt strengthen the ASEAN capacity for environment protection and management.

Global environmental responsibility

The recent ASEAN Declaration on Environmental Sustainability adopted in November 2007 honours and makes commitments to implement multilateral sustainable development and environmental agreements.[29] China and ASEAN countries are parties to numerous international treaties. The most important global environmental treaties in the context of East Asia include inter alia, the UN Convention on the Law of the Sea (1982), Vienna Convention for the Protection of Ozone Layer (1985), Montreal Protocol on Substances That Deplete the Ozone Layer (1987), the Convention on Biological Diversity (CBD; 1992), the Convention to Combat Desertification in Those Countries Experiencing Serious Drought and/or Desertification (1994), the Framework Convention on Climate Change (UNFCCC) (1992) and the Kyoto Protocol to the UN Framework Convention on Climate Change (1997). The majority, if not all, of the East Asian countries have become parties to these global environmental treaties. Table 6.1 is an illustration of their accession to the UNFCCC and the Kyoto Protocol. The following section will discuss the two most important international treaties in the context of China–Southeast Asia relations: the UNFCCC/the Kyoto Protocol and the CBD.

UNFCCC and Kyoto Protocol

The ultimate objective of the UNFCCC is 'to achieve stabilization of greenhouse gas (GHG) concentrations in the atmosphere at a level that would prevent dangerous anthropogenic interference with the climate system' (Article 2). The convention sets forth a number of important principles. First is the principle of inter-generational justice, which emphasises the protection of climate system for the benefit of present and future generations (Article 3.1). Second is the innovative principle of 'common but differentiated responsibilities', that is, the developed countries should take more responsibilities for reduction in GHG emission than developing countries. Following this principle, the convention mandates the developed countries and other parties included in Annex I to

Table 6.1 **East Asian accession to the climate change treaties**

State	Year of accession	
	UNFCCC	Kyoto Protocol
Brunei	2007	
Cambodia	1995	2002
China	1993	2002
Indonesia	1994	2004
Japan	1994	2002
Korea (North)	1995	2005
Korea (South)	1994	2002
Laos	1995	2003
Malaysia	1994	2002
Mongolia	1994	1999
Myanmar	1995	2003
Philippines	1994	1998
Singapore	1997	2006
Thailand	1995	2002
Vietnam	1995	2002

Source: compiled by the author.

bear more responsibilities. For example, they should adopt national policies and take corresponding measures on the mitigation of climate change by limiting their anthropogenic GHG emissions and protecting and enhancing their GHG sinks and reservoirs (Article 4.2). However, during the implementation of the principle of 'common but differentiated responsibilities', the principle of equity should be taken into account. Another principle that is embodied in the convention requires parties to take precautionary measures to anticipate, prevent and minimise the causes of climate change and mitigate its adverse effects (Article 3.3). The last is the principle of sustainable development, which acknowledges that the parties have the right to economic development and provides that policies and measures against climate change 'should be appropriate for the specific conditions of each Party and should be integrated with national development programmes' (Article 3.4).

For implementing the principles of the convention, several institutions have been established in accordance with the relevant provisions of the convention. The most important institution is the Conference of the Parties (COP), which is the 'supreme body' or the highest decision-making authority of the convention.[30] The COP meets annually. A secretariat is established to assist the functions of the COP. In addition, there are two subsidiary bodies: one for scientific and technological advice and another for implementation.

The Kyoto Protocol was adopted in 1997 and came into force in 2005. It further sets forth the quantified emission reduction commitment for Annex I countries, that is developed countries and countries with transitioning economies between 2008 and 2012, but does not impose any emission reduction obligation on developing countries. The compliance regime based on the Kyoto Protocol and established in 2002 is regarded as one of the most comprehensive and rigorous regimes in the international arena. It consists of a *Compliance Committee,* which is made up of two branches: a *Facilitative Branch* and an *Enforcement Branch.* The facilitative branch aims to provide advice and assistance to parties in order to promote compliance, whereas the enforcement branch has the power to determine consequences for parties not meeting their commitments. The Compliance Committee bases its deliberations on reports from expert review teams, subsidiary bodies, parties and other official sources. In case of non-compliance with emission targets, the party can lodge an appeal in the Conference of the Parties/Meeting of the Parties (COP/MOP) if that party believes it has been denied due process by the Compliance Committee.[31]

As shown in Table 6.1, Singapore is the latest country among the Asian signatories to accede to the Kyoto Protocol. It changed its policy after a reassessment of economic costs and benefits.[32] But Singapore is an island country with insignificant GHG emissions at the global level. On the contrary, China is the country with the second highest GHG emission next to the United States. It is well predicted that China's emission will surpass that of the United States in coming years. In 2006, the Netherlands Environmental Assessment Agency (MNP) remarked that 'China topped the list of CO_2 emitting countries, surpassing the USA by an estimated 8%'.[33] Thus, China is the most important player in the establishment and implementation of the legal regime of global climate change. Although as a developing country, it has no compulsory duty to reduce GHG emissions under the existing international climate change regime, domestically it has undertaken a series of reduction efforts.

In June 2007 China published a long and perhaps the most significant document, *the National Climate Change Programme.*[34] Following this,

China established the Leading Work Group on Climate Change Adaptation, Energy Saving and Emission Reduction, with Premier Wen Jiabao as its head. The group has the following responsibilities: (a) to study and work out important state strategy, policy and countermeasures in response to climate change, (b) to coordinate for solving big issues related to climate change, (c) to organise and carry out the policy made by the State Council on energy saving and emission reduction and (d) to unify and implement the energy saving and emission reduction work.[35] It held its first meeting on 9 July 2007 in Beijing, requesting its member units to strictly implement the programme (action plan) and the Work Programme on Comprehensive Energy Saving and Emission Reduction, and deliberated the documents on departmental division of labour in the implementation of these two programmes.[36]

In response to international pressure, China emphasises the principle of 'common but differentiated responsibilities' embodied in the UNFCCC and the Kyoto Protocol. It was recently expounded by the Chinese Foreign Minister Yang that the basic principles embodied in the UNFCCC and the Kyoto Protocol, including the 'common but differentiated responsibilities', constitute the basis for climate change cooperation in the world community. As he said, the global climate change is caused mainly by long-term emissions in the past as well as the current high per capita emissions from the developed countries. Thus, after 2012 the developed countries should continue to bear the emission reduction obligation and to strengthen technology transfer to developing countries. Past GHG emissions from developing countries are not much, and their current emissions are survival emission and development emissions; thus, to adapt to the global climate change, they need to create and implement sustainable development strategy as well as participate in Clean Development Mechanism (CDM) cooperation.[37] It is unknown whether China would accept the compulsion to reduce GHG emission under the post-Kyoto regime, which is yet to be negotiated among the world community members.

As for China and ASEAN, climate change is a new area of cooperation. In November 2007, ASEAN issued a declaration to express the ASEAN concerted attitude towards the establishment of a new legal regime for global climate change by actively and constructively participating in ensuring a successful outcome of the negotiation on a comprehensive agreement.[38] Meanwhile, a declaration was issued on climate change by the participants of the third East Asian Summit, including ASEAN members, Australia, China, India, Japan, South Korea and New Zealand.[39] In the ASEAN Plus Three Cooperation Work Plan 2007–17, the ASEAN members, China, Japan and South Korea agreed to forge closer cooperation among themselves to 'mitigate and adapt to climate change' and strengthen cooperation 'in the development, transfer and diffusion of technologies to raise the capacity of ASEAN Plus Three countries to respond to climate change'.[40]

CBD

The CBD was adopted at the Rio Earth Summit on 5 June 1992 and came into force on 29 December 1993. Its objective is to conserve biological diversity, sustainably use its components, and fairly and equally share the benefits of the utilisation of genetic resources (Article 1). The convention requires state parties to follow its provisions, take necessary measures for biodiversity conservation and sustainable use, and cooperate among themselves to serve this purpose. The CBD contains provisions on dispute settlement first through negotiation, and then through mediation by a third party such as an international organisation. During ratification, state parties may declare to submit their disputes to arbitration or the International Court of Justice (ICJ).[41] The CBD accordingly establishes the procedures for arbitration and conciliation in its annexes. The mechanism is almost identical to the one under the UNFCCC. What is different is that the CBD does not have a comprehensive compliance regime and its protocol adopted in January 2000 deals only with biosafety,[42] one of the issues in the overall biodiversity field. The Strategic Plan for the Convention on Biological Diversity thus openly admits that there are legal and judicial impediments in implementing the convention.[43] As of June 2008, it had 191 state parties, while the Cartagena Protocol on Biosafety had 147 parties. All East Asian countries have acceded to the CBD (see Table 6.2), but there is an impression that the capacity 'to address biodiversity loss and appropriate scientific manpower is generally low'[44] in East Asia, a region with rich biodiversity, including tropical and mangrove forests, wetlands and mountain ranges.

After joining the CBD, China prepared its national *Biodiversity Conservation Action Plan* in May 1994,[45] funded by the Global Environment Facility (GEF). As described by the CBD Secretariat, '[t]he overall objective of China's NBSAP is to undertake effective measures expeditiously to avoid further damage to the natural environment and resources in China and mitigate or reverse this serious situation. Specifically, the action plan has identified seven major objectives, including strengthening the fundamental studies of biodiversity; improving networks of protected areas; protecting wild species with biodiversity

Table 6.2 **Asian accession to CBD and the Cartagena Protocol**

Country	Convention on Biological Diversity			Cartagena Protocol on Biosafety			
	Signed	Party		Signed	Ratification		Party
Brunei Darussalam		2008-07-27	acs				
Cambodia		1995-02-09	acs		2003-09-17	acs	2003-12-16
China	1992-06-11	1993-01-05	rtf	2000-08-08	2005-06-08	apv	2005-09-06
Democratic People's Republic of Korea	1992-06-11	1994-10-26	apv	2001-04-20	2003-07-2	rtf	2003-10-27
Indonesia	1992-06-05	1994-08-23	rtf	2000-05-24	2004-12-03	rtf	2005-03-03
Japan	1992-06-13	1993-05-28	acp		2003-11-21	acs	2004-02-19
Lao People's Democratic Republic		1996-09-20	acs		2004-08-03	acs	2004-11-01
Malaysia	1992-06-12	1994-06-24	rtf	2000-05-24	2003-09-03	rtf	2003-12-02
Mongolia	1992-06-12	1993-09-30	rtf		2003-07-22	acs	2003-10-20
Myanmar	1992-06-11	1994-11-25	rtf	2001-05-11	2008-02-13	rtf	2008-05-13
Philippines	1992-06-12	1993-10-08	rtf	2000-05-24	2006-10-05	rtf	2007-01-03
Republic of Korea	1992-06-13	1994-10-03	rtf	2000-09-06	2007-10-03	rtf	2008-01-01
Singapore	1992-06-12	1995-12-21	rtf				
Thailand	1992-06-12	2004-01-29	rtf		2005-11-10	acs	2006-02-08
Vietnam	1993-05-28	1994-11-16	rtf		2004-01-21	acs	2004-04-20

Note: rtf = ratification, acs = accession, acp = acceptance, apv = approval.

Source: adapted from *http://www.cbd.int/convention/parties/list.shtml* (accessed 3 June 2008).

importance; protecting the genetic resources of crops and domesticated animals; in-situ conservation outside protected areas; establishing national networks of biodiversity monitoring and information; and coordinating between biodiversity conservation and sustainable development. Twenty-six priority activities and eighteen priority programmes have been identified, including assessment of status of biodiversity and its economic values; assessment of representativeness and effectiveness of protected areas and identifying needs for establishing new protected areas; identifying priority wild animals for protection based on their biodiversity importance and level of their risks to endangerment; mainstreaming biodiversity into national economic development plan; promoting eco-farming; establishing standardized monitoring techniques; and setting up model areas for well-coordinated biodiversity protection and sustainable development. China has also developed sectoral plans for conservation and sustainable use of agricultural, forest, marine and coastal and wetland biodiversity'.[46] In addition, China has taken measures to achieve its target by 2010 in accordance with the consensus reached in April 2002 by the CBD state parties 'to achieve by 2010 a significant reduction of the current rate of biodiversity loss at the global, regional and national level as a contribution to poverty alleviation and to the benefit of all life on Earth'.[47] However, in its action plan, China admitted that it 'is still in the primary stage of biodiversity conservation. It still faces many problems and difficulties, and has a long way to go to achieve effective conservation of its biodiversity'.[48]

In addition to the efforts that individual ASEAN states make under the legal framework of the CBD, they conduct collective undertakings for biodiversity conservation and sustainable use of biological resources. For this, the ASEAN Centre for Biodiversity (ACB) was established in September 2005. It 'aims to create, promote, and develop links with the public, private sector, civil society, international development institutions, and donor community for the sustainable use of biodiversity'.[49] According to the ASEAN Declaration on Environmental Sustainability adopted in November 2007, the ACB will be promoted as 'a regional centre for biodiversity conservation and management' in East Asia.[50] In April 2008, environment officials from ASEAN member countries met to identify the core concerns and issues of biodiversity conservation, which will serve as a basis for ACB's long-term frame of action.[51]

In respect of China–ASEAN cooperation, the Singapore Declaration on Climate Change, Energy and the Environment adopted in 2007 at the 13th ASEAN Summit mentions the protection of biodiversity, and conservation and sustainable management of coastal and marine ecosystems.[52] In the ASEAN Plus Three Cooperation Work Plan 2007–17, the ASEAN members, China, Japan and South Korea agreed to forge closer cooperation among themselves in the area of biodiversity and natural heritage conservation.[53] In addition, a biodiversity conservation corridor has been established in the GMS as discussed in Chapter 5.

Regional environmental issues

With regard to particular regional environmental issues in the context of China–ASEAN relations, two important cases are worth addressing: the haze pollution in Southeast Asia and the marine environment protection and marine pollution prevention and control in East Asia.

Indonesian haze

The Indonesian haze is an annual phenomenon caused mainly by the burning of forests and bushes for cultivation – a traditional slash-and-burn method of farming – particularly in the localities of Kalimantan and Sumatra. The haze causes serious harm to human life and health.[54] The most serious consequences of the haze occurred in 1997, which was depicted as 'an environmental disaster'.[55] During the 1997 fires, the Pollution Standard Index (PSI) in the worst affected areas frequently went over the 300 mark (graded as hazardous for human health), and peaked sometimes to 650 PSI.[56] The haze became transboundary and spread to Malaysia, Singapore and to parts of Brunei, the Philippines and Thailand.

Some arrangements have been made to fight haze after it triggered the signing of the MOU between Indonesia and Malaysia in December 1997 for joint operations to deal with disasters that affect both countries, including the haze problem.[57] In the same year, Malaysia, Indonesia, Singapore and Brunei agreed to step up their efforts to control ground and forest fires under the auspices of the ASEAN Task Force on transboundary haze pollution. In addition, Malaysia and Singapore agreed to share the cost of providing water bombers to Indonesia.[58] However, such bilateral and multilateral efforts were not effective enough to curb transboundary haze pollution. To maintain a good neighbourhood policy and the spirit of the 'ASEAN way', governments of Malaysia and Singapore, the two most affected neighbours, did not publicly complain to Indonesia, nor did they claim any legal rights against Indonesia or pursue any legal approaches to seek compensation.[59] When another serious haze pollution occurred in October 2002, Malaysia simply asked Indonesia to take tougher measures to contain fires caused due to land clearing and slash-and-burn farming.[60]

The ineffectiveness of the multilateral cooperation finally invited the involvement of the ASEAN. In December 1997, the ASEAN Environment Ministers agreed on a Regional Haze Action Plan, which sets out cooperative measures needed by ASEAN member countries to address the problem of smoke haze arising from land and forest fires.[61] The primary objectives of the plan are: 'to prevent land and forest fires through better management policies and enforcement; to establish operational mechanisms to monitor land and forest fires; and to strengthen regional land and forest fire-fighting capability and other mitigating measures'.[62] Regional monitoring mechanisms should be established. The Haze Technical Task Force established under the plan meets monthly to review the progress of the plan, and the ASEAN Environment Ministers meet regularly to provide guidance in this respect. Since the plan is simply within the domain of 'soft law' without legal binding force, it cannot alone provide an adequate mechanism to combat haze pollution. Therefore, the ASEAN members have made big strides for a regional treaty.

The ASEAN Agreement on Transboundary Haze Pollution was officially signed in Kuala Lumpur on 10 June 2002.[63] The agreement defines 'haze pollution' as 'smoke resulting from land/or forest fire which causes deleterious effects of such a nature as to endanger human health, harm living resources and ecosystems and material property and impair or interfere with amenities and other legitimate uses of the environment'.[64] In accordance, the 'transboundary haze pollution' refers to 'haze pollution whose physical origin is situated wholly or in part within the area under the national jurisdiction of one Member State and which is transported into the area under the jurisdiction of another Member State'.[65] The purpose of the agreement is to prevent and monitor any pollution which can be mitigated through concerted national efforts and intensified regional and international cooperation. The parties should take the responsibility to ensure that activities within their jurisdiction or control do not cause damage to the environment or harm to human health in other states or in areas beyond the limits of national jurisdiction. They should take precautionary measures to minimise the adverse effects of haze pollution.[66] The cooperative efforts are reflected in the establishment of the ASEAN Coordinating Centre for Transboundary Haze Pollution Control, which provides assistance when a national authority declares an emergency situation. The centre maintains regular contact with the respective National Monitoring Centers maintaining data on fires and resultant haze.[67] The parties agree to resolve any dispute resulting from the implementation of the agreement through 'consultation or negotiation'.[68]

The agreement does not contain any third-party settlement procedure. This again reflects the traditional 'ASEAN way' of not interfering with domestic affairs of a member state; instead it emphasises harmony and shuns conflict.[69] Resorting to a third-party mechanism might be considered unfriendly by some member states. A similar regional treaty on air pollution – Article 13 of the Convention on Long-Range Transboundary Air Pollution – concluded among the European States in 1979 contains the same provision of 'negotiation' as a major means to settle disputes.[70] Yet it differs from the ASEAN agreement in that the parties can seek a solution 'by any other method of dispute settlement acceptable to the parties to the dispute'. That is to say, the means of dispute settlement are not limited only to 'negotiation or consultation'.

The conclusion of the anti-haze agreement has further strengthened the capacity to fight haze pollution in Southeast Asia, though the actual effect could be seen after 25 November 2003 when the agreement was enforced. Another significance of the agreement lies in the fact that for the first time, the problem was put under a regional legal framework, which prevents its exacerbation to an ostensible dispute. Although haze pollution does not seriously affect the environment of China and Northeast Asia, the ASEAN Plus Three Cooperation Work Plan 2007–17 lists 'transboundary haze pollution' as one of the cooperative areas.[71]

Regional marine environmental protection and pollution control

As we know, all the seas in East Asia can be categorised as 'semi-enclosed seas' under the 1982 United Nations Convention on the Law of the Sea (LOS Convention). All the coastal states bordering a particular sea are thus required 'to co-ordinate the implementation of their rights and duties with respect to the protection and preservation of the marine environment'.[72] Some kind of regional arrangement seems necessary in this regard. Regional cooperation and institutions for marine environment protection are not new in state practice. Under the sponsorship of the UNEP, several regional arrangements have been made for different sea areas throughout the world: the Wider Caribbean Region, the Southeast Pacific Region, the Mediterranean Region, the West and Central African

Region, the Red Sea and Gulf of Aden Region, the Kuwait Action Plan Region, the Eastern African Region, the South Asian Seas Region, the South Pacific Region and the Black Sea Region.[73] All of these bear some common characteristics; for example they were sponsored by the UNEP; they have an action plan as well as a treaty.

In 1989, the UNEP Governing Council designated the Northwest Pacific (NOWPAP) as a new area where first a regional action plan and later a regional sea treaty needed to be developed. The geographical coverage includes the marine environment and coastal zones of China, North Korea, South Korea, Japan and Russia. Interested countries around the Northwest Pacific sent their representatives to attend the initial contact meeting held in Nairobi shortly thereafter.[74] Subsequent developments showed that establishing a regional programme in East Asia was not as easy as in other regions. The main culprit could be abnormal political relations among the coastal states of the East Asian region.[75] The tension in the Korean Peninsula and the Taiwan issue are obstacles for smooth regional cooperation for marine environment protection. For example, when the first meeting of National Focal Points and experts convened in Vladivostok in October 1991, North Korea did not send its representative.[76]

In 1994 the action plan was finally adopted with five objectives: monitoring and assessing environment conditions, creating an efficient and effective information base, integrating coastal area planning, integrating coastal area management and establishing a collaborative and cooperative framework.[77] To implement the action plan, a number of projects have been designed and carried out in parallel by national institutions with the support of relevant regional and international organisations. In the case of multiple projects, the scattered nature of various activities, as well as the wide scope of input possible from both within and outside the region, necessitates the establishment of a network of participating institutions coordinated by regional activity centres. Besides, a Regional Coordination Unit (RCU) needed to be established to ensure integrated and well-managed execution from within the region of the projects under the action plan. For the meantime, the member governments had designated the UNEP as the organisation responsible for the coordination for implementing the action plan.[78] The RCU was finally established in 2000 and was co-hosted by Japan and South Korea. It served as a nerve centre and command post for executing the action plan. Two RCU offices started their operations in January 2005. A network of regional activity centres was established for the implementation of the action plan. China hosts the Data and Information Network Regional Activity Center located in Beijing.[79]

In October 2004, a significant legal achievement was made with the signing of the MOU on Regional Cooperation Regarding Preparedness and Response to Oil Spills in the Marine Environment of the Northwest Pacific Region.[80] However, no formal treaty has been negotiated among the states concerned as other regional seas programmes managed under the UNEP.

Another regional marine environmental programme involving both ASEAN members and China is the Regional Programme on Partnerships in Environmental Management for the Seas of East Asia (PEMSEA) jointly sponsored by the International Maritime Organization (IMO), the United Nations Development Programme (UNDP), the Global Environmental Facility (GEF) and the World Bank. It was implemented in 1994 with a mission 'to build interagency, intersectoral, and intergovernmental partnerships for achieving the sustainable development of the Seas of East Asia'.[81] Its official partners include Cambodia, China, Indonesia, Japan, Laos, North Korea, the Philippines, Singapore, South Korea, Timor-Leste and Vietnam. Other ASEAN countries such as Brunei, Malaysia and Thailand also participate in activities sponsored by the PEMSEA. Its geographical coverage is thus broader than that of the NOWPAP. Its overall objective is to support the efforts of the participating countries in the prevention and management of marine pollution at both the national and sub-regional levels on a long-term and self-reliant basis.[82] In order to institutionalise integrated coastal management (ICM), the regional program established two sites for demonstrating the application of ICM: one is in Xiamen, China, and another in Batangas Bay, the Philippines. Similar sites were set up subsequently in Cambodia, Indonesia, North Korea and Vietnam. Another kind of demonstration site for sub-regional sea areas and pollution hot spots were also established in China (Bohai Sea), the Philippines (Manila Bay), Malaysia/Singapore (Malacca Straits) and Thailand (Gulf of Thailand).[83] The programme launched the Marine Pollution Monitoring and Information Management Network to help build linkages with participating countries to notify each other of the status of the marine environment in the East Asian seas (EAS). The programme has four operating mechanisms: the EAS Congress, the EAS Partnership Council, the PEMSEA Resource Facility and the Regional Partnership Fund.[84] During the second East Asian Seas Congress held in Haikou, China, in December 2006, the partners signed the Haikou Partnership Agreement on the Implementation of Sustainable Development Strategy for the Seas of East Asia.[85]

In parallel to the PEMSEA, there is another programme for EAS managed by the UNEP – the 'Coordinating Body on the Seas of East Asia' (COBSEA), which was established in 1994 with 10 member states, namely Australia, Cambodia, China, Indonesia, Malaysia, the Philippines, the Republic of Korea, Singapore, Thailand and Vietnam.[86] According to the 1994 action plan, it is designed to assess the effects of human activities on the marine environment; to control coastal pollution; to protect mangroves, seagrasses and coral reefs; and to manage wastes.[87] Its current activities focus on three areas: marine and land-based pollution, coastal and marine habitat conservation, and management and response to coastal disasters following the New Strategic Direction of COBSEA (2008–12) adopted in January 2008.[88]

It should be noted that the implementation of these three regional programmes depends solely on the willingness and good faith of the participating states, since there is no general legal document binding the states, and not all ASEAN members have joined them. But the existence of these programmes per se can in fact avoid and even prevent environmental disputes resulting from marine pollution and conflicting uses of marine resources. Unlike a regional organisation such as ASEAN, the marine programmes involve cooperation and coordination of international organisations such as the UNEP as well as states of East Asia. The China–ASEAN cooperation for the marine environment protection is mainly undertaken under these regional programmes. Therefore, in the ASEAN Plus Three Cooperation Work Plan 2007–17, the ASEAN members, China, Japan and South Korea identified coast and marine environment as one of the areas that needed their cooperation.[89]

Earthquake-generated tsunami warning

After the Asian tsunami disaster, China and ASEAN adopted a plan of action in January 2005 to formulate a Technology Platform for Earthquake-Generated Tsunami Warning System.[90] It urges to establish a tsunami warning system for the Indian Ocean and the Southeast Asian region, to establish an Asian Regional Seismographic Network (ARSN) and to enhance capacity building and Asian confidence on disaster reduction. China agreed to provide 'the parameters of destructive earthquake events (such as magnitude, location, focal mechanism, etc.) occurring in the ASEAN and South Asia regions to the interested countries and parties as soon as these events are detected by the China National Seismic Network'.[91]

Environmental dispute settlement

Black's Law Dictionary defines a dispute as 'a conflict or controversy, esp[ecially] one that has given rise to a particular lawsuit'.[92] Environmental disputes involve environmental elements. Cesare Romano once discussed the definition of international environmental disputes in considerable length.[93] Peter Sand divides environmental disputes into two major categories: one over reciprocal obligations and one over collective obligations. According to him, the former refers to environmental disputes that occur 'between specific victims (e.g. of pollution) and specific villains (e.g. polluters)' and the latter refers to those which 'owed to the international community or to humankind as a whole'.[94] From this categorisation, it is understood that there are two kinds of disputes: one between/among states and another with global implications. However, some disputes that are not directly related to the environment also have environmental implications. The most notorious example in East Asia is the dispute over the Spratly Islands in the South China Sea, which can be defined as a territorial dispute and/or subsequent maritime boundary dispute. But it has caused a chaotic situation regarding marine resource uses and marine environment protection.

International law has a number of mechanisms for avoiding and settling environmental disputes, including such political means as negotiation and consultation, mediation and good offices, conciliation and investigation, and such judicial means as arbitration and international adjudication. Most of them are listed in the UN Charter.[95] In addition, international organisations, whether universal or regional, have played an active role in dispute avoidance and settlement. However, for avoiding and settling environmental disputes, judicial settlement is the most effective.

Judicial settlement refers to the settlement made by the international judiciary that mainly comprises the ICJ and the International Tribunal for the Law of the Sea (ITLOS). In view of recent developments in the field of environmental law and protection, the ICJ, in July 1993, decided to establish the Chamber for Environmental Matters. The chamber at present has seven members.[96] Among the cases the ICJ has handled, some are directly related to environmental disputes. The most salient case probably is the *Gabcíkovo-Nagymaros Project (Hungary/Slovakia)*, which was submitted by the concerned parties in 1993. The final decision of the court was made in 1997.[97]

The ITLOS was established in October 1996 in Hamburg, Germany, under the framework of the LOS Convention. It has jurisdiction over any dispute that is submitted to it concerning the interpretation or application of the LOS Convention and the agreement relating to the implementation of Part XI of the convention. In addition, it can adjudicate cases submitted by parties to other international treaties, if such treaties allow it to do so.[98] ITLOS has established two special chambers to deal with marine environmental disputes within the tribunal: the Chamber for Fisheries Disputes, which deals with disputes concerning the conservation and management of marine living resources, which parties may agree to submit, and the Chamber for Marine Environment Disputes, which deals with disputes relating to the protection and preservation of the marine environment, which parties may agree to submit. Each chamber consists of seven members. The ITLOS has dealt with a number of cases and some of them are particularly related to marine environment protection, such as the case concerning *the Conservation and Sustainable Exploitation of Swordfish Stocks in the South-Eastern Pacific Ocean (Chile/European Community)* and *the Southern Bluefin Tuna Cases (New Zealand v. Japan; Australia v. Japan)(Provisional Measures).*[99]

As discussed in Chapter 2, China prefers bilateral negotiation and consultation for dispute settlement between states. After the 1980s, China has consented to arbitration in treaties it concluded and acceded to, but confined it only to economic, trade, scientific, transport, environment and health areas. In this context, there should be no problem for China to submit environmental disputes for arbitration, though in practice China has to evaluate whether such a submission would endanger its national interest and sovereignty, and other factors that might not be in its favour. China's hesitation in this respect can be seen in its attitude towards the dispute settlement mechanism set forth in the 1997 Convention on the Law of the Non-Navigational Uses of International Watercourses. During the negotiations, China expressed its concerns over any arrangement for compulsory mechanism. The Chinese representative stated that 'China was not opposed to binding procedures, only to the adoption of such procedures without the consent of the parties'.[100] This means that China will not accept any compulsory mechanism. China's attitude towards the role of international courts in dispute settlement is even more passive. It has usually made a reservation about the clause of judicial settlement by the ICJ in the treaties to which it is a party.

The case of *Sovereignty over Pulau Litigan and Pulau Sipadan (Malaysia/Indonesia)* (1998–2002) before the ICJ, which concerns territorial disputes, has some implications for environmental law developments. In the judgement on *Sovereignty over Pulau Litigan and Pulau Sipadan*, ICJ granted the disputed islands to Malaysia. The court, when addressing the issue of *effectivités*, confirmed the validity of Malaysia's regulations concerning the control of collecting turtle eggs and the establishment of a bird reserve and regarded them as 'regulatory and administrative assertions of authority over territory which is specified by name'.[101] The recognition of domestic environmental legislations by the ICJ as evidences of effective occupation of a certain territory will inspire the individual states to pay more regard to this category of laws and, in turn, strengthen environment protection in reality.

Another case which is directly caused by environmental concerns is the *Case Concerning Land Reclamation by Singapore in and around the Straits of Johor (Malaysia v. Singapore)*. The case was first submitted to the ITLOS in September 2003 by Malaysia requesting the tribunal to prescribe provisional measures to stop Singapore's land reclamation activities in the vicinity of the maritime boundary between the two states or of areas claimed as territorial waters by Malaysia pending the decision of the arbitral tribunal.[102] In this case, the tribunal reiterated its statement expressed in the *Case of MOX Plant* that 'the duty to cooperate is a fundamental principle in the prevention of pollution of the marine environment under Part XII of the Convention and general international law'.[103] The tribunal issued an order prescribing that Malaysia and Singapore should cooperate to establish a group of independent experts to study and prepare an interim report on the subject matter, directing that Singapore should not 'conduct its land reclamation in ways that might cause irreparable prejudice to the rights of Malaysia or serious harm to the marine environment, taking especially into account the reports of the group of independent experts' and deciding that 'Malaysia and Singapore shall each submit the initial report referred to in article 95, paragraph 1, of the Rules, not later than 9 January 2004 to this Tribunal and to the Annex VII arbitral tribunal, unless the arbitral tribunal decides otherwise'.[104] Following the Order of the ITLOS, the two sides jointly established a group of experts who submitted their final report to the two sides on 5 November 2004. Based on the report, the two sides reached an agreement for resolving the dispute on 26 April 2005. Both sides agreed to terminate the case by several arrangements, including Singapore's modification of its final design of the shoreline of its land reclamation, its compensation to the affected Malaysia fishermen, and the discussion and monitoring of the environmental impacts in the Straits of Johor by the Malaysia–Singapore Joint Committee on the Environment (MSJCE).[105]

Generally speaking, judicial organs are under-used in settling environmental disputes not only in East Asia, but also in the rest of the world. Because of this, in recent years legal experts have begun to discuss how the role of judicial organs could be strengthened. In May 2003, judges and legal experts from around the world met in Rome, Italy, to advance the implementation of the World Summit on Sustainable Development's Johannesburg Plan of Implementation, as it relates to the role of the judiciary in achieving sustainable development. The meeting also centred around the UNEP Global Judicial Symposium and on furthering the recommendations made at the IUCN/UNEP European Judges Symposium held in London in October 2002. Specific outcomes included the first meeting of the European Judges Forum and the IUCN Commission on Environmental Law Judicial Specialist Group and further support for the IUCN/UNEP Judicial Portal and consideration of the content of the UNEP Judges Handbook.[106]

Experiences of individual states in resolving environmental disputes are sometimes a decisive factor for Asian countries to accept or refuse third-party settlement mechanisms including adjudication. The dispute between Malaysia and Singapore over Pedra Branca illustrates this. Inspired by its victory in the case of *Sovereignty over Pulau Litigan and Pulau Sipadan*, Malaysia quickly signed a special agreement with Singapore to submit the Pedra Branca dispute to ICJ, confidently thinking that it would win again. Before submitting a dispute to a certain settlement institution, states will evaluate the degree of chances of its winning. If Asian states can benefit from international dispute settlement mechanisms, their confidence will grow and they will be more likely to use them. As one scholar puts it, 'where states involved in a transboundary environmental dispute perceive there to be an objective institution capable of competently applying the principles and rules of international law to their dispute, those states may be more inclined to use international law to promote a resolution of that dispute. Although the existence of an adequate international dispute resolution mechanism is not necessarily sufficient to lead to the resolution of a transboundary environmental dispute, its existence substantially enhances the utilisation of international law, and its absence lessens the chances of the proper application of international law'.[107] Thus, legal control of environmental disputes in East Asia is not only concerned with East Asian countries, but also with the whole world community. It would be a positive sign if other members of the world community could encourage and support Asian states to use international mechanisms.

Although environmental disputes do not happen very often in East Asia, there is a tendency for increasing number of environment-related trade/commercial disputes in the region. In recent years, trade disputes between China and developed countries often involve trade-related environmental measures (TREMs), which are regarded as 'green protection' for import countries and 'green barrier' for export countries. Ostensibly, some of the trade disputes between China and Japan arose from the tough enforcement of domestic environmental regulations. It is perceived that many of such disputes may be settled under the framework of the WTO mechanisms. As is reported, one of the major reasons for China to enter into the WTO is to settle its disputes (including those related to the environment) with other countries under the WTO settlement system so as to avoid trade sanctions.[108] ASEAN developing countries may face the same problem.

Conclusion

Environment protection is critical for the survival of human beings. In this respect, international law is indispensable for the effective implementation of any environmental regimes and for carrying out any international environmental cooperation. Although environment protection was not a priority in the early stage of China–ASEAN cooperation, the two sides have realised its ever-increasing importance and made it one of the priorities in their current and future cooperation. It is perceived that the bilateral cooperation in this area will be strengthened with the development of the China–ASEAN relations.

As a final note, it should be pointed out that apart from global responsibilities, regional and sub-regional cooperative activities, bilateral cooperation between China and individual ASEAN states in the field of environment protection cannot be ignored.

Notes

1. Japan Environmental Council (ed.), *The State of the Environment in Asia 1999/2000* (Tokyo: Springer-Verlag, 2000), p. v.
2. Guatam Kaji, 'Challenges to the East Asian Environment', *Pacific Review*, vol. 7, 1994, p. 210; reprinted in Alexander J. Bolla and Ted L. McDorman, *Comparative Environmental Law Anthology* (Durham, North Carolina: Carolina Academic Press, 1999), p. 31.
3. Though the real cause of SARS is not yet known, it has probably two main causes: human-produced chemical pollutants that may lead to its creation and/or human behaviour of eating animals that may carry such virus and spread it to human beings. For details, see Li Hao, 'Close Connection of SARS to Environmental Behavior', *People's Daily* (in Chinese), 20 May 2003, p. 16.

4. Asian Development Bank, *Emerging Asia: Changes and Challenges*, 1997, p. 222.
5. Report of the World Commission on Environment and Development: Our Common Future, available at *http://www.un-documents.net/wced-ocf.htm* (accessed 5 June 2008). For relevant references, see Alan E. Boyle and David Freestone (eds.), *International Law and Sustainable Development: Past Achievements and Future Challenges* (Oxford: Oxford University Press, 1999).
6. For reference, see Chapter 7.
7. 'Database on the Cooperation Progressing in the ASEAN Plus Three and ASEAN Plus One Cooperation Frameworks' (11 January 2008), p. 26, available at *http://www.aseansec.org/* (accessed 20 May 2008).
8. 'Chairman's Statement of the 11th ASEAN-China Summit', Singapore, 20 November 2007, available at *http://www.aseansec.org/21105.htm* (accessed 20 May 2008).
9. ibid.
10. Text is available at *http://www.aseansec.org/6080.htm* (accessed 30 May 2008).
11. Article 1 of the agreement.
12. 'ASEAN Vision 2020', 15 December 1997, available at *http://www.aseansec.org/1814.htm* (accessed 20 May 2008).
13. 'Environment', available at *http://www.aseansec.org/8914.htm* (accessed 30 May 2008).
14. Gregory Rose, 'Regional Environmental Law in South East Asia', RECIEL, vol. 4 (1), 1995, p. 41.
15. For details, see 'Working Groups on Environment', available at *http://www.aseansec.org/14538.htm* (accessed 30 May 2008).
16. Simon S.C. Tay, 'South East Asian Forest Fires: Haze over ASEAN and International Environmental Law', RECIEL, vol. 7 (2), 1998, p. 204.
17. Rose, supra note 14, p. 43.
18. Ben Boer, Ross Ramsay and Donald R. Rothwell, *International Environmental Law in the Asia Pacific* (London: Kluwer Law International, 1998), p. 228.
19. Text is available at *http://www.aseansec.org/3636.htm* (accessed 30 May 2008).
20. Article 1 (a) of the treaty.
21. Article 3 (3) of the treaty.
22. Article 8 (3) of the treaty.
23. Article 10 of the treaty.
24. Article 14 of the treaty (In case the Executive Committee decides in accordance with the Annex that there is a breach of this treaty by a state party, that state party shall, within a reasonable time, take all steps necessary to bring itself in full compliance with this treaty and shall promptly inform the Executive Committee of the action taken or proposed to be taken by it. Where a state party fails or refuses to comply with the provisions of Paragraph 1 of this article, the Executive Committee shall request the commission to convene a meeting in accordance with the provisions of Paragraph 3(e) of Article 9. At the meeting convened pursuant to

Paragraph 2 of this Article, the commission shall consider the emergent situation and shall decide on any measure it deems appropriate to cope with the situation, including the submission of the matter to the IAEA and, where the situation might endanger international peace and security, the Security Council and the General Assembly of the United Nations. In the event of breach of the protocol attached to this treaty by a state party, the Executive Committee shall convene a special meeting of the commission to decide on appropriate measures to be taken).

25. Indonesia passed its Nuclear Energy Law in 2006.
26. Dong Li, 'Southeast Asia Beefing Up Nuclear Energy Plans', *People's Daily* (in Chinese), 24 September 2007, p. 7.
27. For reference, see Joint Declaration of the Heads of State/Government of the Association of Southeast Asian Nations and the People's Republic of China on Strategic Partnership for Peace and Prosperity, 18 October 2003, available at *http://www.aseansec.org/15265.htm* (accessed 5 July 2008).
28. UNEP, 'Sub-regional Mechanisms of Cooperation', available at *http://www.unep.org/unep/regoffs/roap/Cooperation.html* (accessed 30 May 2003).
29. ASEAN Declaration on Environmental Sustainability, available at *http://www.aseansec.org/21060.htm* (accessed 4 June 2008).
30. 'Convention Bodies', available at *http://unfccc.int/essential_background/convention/convention_bodies/items/2629.php* (accessed 24 August 2007).
31. UN Doc. FCCC/CP/2001/13/Add.3, 21 January 2002, available at *http://unfccc.int/resource/docs/cop7/13a03.pdf* (accessed 5 June 2003); also see 'Issues in the Negotiation Process: Compliance Under the Kyoto Protocol', available at *http://unfccc.int/issues/comp.html* (accessed 2 June 2003).
32. For details, see Natasha Hamilton-Hart, 'Singapore's Climate Change Policy: The Limits of Learning', *Contemporary Southeast Asia*, vol. 28 (3), 2006, pp. 363–84.
33. 'Chinese CO_2 Emissions in Perspective: Intercomparison of CO_2 Emissions of Countries and Burden Sharing of Emission Reductions', Press release, 22 June 2007, from 'Climate Change Info Mailing List'climate-I@lists.iisd.ca, 22 June 2007.
34. The English version of this document is available at *http://en.ndrc.gov.cn/newsrelease/P020070604561191006823.pdf* (accessed 22 July 2007).
35. 'Wen Jiabao Chaired the First Meeting of the National Leading Work Group on Climate Change Adaptation, Energy Saving and Emission Reduction', *People's Daily* (in Chinese), 10 July 2007, p. 1.
36. Ibid.
37. 'Our Foreign Minister Expounds China's Position on the Issues of North Korean Nuclear and Climate Change', *People's Daily* (in Chinese), 2 August 2007, p. 3. For reference on the principle of 'common but differentiated responsibilities', see Anita M. Halvorssen, 'Climate Change Regime – Amending the Kyoto Protocol to Include Annex C and the Annex D Mitigation Fund', *Colorado Journal of International Environmental Law and Policy*, vol. 18 (2), 2007, pp. 247–65.

38. 'ASEAN Declaration on the 13th Session of the Conference of Parties (COP) to the UN Framework Convention on Climate Change (UNFCCC) and the 3rd Session of the Conference of the Parties Serving as the Meeting of the Parties (CMP) to the Kyoto Protocol', Singapore, 20 November 2007, available at *http://www.aseansec.org/21078.htm* (accessed 27 May 2008).
39. 'Singapore Declaration on Climate Change, Energy and the Environment', available at *http://www.aseansec.org/21116.htm* (accessed 27 May 2008).
40. 'ASEAN Plus Three Cooperation Work Plan 2007-2017', available at *http://www.aseansec.org/21054.htm* (accessed 27 May 2008).
41. Article 27 of the CBD. Text is available at *http://www.biodiv.org/convention/articles.asp?lg=0&a=cbd-27* (accessed 5 June 2003).
42. Text is available at *http://www.biodiv.org/biosafety/protocol.asp* (accessed 5 June 2003).
43. Decision VI/26, available at *http://www.biodiv.org/decisions/default.asp?lg=0&dec=VI/26* (accessed 5 June 2003).
44. 'MEAs and Non-Binding Agreements', available at *http://www.grida.no/geo2000/english/0159.htm* (accessed 6 June 2003).
45. Text is available at *http://www.cbd.int/countries/profile.shtml?country=cn#thematic* (accessed 3 June 2008).
46. 'China – Details', available at *http://www.cbd.int/countries/profile.shtml?country=cn#thematic* (accessed 3 June 2008).
47. '2010 Biodiversity Target', available at *http://www.cbd.int/2010-target/* (accessed 3 June 2008).
48. China's *Biodiversity Conservation Action Plan*, p. iii.
49. 'About ACB', available at *http://www.aseanbiodiversity.org/about.htm* (accessed 3 June 2008).
50. 'ASEAN Declaration on Environmental Sustainability', available at *http://www.aseansec.org/21060.htm* (accessed 4 June 2008).
51. 'ASEAN to Develop Long-Term Strategic Plan to Save Biodiversity', available at *http://www.aseanbiodiversity.org/news/2008/news_long_term_strategic_plan.htm* (accessed 3 June 2008).
52. 'The Singapore Declaration on Climate Change, Energy and the Environment', available at *http://www.aseansec.org/21116.htm* (accessed 3 June 2008).
53. 'ASEAN Plus Three Cooperation Work Plan 2007-2017', available at *http://www.aseansec.org/21054.htm* (accessed 27 May 2008).
54. Haze consists of sufficient smoke, dust, moisture and vapor suspended in air to impair visibility. Haze pollution can be said to be 'transboundary' if its density and extent are so great at source that it remains at measurable levels after crossing into another country's air space. At *http://www.haze-online.or.id/help/firehaze.php?PHPSESSID=b772ae92efcb763b972d241c724ff8ba* (accessed 28 May 2003).
55. Between 800,000 and 1.7 million hectares of forests and bushes in the Indonesian islands of Sumatra and Kalimantan were burnt. See Tay, supra note 16, p. 202.
56. Ibid.

57. 'KL, Jakarta to sign MOU on Handling Disasters', *Straits Times*, 10 December 1997, available at *http://www.icsea.or.id/sea-span/0497/TP1211LL.htm* (accessed 28 May 2003).
58. 'Nations Agree to Share Costs in Controlling Haze', available at *http://www.icsea.or.id/sea-span/0497/TP0821LL.htm* (accessed 28 May 2003).
59. Tay, supra note 16, at 206.
60. 'Indonesian Forest Fire Haze Covers Singapore and Malaysia', available at *http://asia.news.yahoo.com/021017/reuters/asia-130002.html* (accessed 28 May 2003).
61. Text is available at *http://www.aseansec.org/8953.htm* (accessed 29 May 2003).
62. Item 4 of the plan.
63. Text is available at *http://www.aseansec.org/6086.htm* (accessed 29 May 2003).
64. Article 1 (6) of the agreement.
65. Article 1 (13) of the agreement.
66. Article 3 of the agreement.
67. The functions of the ASEAN Centre are stipulated in the Annex to the Agreement: Terms of Reference of the ASEAN Coordinating Centre for Transboundary Haze Pollution Control.
68. Article 27 of the agreement.
69. M. Sornarajah, 'The Haze over Southeast Asia', *Singapore Journal of International and Comparative Law*, vol. 1, 1997, p. 641.
70. Text is available at *http://www.unece.org/env/lrtap/conv/lrtap_c.htm* (accessed 30 May 2003).
71. 'ASEAN Plus Three Cooperation Work Plan 2007-2017', available at *http://www.aseansec.org/21054.htm* (accessed 27 May 2008).
72. Article 123 (b), LOS Convention, in United Nations, *The Law of the Sea: Official Text of the United Nations Convention on the Law of the Sea with Annexes and Index* (New York: United Nations, 1983), p. 39.
73. Patricia W. Birnie and Alan E. Boyle, *International Law and the Environment* (Oxford: Clarendon Press, 1992), pp. 260–3. For reference, see Peter H. Sand, *Marine Environment Law in the United Nations Environment Programme* (London: Tycooly Publishing, 1988), pp. 1–225.
74. BSAP and NOWPAP – Now We Are 12, *The Siren* (UNEP's Oceans and Coastal Area Program), no. 43, at.1 (December 1991); as cited in Jon M. van Dyke, 'Promoting Maritime Co-operation in the Asia-Pacific Era', in Dalchoog Kim *et al.* (eds.), *Exploring Maritime Co-operation in Northeast Asia* (Seoul: Institute of East and West Studies, Yonsei University, 1993), p. 204.
75. Jin-Hyun Paik, 'East Asia and the Law of the Sea', in James Crawford and Donald R. Rothwell (eds.), *The Law of the Sea in the Asia-Pacific Region: Developments and Prospects* (Dordrecht: Martinus Nijhoff, 1995), p. 7.
76. Sang-Don Lee, 'A Framework for Co-operation for the Protection of the Marine Environment in the Yellow Sea: A Korean View', in Dalchoog Kim *et al.* (eds.), *Exploring Maritime Co-operation in Northeast Asia* (Seoul: Institute of East and West Studies, Yonsei University, 1993), p. 73.

77. 'Action Plan for the Protection, Management and Development of the Marine and Coastal Environment of the Northwest Pacific Region', available at *http://www.nowpap1.org/2-NOWPAP.htm* (accessed 2 June 2003).
78. 'Action Plan for the Protection, Management and Development of the Marine and Coastal Environment of the Northwest Pacific Region', available at *http://www.nowpap1.org/2-NOWPAP.htm* (accessed 22 May 2003). The full text of the Action Plan is available at *http://www.unep.org/regionalseas/programmes/unpro/nwpacific/instruments/action_plan_nowpap.pdf* (accessed 6 June 2008).
79. For details, see its website: *http://dinrac.nowpap.org/* (accessed 5 June 2008).
80. Text is available at *http://merrac.nowpap.org/new/plan01.asp* (accessed 5 June 2008). It is to be noted that North Korea is not a signatory to this MOU.
81. 'PEMSEA at a Glance', available at *http://www.pemsea.org/about-pemsea/pemsea-at-a-glance/* (accessed 5 June 2008).
82. 'Fighting Pollution in the East Asian Seas', IMO News 4/97, available at *http://www.imo.org/imo/news/3&497/drchua2.htm* (27 February 1998).
83. For details, see *http://www.pemsea.org/* (accessed 2 June 2003).
84. 'EAS Partnership Operating Arrangements', available at *http://www.pemsea.org/about-pemsea/operating-mechanism/portfolio-19.gif/view* (accessed 5 June 2008).
85. Text is available at *http://www.pemsea.org/partnerships/overview/* (accessed 5 June 2008).
86. It is recalled that the first East Asian Seas Action Plan was approved in 1981 with only five countries (Indonesia, Malaysia, the Philippines, Singapore and Thailand).
87. The Action Plan for the Protection and Sustainable Development of the Marine and Coastal Areas of the East Asian Region, available at *http://www.cobsea.org/documents/action_plan/ActionPlan1994.pdf* (accessed 5 June 2008).
88. For details, see 'Current Activities', available at *http://www.cobsea.org/activities/current_activities.html* (accessed 5 June 2008).
89. 'ASEAN Plus Three Cooperation Work Plan 2007–2017', available at *http://www.aseansec.org/21054.htm* (accessed 27 May 2008).
90. Text is available at *http://www.aseansec.org/17249.htm* (accessed 20 May 2008).
91. 'Action Plan to Formulate a Technology Platform for Earthquake-Generated Tsunami Warning System', ibid.
92. *Black's Law Dictionary*, 7th Edition (St. Paul, Minn.: West Group, 1999), p. 485.
93. Cesare P. R. Romano, *The Peaceful Settlement of International Environmental Disputes: A Pragmatic Approach* (The Hague: Kluwer Law International, 2000), pp. 1–33.
94. Peter H. Sand, *Transnational Environmental Law: Lessons in Global Change* (The Hague: Kluwer Law International, 1999), p. 46.
95. Article 33, paragraph 1 of the UN Charter.

96. 'International Court of Justice 1946–1996', available at *http://www.icj-cij.org/icjwww/igeneralinformation/ibbook/Bbookframepage.htm* (accessed 16 May 2002).
97. For details, see *http://www.icj-cij.org/docket/index.php?p1=3&p2=3&code=hs&case=92&k=8d* (accessed 18 May 2008). For relevant literature, see Paul R. Williams, 'International Environmental Dispute Resolution: The Dispute Between Slovakia and Hungary Concerning Construction of the Gabcíkovo and Nagymaros Dams', *Columbia Journal of Environmental Law*, vol. 19 (1), 1994, pp. 1–57.
98. Articles 21–22 of the Statute of the ITLOS.
99. For details, see *http://www.itlos.org/start2_en.html* (accessed 3 June 2003).
100. UN Doc. A/C.6/51/SR.59 (1997), paragraph 3, p. 3; cited in Attila Tanzi, 'Recent Trends in International Water Law Dispute Settlement', in International Bureau of the Permanent Court of Arbitration (ed.), *International Investments and Protection of the Environment: The Role of Dispute Resolution Mechanisms* (The Hague: Kluwer Law International, 2001), p. 139.
101. The ICJ Judgment, paragraph 145, available at *http://www.icj-cij.org/icjwww/idocket/iinma/iinmajudgment/iinma_ijudgment_20021217.PDF* (accessed 9 June 2003).
102. Due to its land scarcity, Singapore actively carries out land reclamation. According to a statistic, Singapore's land area increased from 581 km^2 in 1966 to 695 km^2 in 2003. See Kog Yue-Choong, 'Environmental Management and Conflict in Southeast Asia: Land Reclamation and Its Political Impact', IDSS Working Paper No. 101 (Institute for Defence and Strategic Studies, Nanyang Technological University, Singapore), January 2006, p. 7.
103. Order on the *Case Concerning Land Reclamation by Singapore in and around the Straits of Johor (Malaysia v. Singapore)*: Request for Provisional Measures, 8 October 2003, paragraph 92, available at *http://www.itlos.org/start2_en.html* (accessed 22 May 2008).
104. Order on the *Case Concerning Land Reclamation by Singapore in and around the Straits of Johor (Malaysia v. Singapore)*: Request for Provisional Measures, ibid., paragraph 102.
105. Case Concerning Land Reclamation by Singapore in and around the Straits of Johor (Malaysia v. Singapore): Settlement Agreement (on file with the author).
106. Available at *http://www.iisd.ca/recent/recentmeetings.asp?id=1* (accessed 21 May 2003).
107. Paul R. William, *International Law and the Resolution of Central and East European Transboundary Environmental Disputes* (Macmillan Press, 2000), p. 157.
108. Zhang Ruosi, 'Settlement of Disputes over TREMs in the WTO, and Environmental Challenges to China's Foreign Trade', in Tao Zhenghua and Rüdiger Wolfrum (eds.), *Implementing International Environmental Law in Germany and China* (London: Kluwer Law International, 2001), p. 192.

7

Law tackling non-traditional security issues

Introduction

After the 9/11 terrorist attacks, non-traditional security issues have caught the attention of the international community, because these issues pose (potential) threats to world peace and security. There is no accurate definition of 'non-traditional security issues'. The term usually refers to emerging issues concerning security, such as terrorism, human trafficking and epidemics, among others.[1] The so-called non-traditional security issues may cause some type of confusion because many of these are in fact considered transnational crimes in the criminal and penal sense, such as in the China–ASEAN (Association of Southeast Asian Nations) Joint Declaration on Cooperation in the Field of Non-Traditional Security Issues. However, it may cover other non-criminal issues such as natural disasters, epidemics, and food and water shortage.

After the collapse of the Soviet Communist Bloc, China gradually revised its security concept in response to the changed situation of the post–Cold War era. In the 1990s, a new security concept was formulated, which is reflected in China's white papers on defence. The 1998 White Paper was the first to put forward this new concept, and the 2000 White Paper detailed the concept by adding to it four core components: mutual trust, mutual benefit, equality and cooperation.[2] These white papers recognise that non-traditional security issues are salient and threatening issues. The latest white paper has put more emphasis on these issues than its previous counterparts, because these issues have become more prominent.[3]

In the China–ASEAN relations, China adheres to the policy to 'maintain its own stability and development, uphold peace and security in the neighborhood areas, promote dialogue and cooperation, and foster harmony and common prosperity in the region'.[4] It has been attending the conferences of the ASEAN Regional Forum (the ARF) since 1995. The ARF, officially launched in 1994, is an important regional mechanism that deals with security issues. China openly supports the positive role played by the ARF in maintaining regional peace and stability, and in exploring and developing dialogue and cooperation in the area of non-traditional security, including counterterrorism. It has been commented: 'China also supports ASEAN in continuing to play a leading role within ARF'.[5] During the ARF foreign ministers' meeting in 1996, China called for the first time 'for the abandonment of the Cold-War mentality and the introduction of a new security concept'.[6] At the ARF Senior Officials Meeting (SOM) held in May 2002, China distributed its Position Paper on Enhanced Cooperation in the Field of Non-Traditional Security Issues. Besides, these issues have also been discussed at the ASEAN+1 forums and the ASEAN plus China meetings.

Legal arrangements in China–ASEAN relations

In November 2002, the Joint Declaration of ASEAN and China on Cooperation in the Field of Non-Traditional Security Issues (the Joint Declaration) was adopted, which initiated full cooperation between ASEAN and China in the area of non-traditional security issues and listed the priority and form of cooperation. The two sides pledge to formulate measures and modalities to enhance their capacity to handle non-traditional security issues so as to safeguard regional peace and security. They agree to cooperate in information exchange, personnel exchange and training, capacity building, joint research and other areas. Their current cooperation priorities include 'combating trafficking in illegal drugs, people-smuggling including trafficking in women and children, sea piracy, terrorism, arms-smuggling, money-laundering, international economic crime and cyber crime.'[7]

Following the Joint Declaration, on 10 January 2004, China and ASEAN (under the authorisation of the governments of its member states) signed the Memorandum of Understanding on Cooperation in the Field of Non-Traditional Security Issues (MOU on Non-Traditional Security Issues) in Bangkok. The MOU was signed between the governments of the member countries of the ASEAN and the government of the People's Republic of China,[8] with an attempt to make the objectives and principles contained in the declaration worth implementing. The two sides pledged to develop practical strategies to 'enhance the capacity of each individual country and the region as a whole in dealing with such non-traditional security issues', but 'in accordance with their national laws and regulations' (Article 1).[9] They identified the following four areas of cooperation: (1) information exchange, (2) personnel exchange and relevant workshops and training courses in China, (3) law-enforcement cooperation for 'evidence gathering, tracing of crime proceeds, apprehension and repatriation of criminal fugitives and return of crime proceeds' and (4) joint research by experts and scholars.[10] The MOU came into effect the same day it was signed and would remain in force for 5 years from the date of its signing. It may be extended subject to approval by the two parties. In November 2007, China and ASEAN member states held a consultative ministerial meeting in Bandar Seri Begawan and agreed to review and revise the MOU in 2009.[11]

In addition, non-traditional security issues are also mentioned in the 2002 Declaration on the Conduct of the Parties in the South China Sea.[12] Finally, it is notable that relevant international treaties are applicable to the legal arrangements between ASEAN and China in dealing with non-traditional security issues such as the treaties sponsored by the United Nations for tackling terrorism and transnational crimes, which is discussed next.

In terms of extradition and judicial assistance, China began to negotiate with its foreign counterparts of bilateral treaties on judicial assistance and/or extradition in 1985. As of March 2008, China had signed 99 such treaties with more than 50 countries.[13] Table 7.1 shows judicial assistance/extradition treaties signed between China and other East Asian countries. Domestically, China promulgated the Extradition Law in December 2000. The law enables China to deal with extradition cases of transnational crimes even without the need for conclusion of extradition treaties.[14]

On the ASEAN side, in May 2002, a significant step was taken by Indonesia, Malaysia and the Philippines with the signing of the Agreement on Information Exchange and Establishment of Communication Procedures[15] with a view to preventing any nation from utilising their land–air–sea territories for the purpose of committing or encouraging terrorism, money laundering, smuggling, piracy, hijacking, intrusion, illegal entry, drug trafficking, theft of marine resources, marine pollution and illicit trafficking of arms.[16] The agreement is open to other ASEAN countries. Following this agreement, the ASEAN ministerial meeting held in Kuala Lumpur in early May 2002 adopted the Work Programme to

Table 7.1 **Bilateral judicial assistance/extradition treaties between China and other East Asian countries (as of 31 March 2008)**

State	Type of treaty	Signed	Came into force (day/month/year)
Cambodia	Extradition	09/02/1999	13/12/2000
Indonesia	Civil and criminal	24/07/2000	28/07/2006
Japan	Criminal	01/12/2007	
Laos	Civil and criminal	25/01/1999	15/12/2001
	Extradition	04/02/2002	13/08/2003
Mongolia	Civil and criminal	31/08/1989	29/10/1990
	Extradition	19/08/1997	10/01/1999
North Korea	Civil and criminal	19/11/2003	21/01/2006
Philippines	Criminal	16/10/2000	
	Extradition	30/10/2001	12/03/2006
Singapore	Civil and commercial	28/04/1997	27/06/1999
South Korea	Criminal	12/11/1998	24/03/2000
	Extradition	18/10/2000	12/04/2002
	Civil and commercial	07/07/2003	27/04/2005
Thailand	Civil and commercial	16/03/1994	06/07/1997
	Extradition	26/08/1993	07/03/1999
	Criminal	21/06/2003	20/02/2005
Vietnam	Civil and criminal	19/10/1998	25/12/1999

Source: Compiled by the author based on *http://www.fmprc.gov.cn/chn/wjb/zzjg/tyfls/tfsckzlk/zgywgsbtyylb/t422584.htm.*

Implement the ASEAN Plan of Action to Combat Transnational Crime, which focuses on eight 'priority areas': illegal drug trafficking, trafficking of personnel, sea piracy, arms smuggling, money laundering, terrorism, international economic crime and cyber crime.[17] The ASEAN member states agreed to work towards the harmonisation of laws among themselves in order to effectively deal with the issues of transnational crime, and also agreed to develop programmes for joint exercises and simulations in various areas to enhance cooperation and coordination in law enforcement and intelligence sharing.[18] Two institutional arrangements were made by the ASEAN members: the ASEAN Ministerial Meeting on Transnational Crime (AMMTC), which is the highest policy-making body on ASEAN cooperation in combating transnational crime, and the Senior Officials Meeting on Transnational Crime (SOMTC), which is the implementing body.[19] For implementing the MOU on Non-Traditional Security Issues, China joined the existing ASEAN cooperative actions on the fight against transnational crime, including the ASEAN Action Plan on the Fight Against Transnational Crime and its Work Program.

Issues tackled

According to the ASEAN–China Declaration as well as the MOU, non-traditional security issues that need to be tackled include trafficking of illegal drugs, people smuggling including trafficking of women and children, sea piracy, terrorism, arms smuggling, money laundering, international economic crime and cyber crime.

Terrorism

Terrorism has become a global threat, particularly after the 9/11 terrorist attacks. It remains a major concern for the world community, including Asian countries. There is no universally accepted definition of terrorism because different states may hold different views and understandings on what exactly constitutes terrorist acts. Therefore, the international treaties adopted under the auspices of the United Nations avoid defining the term.[20] The UN Security Council has only declared that any acts of terrorism 'constitute a threat to international peace and security'.[21] However, some regional conventions contain the definition on terrorism as is shown by the Convention of the Organization of the Islamic Conference on Combating International Terrorism, adopted at Ouagadougou on 1 July 1999, which provides that 'terrorism means any act of violence or threat thereof notwithstanding its motives or intentions perpetrated to carry out an individual or collective criminal plan with the aim of terrorizing people or threatening to harm them or imperiling their lives, honour, freedoms, security or rights or exposing the environment or any facility or public or private property to hazards or occupying or seizing them, or endangering a national resource, or international facilities, or threatening the stability, territorial integrity, political unity or sovereignty of independent States'.[22] Moreover, the draft statute of the

International Criminal Court (ICC) defines 'crimes of terrorism' as the 'undertaking, organizing, sponsoring, ordering, facilitating, financing, encouraging or tolerating acts of violence against another State directed at persons or property and of such a nature as to create terror, fear or insecurity in the minds of public figures, groups of persons, the general public or populations, for whatever considerations and purposes of a political, philosophical, ideological, racial, ethnic, religious or such other nature that may be invoked to justify them'.[23] But in the end the attempt to include the crime of terrorism under the jurisdiction of the ICC failed. Nevertheless, the lack of a universally accepted definition on terrorism does not significantly adversely affect and hinder the efforts made by the world community in the fight against terrorism.[24]

The transnational terrorist organisation Al-Qaeda (the base) has links with terrorist groups in Southeast Asia and China. It plotted and carried out the 2000 Christmas eve bombings in Indonesia in conjunction with Jemaah Islamiyah (JI), a Southeast Asian terrorist group.[25] After 2001, ASEAN member states started intensifying their joint anti-terrorist efforts, marked by the adoption of the ASEAN Declaration on Joint Action to Counter Terrorism at the seventh ASEAN Summit on 5 November 2001. They expressed their commitment to combat terrorism in accordance with the UN Charter, relevant international laws and UN resolutions, and to take practical measures for that purpose.[26] As commented, prior to 2001 there was no unified threat perception among the ASEAN members, but this declaration signified the formulation of a unified ASEAN threat perception of terrorism.[27] The following year, the eighth ASEAN Summit adopted another declaration on terrorism to enhance regional cooperation, including the establishment of a Regional Counter-Terrorism Center in November 2002 in Kuala Lumpur.[28] ASEAN also made a joint declaration with the European Union on counterterrorism in 2003. These declarations aim at not only terrorism but also other transnational crimes. Because these declarations are soft law, the effectiveness of their implementation is doubtful. Hence, there was a need for a regional treaty on terrorism for ASEAN as in other regions.[29] One source has listed four justifications for an ASEAN counterterrorism treaty: (1) lack of an effective international convention to suppress terrorism, (2) existence of active terrorist groups in ASEAN member countries, (3) fear of an Asian connection to international terrorist organisations and (4) threat posed by terrorism to regional stability and economic growth.[30]

Partly in response to these calls, the ASEAN member states finally adopted the ASEAN Convention on Counter Terrorism in January 2007.

It serves as the legal framework 'for regional cooperation to counter, prevent and suppress terrorism in all its forms and manifestations and to deepen cooperation among law enforcement agencies and relevant authorities of the Parties in countering terrorism'.[31] Although it does not define terrorism, it recognises the criminal acts of terrorism prescribed in the 13 UN anti-terrorism treaties. With the condition that state sovereignty is preserved, the contracting parties identify a series of cooperative areas including, inter alia, taking necessary steps to prevent terrorist acts, use of facilities and financing.[32] Besides, the convention provides for the establishment of state jurisdiction over terrorism, fair treatment and the grant of refuge status, mutual legal assistance and extradition, and rehabilitation programmes. It is a significant step taken by the ASEAN in the fight against terrorism. Legally, it is a milestone that signifies a decisive turn from 'soft law' to 'hard law' in the ASEAN anti-terrorism efforts, since before its adoption there had been only political declarations and statements without a legally binding force. Nevertheless, some legal documents related to counterterrorism did exist, for example the 2004 Treaty on Mutual Legal Assistance in Criminal Matters and the 2002 Agreement on Information Exchange and Establishment of Communication Procedures. Even though not all ASEAN members are signatories to these two treaties, the treaties cover all transnational crimes, including terrorism.

Sea piracy

Sea piracy in Southeast Asia is not something new. History records that as early as the fourteenth century, piracy was existent in the waters of Southeast Asia.[33] In the late twentieth century, Southeast Asia was categorised as one of the most active piracy zones in the world, with seven key 'pirate-prone areas'.[34] The figure for 2000 showed that piracy in the region accounted for 65 per cent of the piracy worldwide. From January through March 2002, Indonesia was the country most affected by piracy, facing 22 of the 87 attacks reported worldwide (32 in the Southeast Asian seas).[35] Due to joint efforts of the littoral states, the number of piracy incidents in Southeast Asia has significantly reduced,[36] though piracy still remains a challenging problem for maritime safety and security.

The security of navigation through sea lanes in Southeast Asia is a vital concern for East Asian countries. More than half the world's merchant fleet capacity sails through the Straits of Malacca, Sunda and Lombok and the South China Sea.[37] Annually, more than 10,000 vessels weighing more than 10,000 dwt move southward through the South China Sea, with over 8000 proceeding in the opposite direction.[38]

Traditionally, piracy is regarded as *hostis humani generis*, the enemy of the human race. Pirates commit murder, robbery, plunder, rape or other villainous deeds in the sea. Thus, this offence is punishable in the court of law.[39] The 1982 United Nations Convention on the Law of the Sea (the LOS Convention) defines that piracy 'consists of any of the following acts: (a) any illegal acts of violence or detention, or any act of depredation, committed for private ends by the crew or the passengers of a private ship or a private aircraft, and directed to: (i) on the high seas, against another ship or aircraft, or against persons or property on board such ship or aircraft; (ii) against a ship, aircraft, persons or property in a place outside the jurisdiction of any State; (b) any act of voluntary participation in the operation of a ship or of an aircraft with knowledge of facts making it a pirate ship or aircraft; (c) any act of inciting or of intentionally facilitating an act described in subparagraph (a) or (b).'[40]

However, this definition has limitations with respect to the phenomenon of piracy, as it regards 'piracy' as being committed only for 'private ends' and covers acts of piracy on the high seas or places outside the jurisdiction of states. Thus, after the *Achille Lauro* incident in 1988,[41] the world community needed the Convention on the Suppression of Unlawful Acts Against the Safety of Maritime Navigation (SUA Convention). The Piracy Reporting Center of the International Maritime Bureau of the International Chamber of Commerce (IMB-PRC) suggested another definition of piracy: 'an act of boarding any vessel with the intent to commit theft or any other crime and with the intent or capability to use force in the furtherance of that act'.[42] This definition seems to be accepted by the shipping industry but has not been recognised either in international law and or in domestic law. The International Maritime Organization (IMO) divides act of piracy into two categories on the basis of geographical and legal division of maritime zones: piracy on the high seas is 'piracy' in accordance with the LOS Convention, while that in ports or national waters (internal waters and territorial sea) is 'armed robbery against ships'.[43]

International law has established an obligation on states to cooperate in suppressing piracy. It grants the states certain rights to seize pirate ships and criminals. The LOS Convention is a major anti-piracy treaty in contemporary era with the following relevant provisions:

- *Obligation to cooperate*: Article 100 of the LOS Convention provides that 'All States shall cooperate to the fullest possible extent in the repression of piracy on the high seas or in any other place outside the jurisdiction of any State'.

- *Right to seize pirate ships and criminals*: Article 105 provides that 'on the high seas, or in any other place outside the jurisdiction of any State, every State may seize a pirate ship or aircraft, or a ship or aircraft taken by piracy and under the control of pirates, and arrest the persons and seize the property on board'.
- Only warships or military aircrafts or similar government-authorised ships or aircrafts have the power to seize a pirate ship or aircraft.
- These provisions are also applicable to the exclusive economic zone (EEZ).

In addition, there are supplementary anti-piracy treaties, including the 1988 SUA Convention and the Protocol, which takes care of the following aspects:

- It covers unlawful acts, irrespective of whether they are for political or private ends.
- It aims to punish any person who commits an unlawful offence of intentionally seizing or exercising control over a ship by force or threat, or of performing an act of violence against a person on board a ship, or of destroying a ship or causing damage to it or to its cargo. All such acts that are likely to endanger the safe navigation of a ship are punishable.
- Each contracting party should take necessary measures to establish its jurisdiction over such offences or should extradite the offender or the alleged offender to the contracting party that has the jurisdiction over the offence.
- The convention applies to offences committed in a ship which is navigating or is scheduled to navigate in or through the waters beyond the outer limit of the territorial sea of a coastal state, or applies when the offender or the alleged offender is found in the territory of a contracting party other than the case discussed in the preceding point.
- The 1988 Protocol for the Suppression of Unlawful Acts Against the Safety of Fixed Platforms Located on the Continental Shelf (the SUA Protocol) contains similar provisions.

China borders the South China Sea, which is located in Southeast Asia. The sea area with its coasts in Hong Kong, Luzon Island and Hainan Island is called 'the Hainan Triangle'. It is a pirate resort. China signed the LOS Convention in 1982 and ratified it in 1996. In addition, China has also ratified the two 1988 Rome legal documents against maritime terrorism. Piracy is subject to the Chinese law and law enforcement via its criminal code. According to its recently amended criminal law, certain crimes, particularly those that endanger public security, are related to piracy, so piracy can be punishable under its law. This law also allows China to enforce anti-piracy conventions within its territory.

Other pertinent laws are Maritime Traffic Safety Law, 1984 (concerns the safety of navigation); the Law on the Territorial Sea and the Contiguous Zone, 1992 (establishes the territorial sea and contiguous zone in China and provides the right of hot pursuit to chase and arrest suspected piracy vessels); and the Law on the Exclusive Economic Zone and the Continental Shelf, 1998 (establishes China's jurisdiction in its EEZ and on its continental shelf, including the right of hot pursuit). In addition, the Opinion on Strengthening the Safety of Navigation and Fishery in the East China Sea adopted in 1993 is particularly relevant to the suppression of piracy within China's jurisdictional waters. Despite these efforts, law enforcement is still weak due to various factors such as lack of effective coast guard, vastness of sea areas and local protectionism of interest.[44]

With the rapid growth of its economy, China has become more dependent on energy resources from abroad. Transportation of petroleum products to China through sea lanes in East Asia, in particular through the Malacca Strait, has become more frequent. Eighty per cent of its imported oil is shipped to China through this sea lane. Thus, China recently expressed its deep concerns with the navigational safety of the Malacca Strait and its strong interests in strait affairs. As reported, China expressed its willingness to help strengthen maritime security in straits.[45]

The ASEAN member states Indonesia, Malaysia and Singapore ratified the LOS Convention, but only Singapore is the signatory to the SUA Convention. Indonesia suffers the most serious problem of piracy in the whole Southeast Asian region. It has been long criticised for its slow and ineffective response to piracy. In order to strengthen its fight against piracy, it has established a number of anti-piracy centres in Medan on Sumatra, on Batam Island and in Bangka on Sumatra.[46] In Malaysian waters, in particular in the Strait of Malacca, recent strong anti-piracy measures achieved good results. For example, in 2000, there were 75 attacks in Malaysia waters, but after the Malaysian authorities took measures, the number was reduced to 17 in 2001.[47] Due to the severity of piracy in the Strait of Malacca, these three countries have intensified the degree of their trilateral cooperation. In the end of July 2005, a scheme of maritime air surveillance was discussed, which aimed to strengthen the crackdown of piracy in this critical international waterway.[48] In August 2005, the three countries agreed to implement the scheme of air patrol over the Malacca Strait from September 2005 and also agreed to establish a Tripartite Technical Experts Group on Maritime Security.[49] All these tripartite cooperative operations, whether in the sea or in air, are called 'coordinated', rather than joint, patrols.

Other ASEAN countries such as the Philippines, Vietnam, Myanmar, Thailand and Cambodia are affected with piracy, but not so seriously as Malaysia and Indonesia. Since Cambodia and Thailand have not yet ratified the LOS Convention, they are not bound by the treaty obligation under the convention, including the suppression of piracy. However, when the provisions on piracy in the LOS Convention are regarded as rules of international customary law, countries outside the convention should also abide by them. Though not a party member of the LOS Convention, Thailand expressed its willingness to join the recently adopted anti-terrorism agreement among Indonesia, Malaysia and the Philippines.

Cooperation has already begun at the regional level, such as the tripartite cooperation among Indonesia, Malaysia and Singapore. The IMB Piracy Reporting Center was established in Kuala Lumpur in October 1992. It acts as a focal point for the industry. It liaisons with the law-enforcement authorities in the region as well as in the world. Its functions include: (1) to receive reports of suspicious or unexplained craft movements, boarding and armed robbery from ships and to alert other ships and law-enforcement agencies, (2) to issue regular status reports of piracy and armed robbery via broadcasts on Inmarsat-C through its SafetyNET service and (3) to collate and analyse all information received and to issue consolidated reports to interested bodies, including the IMO.[50]

The most significant development is the Regional Cooperation Agreement on Combating Piracy and Armed Robbery Against Ships in Asia (ReCAAP), which was adopted in 2004 by 16 Asian countries, including 10 ASEAN member states, China together with Bangladesh, India, Japan, Sri Lanka and South Korea. The agreement mandates the contracting states (a) to prevent and suppress piracy and armed robbery against ships, (b) to arrest pirates who have committed armed robbery against ships, (c) to seize ships or aircrafts used for committing piracy or armed robbery against ships and (d) to rescue ships and people who are victims of piracy or armed robbery.[51] For cooperation, the contracting parties should endeavour to render mutual legal assistance as well as extradition for piracy suppression and punishment. The agreement came into force in September 2006 and the ReCAAP Information Sharing Center (ISC) was accordingly established in Singapore.[52]

Illegal human trafficking

There are similar as well as different terms related to human trafficking. The Protocol Against the Smuggling of Migrants by Land, Sea and Air (the Smuggling Protocol) to the United Nations Convention Against Transnational Organized Crime (the Palermo Convention)[53] uses the term 'smuggling of migrants', which refers to 'the procurement, in order to obtain, directly or indirectly, a financial or other material benefit, of the illegal entry of a person into a State Party of which the person is not a national or a permanent resident'.[54] Related to this is the definition of 'trafficking of persons', which is contained in the Protocol to Prevent, Suppress and Punish Trafficking in Persons, Especially Women and Children to the Palermo Convention (the Trafficking Protocol). It refers to 'the recruitment, transportation, transfer, harbouring or receipt of persons, by means of the threat or use of force or other forms of coercion, of abduction, of fraud, of deception, of the abuse of power or of a position of vulnerability or of the giving or receiving of payments or benefits to achieve the consent of a person having control over another person, for the purpose of exploitation'.[55] The definition in the Trafficking Protocol is widely accepted by the world community as an operational definition.

In the late 1990s, the issue of human smuggling was put on the UN agenda, and the discussion culminated with the adoption of the Palermo Convention in New York on 15 November 2000, together with three protocols, of which two directly concern with the illegal human trafficking issue. The convention came into force on 29 September 2003. As of May 2008, 143 countries ratified or acceded to the convention. In East Asia, eight countries – Brunei, Cambodia, China, Laos, Malaysia, Myanmar, the Philippines and Singapore – joined the treaty (see Table 7.2). Besides, Cambodia, Laos, Myanmar and the Philippines acceded to the Trafficking Protocol and the Smuggling Protocol.

The Palermo Convention, which was the first comprehensive multilateral legal instrument in this regard, aims to promote international cooperation so as to prevent and combat transnational organised crime. It contains specific provisions for the prevention, investigation and prosecution of organised transnational crimes. The main area which requires cooperation among state parties is the provision on mutual legal assistance, which can be undertaken through competent authorities of the states parties.

The Smuggling Protocol, which entered into force on 28 January 2004, aims at preventing and combating smuggling, promoting cooperation among state parties and protecting the rights of smuggled migrants.

Table 7.2 United Nations Convention Against Transnational Organized Crime in East Asia (as of 10 May 2008)

State	Signature	Ratification/accession
Brunei		25 Mar 2008
Cambodia	11 Nov 2001	12 Dec 2005
China	12 Dec 2000	27 Aug 2003
Indonesia	12 Dec 2000	
Japan	12 Dec 2000	
Laos		26 Sept 2003
Malaysia	26 Sep 2002	24 Sept 2004
Mongolia		
Myanmar		30 Mar 2004
North Korea		
Philippines	14 Dec 2000	28 May 2002
Republic of Korea	13 Dec 2000	
Singapore	13 Dec 2000	28 Aug 2007
Thailand	13 Dec 2000	
Vietnam	13 Dec 2000	

Source: Compiled by the author (mainly based on *http://www.unodc.org/unodc/crime_cicp_signatures_convention.html*).

Many of its provisions are intended to ensure that the approaches taken by member states under their domestic legislative and law-enforcement regimes are as coordinated as possible to make collective international measures both efficient and effective.[56] The protocol applies to the prevention, investigation and prosecution of the smuggling of migrants as well as to the protection of the rights of persons who have been the object of such offences. Although states that are parties to the protocol are required to criminalise the smuggling of migrants and other forms of activities that support such smuggling, it is stipulated that migrants should not be liable for being involved in smuggling. State parties are required to strengthen border measures and mandate commercial carriers to check the travel documents of passengers, to raise awareness among the migrants about the dangers of smuggling and to accept repatriated migrants who had residential right in that country before they were smuggled.

The Trafficking Protocol is designed to prevent and combat such crime and facilitate international cooperation against it. The protocol highlights the problems associated with trafficking of persons, that is inhuman, degraded and dangerous exploitation of trafficked persons. Law-enforcement agencies of countries which ratify the protocol should cooperate in identifying offenders and trafficked persons, sharing information about the methods of offenders, and training investigators and enforcement and victim-support personnel. Like the Smuggling Protocol, the Trafficking Protocol also requires state parties to implement security and border controls so as to detect and prevent trafficking, including requirements on commercial carriers to check passports and visas and standards for the technical quality of passports and other travel documents. The Trafficking Protocol came into force on 25 December 2003.

According to the report of the UN Office on Drugs and Crime, 'Asia is mainly an origin region as well as a destination for trafficking in persons'.[57] China (PRC), as one of the biggest and the most populated countries in East Asia, is inevitably haunted by the human trafficking problem. It is often accused of exporting large number of illegal immigrants to Australia, Europe and North America. It is very reasonable that any literature on illegal human trafficking in East Asia cannot neglect the significant influence of China over the emergence as well as the resolution of the issue. In fact, in the East Asian region, most of the illegal immigration cases occur in China.

In comparison, illegal emigration from other countries into China is a much less serious problem. However, with the open-door policy and rapid economic growth, more and more foreigners have moved into China for various reasons. They mainly come from China's neighbouring countries, such as Russia, Cambodia and Vietnam, with the main purpose of making money and improving their living conditions. Most illegal migrants in China are from North Korea. The large-scale illegal emigration from North Korea to China began in 1997 due to food shortages and human rights violations in their home country.[58] It is estimated that China may have hosted 300,000 illegal North Korean immigrants. Some recent cases have revealed that organised criminal organisations are involved in the smuggling of North Korean illegal immigrants to China. A Japanese snakehead Takayuki Noguchi was deported in August 2004 after he had served an 8-month jail sentence for smuggling two North Koreans out of China. He was paid 5 million yen (US$4511) to take the two Koreans from Dalian to Nanning and, with assistance from Chinese collaborators, helped them cross the Chinese border. He was arrested on 13 December 2003 when he made a second attempt to smuggle out two other Koreans.[59]

As a transnational crime, illegal human trafficking is subject to crack-down measures provided in the Palermo Convention, which China ratified on 27 August 2003.[60] In order to fulfill its international treaty obligation, China needs to take necessary measures in this regard, including legal measures. In China's legal system, there are two main categories related to the prevention and suppression of illegal human trafficking: criminal law and border control regulations.

The Chinese criminal law provides that 'for the crimes defined in international treaties, concluded or acceded to by the People's Republic of China, which are under the jurisdiction of the People's Republic of China within the framework of the treaty obligations, this Law shall apply'.[61] It thus establishes the universal jurisdiction of China over transnational crimes including illegal human trafficking, which is a statutory crime under the Chinese criminal law. It is punishable under 'crimes of obstructing national border control'. Accordingly, anyone who organises people to secretly cross the national border is to be sentenced to fixed-term imprisonment from 2 to 7 years, and may also be fined. In serious cases, the penal punishment can be much severe.

Three to ten years of imprisonment can be imposed on those who obtain passports, visas or other exit documents by using false plans of labour export, business transactions or other excuses for the purpose of organising people to secretly cross the national border, or those who provide false or altered passports, visas or other exit documents or sell passports or visas.[62]

In 1994, the National People's Congress (NPC) adopted the Supplementary Rules for Severely Punishing Crimes of Organizing or Transporting Other People to Secretly Cross the National Border.[63] These rules contain three characteristics. First, they reinforce the severity of punishment for those who commit 'crimes of obstructing national border control'. Second, they detail some provisions of the criminal law. Finally, these rules have some new provisions, including imprisonment for civil servants, such as those who work at passport, border control or customs offices, but help illegal crossings.[64] In addition, relevant crimes stipulated in the criminal law include the crime of abducting or selling a woman or a child, since many women are victims of illegal human trafficking.

The second category of laws and regulations which govern the subject is the one concerning control over the entry into and exit from the Chinese border. There are two major laws in this field: the Law on the Management of the Border Entry and Exit of Foreigners and the Law on the Management of the Border Entry and Exit of Chinese Citizens, both promulgated in November 1985.[65] The entry, transit or sojourn of foreigners is subject to the approval of the relevant Chinese authorities and must undergo inspection at the border. Although the legitimate rights and interests of foreigners are protected within the Chinese territory, they have to comply with Chinese laws. Foreigners who illegally enter into, exit from or stay in China may receive a warning, or may be fined or put to custody for less than 10 days by the public security department above the county level. Those who commit crimes are subject to criminal liability, and the Department of Public Security may expel any foreigner who has seriously broken the law. Chinese citizens must hold valid passports or other valid documents when they enter or exit the country, and must accept the inspection of the border control agency; they should not do any harm to China's security, honour and interest when they go overseas.[66]

As for ASEAN, a declaration adopted in 2004 by the ASEAN members has directed their efforts towards the prevention and punishment of illegal human trafficking. Accordingly, ASEAN members agree '(1) to establish a regional focal network to prevent and combat trafficking in persons, particularly women and children, in the ASEAN region; (2) to adopt measures to protect the integrity of their respective passports, official travel documents, identity and other official travel documents from fraud; (3) to undertake regular exchange of views, information sharing on relevant migratory flows, trends and pattern, strengthening of border controls and monitoring mechanisms, and the enactment of applicable and necessary legislations; (4) to intensify cooperation among our respective immigration and other law enforcement authorities; (5) to distinguish victims of trafficking in persons from the perpetrators, and identify the countries of origin and nationalities of such victims and thereafter ensure that such victims are treated humanely and provided with such essential medical and other forms of assistance deemed appropriate by the respective receiving/ recipient country, including prompt repatriation to their respective countries of origin; (6) to undertake actions to respect and safeguard the dignity and human rights of genuine victims of trafficking in persons; (7) to undertake coercive actions/measures against individual and/or syndicate engaged in trafficking in persons and shall offer one another the widest possible assistance to punish such activities; and (8) to take measures to strengthen regional and international cooperation to prevent and combat trafficking in persons'.[67] The ASEAN member states also prepared a plan of action[68] for cooperation on immigration matters. Some relevant agreements within the ASEAN include, inter alia, the 2002 Agreement on Information Exchange and Establishment of Communication Procedures and the 2004 Treaty on Mutual Legal

Table 7.3 **Human trafficking prosecution, conviction and new legislation in East Asia and the Pacific**

Year	Prosecutions	Convictions	New/amended legislation
2003	1727	583	1
2004	438	348	3
2005	2580	2347	5
2006	1,321*	763*	3

Source: US Department of State, *Victims of Trafficking and Violence Protection Act of 2000: Trafficking in Persons Report 2007*, available at *http://www.state.gov/g/tip/rls/tiprpt/2007/* (accessed 14 May 2008).

*The decline in 2006 is largely due to the lack of data provided by China.

Assistance in Criminal Matters as well as the ASEAN Framework Agreement on Visa Exemption.[69] Table 7.3 shows recent laws and law enforcement in East Asia.

In China–ASEAN relations, the two sides cooperate on the basis of the 2002 Joint Declaration and the 2004 MOU on Non-Traditional Security Issues. In October 2003, the AMMTC was in Bangkok with ministerial counterparts from China, Japan and South Korea. China began to train policepersons from Laos, Myanmar and Vietnam. The training course includes criminal investigative techniques, surveillance analyses, ammunitions handling and other criminal investigative technologies.[70] In 2004, China and Vietnam conducted law-enforcement and training activities aimed at combating transboundary child trafficking. Same year in October, China signed an MOU with Cambodia, Laos, Myanmar, Thailand and Vietnam on cooperation to combat human trafficking in the Greater Mekong Sub-Region (GMS).[71]

The six-party MOU established the Coordinated Mekong Ministerial Initiative Against Trafficking (COMMIT). As commented, 'COMMIT is the first regional instrument making a serious effort to institutionalize a multi-sectoral approach to ensure that the obligations and commitments made in the MOU and the subsequent Sub-regional Plan of Action (SPA) are translated into a timely manner and in accordance with agreed international norms and standards'.[72] Its secretariat is located in Bangkok-based UN Inter-Agency Project on Human Trafficking in the GMS (UNIAP).

The COMMIT MOU provides five areas of cooperation among the GMS countries: 'policy and cooperation', 'legal frameworks, law enforcement and justice', 'protection, recovery and reintegration', 'preventive measures' and 'mechanisms for implementation, monitoring and evaluation'. It endorses the definition provided by the Trafficking Protocol. The contracting parties agreed to coordinate the implementation of their national plans of action, to improve regional cooperation, to adopt and enforce national anti-trafficking laws, to cooperate in criminal justice, to adopt policies and mechanisms for the protection of the victims of trafficking, to adopt measures to reduce vulnerability to trafficking, to develop a regional plan of action and to establish a monitoring system for the implementation of the plan of action.[73] The MOU linked itself to a series of international treaties: in addition to the Palermo Convention and the Trafficking Protocol, it links to the UN Convention on the Elimination of All Forms of Discrimination against Women, the UN Convention on the Rights of the Child and its protocols, the ILO Forced Labour Conventions (29 & 105) and the ILO Convention (182) Concerning the Prohibition and Immediate Action for the Elimination of the Worst Forms of Child Labour.

Illegal drug trafficking

Closely related to human trafficking is the issue of drug trafficking in China and Southeast Asia. Drug abuse and trafficking is a serious problem around the world. At the international level, there are two treaties that deal with this non-traditional security issue: the 1971 Vienna Convention on Psychotropic Substances[74] and the 1988 UN Convention Against Illicit Traffic in Narcotics Drugs and Psychotropic Substances.[75] Significantly, this convention has been ratified by all East Asian countries (see Table 7.4). Cannabis, cocaine, heroin and synthetic drugs like amphetamine-type stimulants (ATS) are the four main categories of illicit drugs. In Southeast Asia, drug crimes are severely punishable acts, particularly in Malaysia and Singapore. ASEAN took action as early as 1976 when the ASEAN Declaration of Principles to Combat the Abuse of Narcotics Drugs was issued.[76] In October 1994 it adopted the ASEAN Plan of Action on Drug Abuse and Control, a new effort for tackling the drug problem, which focused on four cooperative areas: preventive drug education; treatment, rehabilitation and social integration; law enforcement; and research.[77] In 1998 and 2000, two declarations on drugs were made by the ASEAN government heads who pledged to seek a drug-free ASEAN by 2015.[78]

In China too, drug crime is considered a serious offence under the Chinese criminal law. In December 2007, China promulgated the Law on the Prohibition of Narcotic Drugs, which came into force on 1 June 2008.[79] Chapter 5 of the law specifically provides for international cooperation against drugs and drug trafficking. As stipulated, under the authorisation of

Table 7.4 **United Nations Convention Against Illicit Traffic in Narcotics Drugs and Psychotropic Substances in East Asia (as of 10 May 2008)**

State	Signature	Ratification/accession
Brunei	26 Oct 1989	12 Nov 1993
Cambodia		7 July 2005
China	20 Dec 1988	25 Oct 1989
Indonesia	27 Mar 1989	23 Feb 1999
Japan	19 Dec 1989	12 Jun 1992
Laos		1 Oct 2004
Malaysia	20 Dec 1988	11 May 1993
Mongolia		25 Jun 2003
Myanmar		11 Jun 1991
North Korea		19 Mar 2007
Philippines	20 Dec 1988	7 Jun 1996
Republic of Korea		28 Dec 1998
Singapore		23 Oct 1997
Thailand		3 May 2002
Vietnam		4 Nov 1997

Source: Compiled by the author (based on *http://www.unodc.org/unodc/en/treaties/illicit-trafficking.html*).

the State Council, the National Narcotics Control Commission (NNCC) is responsible for conducting international cooperation and implementing international treaty obligations (Article 54). Matters related to legal assistance are dealt by judicial organs in accordance with relevant laws (Article 55). Relevant departments of the State Council should enhance information exchange with law-enforcement organs of other countries and with international organisations, and should cooperate in law enforcement to control drug-related crime (Article 56). Illegal gains and proceeds from drug trafficking in criminal cases can be shared by China and other countries (Article 57). China supports cultivation of alternative plants to replace narcotic plants in the involved countries (Article 58).

The China–ASEAN cooperation in dealing with the narcotics problem officially commenced in October 2000 when the two sides adopted the plan of action on the ASEAN and China Cooperative Operation in Response to Dangerous Drugs (ACCORD),[80] with the aim to pursue a drug-free ASEAN and China by 2015. There are four pillars of the plan: civic awareness, demand reduction, law enforcement and alternative development. One scholar considers this institutional arrangement as one that 'presents most of the characteristics of an international regime'.[81] The second Congress of the ACCORD issued the Beijing Declaration in October 2005, which reaffirms 'the significance of the ACCORD mechanism as a unique regional drug control framework encompassing both ASEAN and China', endorses the revised 'ACCORD Plan of Action' and the Regional Joint Action Against ATS-related Crimes Initiative and promotes the development of relevant anti-drug laws and regulations.[82] Since China and ASEAN countries launched the joint action to combat amphetamine-type drug crimes in December 2005, law-enforcement departments from China, the Philippines, Malaysia, Indonesia, Singapore, Myanmar and Thailand have been targetting a group of big drug cases and have formed a highly efficient cooperative mechanism.[83] For example, China and the Philippines cracked down on a number of drug trafficking cases.[84] In 2007, China uncovered three big transborder drug cases involving several countries such as Canada, Japan, Myanmar and the United States.[85]

As for alternative cultivation programmes, China issued a special document in April 2006 to encourage Chinese enterprises to go to Myanmar and Laos to conduct alternative development work. It also established a special fund for alternative development abroad.[86] Since the 1990s, China has invested more than 500 million RMB in alternative development in Myanmar and Laos, covering more than 600,000 mu.[87] The poppy cultivation area reduced by 85 per cent, from 157,900 hectares in 1998 to 24,160 hectares in 2007.[88]

During 19–21 September 2007, the ARF Symposium on Prohibition of Drugs was held in Xi'an, China. It was organised jointly by China and Thailand. Participants from 23 countries examined the implementation of the cooperative consensus and exchanged views on anti-drug policy and experiences. The conference appreciated the active role the ARF has played in pushing forward the dialogue and cooperation in the area of non-traditional security and in enhancing the capacity of the region to face the challenge.[89]

Other non-traditional security areas

As reflected in the MOU on Non-traditional Security Issues, there are other areas of non-traditional security issues to be covered in the

China–ASEAN cooperative framework, for instance money laundering, which is connected to other transnational crimes such as terrorism and illicit human and drug trafficking. China and ASEAN states have made efforts to deter the economic power of criminal or terrorist organisations in accordance with relevant international treaties. The first international legal instrument to embody the concept of money laundering and criminalise it is the 1988 UN Convention Against Illicit Traffic in Narcotics Drugs and Psychotropic Substances. Other treaties include the UN Convention Against Transnational Organized Crime, the UN Convention Against Corruption and the International Convention for the Suppression of the Financing of Terrorism.[90] China is the hub of international money laundering. 'According to statistics provided by the National Statistics Bureau in China, there have been crackdowns in 500 cases of illegal foreign exchanges since 1998, and underground banks have been eradicated in 600 cases; more than $25 million has been confiscated'.[91] In China's legal system, the 1997 amendment of its criminal law contains a specific clause to punish money laundering. In March 2003, the People's Bank of China promulgated the Rules for Anti-Money Laundering by Financial Institutions, Administrative Rules for the Reporting of Large-Value and Suspicious RMB Payment Transactions and Administrative Rules for the Reporting by Financial Institutions of Large-Value and Suspicious Foreign Exchange Transactions, which set forth anti-money-laundering (AML) supervisory requirements for banking institutions and set up the basic framework for China's system of AML reporting and AML information monitoring.[92] In October 2006, China promulgated the Anti-Money Laundering Law, which came into force on 1 July 2007. It contains provisions on international cooperation.[93]

On the other hand, there are some non-traditional security issues which are not covered by the MOU on Non-Traditional Security Issues, but for which China and ASEAN did cooperate, such as the prevention of epidemics. The efforts in the prevention and control of HIV/AIDS made by China and ASEAN began in 1999. In 2002 China proposed and ASEAN accepted the establishment of the ASEAN AIDS Laboratory Network.[94] Since AIDS is particularly related to drug abuse, it is also monitored under the ACCORD. Since 2003, the two sides have been cooperating in the prevention and control of SARS and avian flu. Relevant mechanisms for monitoring and information exchange have been established, among other cooperation activities.[95] As for disaster management, China launched the first ever, the largest of its overseas aid for relief operations for countries (including ASEAN members Indonesia and

Myanmar) which were struck by the Asian tsunami disaster in 2004.[96] Also, in response to the tsunami, the ASEAN members concluded the ASEAN Agreement on Disaster Management and Emergency Response[97] in Vientiane on 26 July 2005.

Conclusion

Non-traditional security issues are common serious concerns for all countries. The concept may cover a broad range of issues affecting human living and progress. The list demonstrated in the MOU on Non-Traditional Security Issues is limited only to transnational and international crimes. Even for transnational and international crimes, the list is not conclusive. As discussed in the chapter, China and ASEAN have put in sincere efforts to solve transnational crimes. However, so far the results are limited. They have not substantially launched cooperative activities in such areas as money laundering and cyber crime, among others. It is perceived that the China–ASEAN cooperation in the area of non-traditional security field will be a long-term endeavour.

Notes

1. According to some statistics, more than 30 issues can be listed under the heading of 'non-traditional security issues'. see Yizhou Wang, 'Defining Non-Traditional Security and Its Implications for China', available at *http://www.iwep.org.cn* (accessed 1 May 2008). As Wang comments, 'almost all issues can be included in the 'big basket' of NTS once they are regarded as serious enough'.
2. 'White Paper on Defence: New Security Concept of Adhering to Mutual Trust, Mutual Benefit, Equality and Cooperation', 27 December 2004, available at *http://www.people.com.cn/GB/shizheng/1027/3082005.html* (accessed 16 May 2008).
3. White Paper on Defence 2006, available at *http://news.sina.com.cn/c/2006-12-29/123911916402.shtml* (accessed 16 May 2008).
4. ARF, *Annual Security Outlook 2007*, p. 26, available at *http://www.aseanregionalforum.org/Default.aspx?tabid=300* (accessed 16 May 2008).
5. 'Speech by Chinese Foreign Minister Tang Jiaxuan at 9th ARF Foreign Ministers' Meeting (8 August 2002)', 19 April 2004, available at *http://www.china-un.ch/eng/ljzg/zgwjzc/t85873.htm* (accessed 1 May 2008).
6. Ibid.
7. Joint Declaration of ASEAN and China on Cooperation in the Field of Non-Traditional Security Issues, 6th ASEAN–China Summit, Phnom Penh, Cambodia, 4 November 2002, available at *http://www.aseansec.org/13185.htm* (accessed 2 July 2004).

8. Text is available at *http://www.aseansec.org/15647.htm* (accessed 1 May 2008).
9. This is difficult to understand, since non-traditional security issues as listed in the MOU are transnational crimes, and international law is indispensable for their prevention and punishment. But only national laws are mentioned here.
10. Article 2 of the MOU on Non-Traditional Security Issues.
11. 'Joint Press Statement – Informal ASEAN Ministerial Meeting on Transnational Crime Plus China Consultation, Bandar Seri Begawan, 7 November 2007', available at *http://www.aseansec.org/21044.htm* (accessed 6 May 2008).
12. The parties agree to explore cooperative activities in 'combating transnational crime, including but not limited to trafficking in illicit drugs, piracy and armed robbery at sea, and illegal traffic in arms'. Text of the declaration is available at *http://www.aseansec.org/13163.htm* (accessed 28 March 2005).
13. *http://www.fmprc.gov.cn/chn/wjb/zzjg/tyfls/wjzdtyflgz/zgywgdsfxzyflhz/t422555.htm* (accessed 9 May 2008).
14. Text is available at *http://162.105.148.239:8082/newlaw2001/ShowLawContent.asp?LinkLawId=&DatabaseName=chl&Id=32110* (accessed 21 July 2003). For further details, see Hu Qian and Chen Qiang, 'China's Extradition Law of 2000', *Chinese Journal of International Law*, vol. 1 (2), 2002, pp. 645–54.
15. Text is available at *http://www.aseansec.org/4964.htm* (accessed 18 May 2008).
16. 'Thailand to Join SE Asian Nations in Terrorism Agreement', *Asia Pulse*, 9 May 2002.
17. 'Work Programme to Implement the ASEAN Plan of Action to Combat Transnational Crime', available at *http://www.aseansec.org/5616.htm* (accessed 18 May 2008).
18. 'Asean plan to fight terror', *The Straits Times*, 18 May 2002.
19. 'ASEAN Plan of Action to Combat Transnational Crime', available at *http://www.aseansec.org/16133.htm* (accessed 18 May 2008).
20. This can be seen in, from example the International Convention for the Suppression of Terrorist Bombings, adopted by the UN General Assembly on 15 December 1997; International Convention for the Suppression of the Financing of Terrorism, adopted by the UN General Assembly on 9 December 1999; and International Convention for the Suppression of Acts of Nuclear Terrorism, adopted on 13 April 2005. For reference, see Reuven Young, 'Defining Terrorism: The Evolution of Terrorism as a Legal Concept in International Law and Its Influence on Definitions in Domestic Legislation', *Boston College International and Comparative Law Review*, vol. 29, 2006, pp. 23–105.
21. UNSC Resolution 1373 (S/RES/1373(2001)), 28 September 2001, available at *http://daccess-ods.un.org/TMP/4662871.html* (accessed 14 May 2008).
22. Article 1 (2) of the convention. Text is available at *http://www.oic-un.org/26icfm/c.html* (accessed 5 May 2008).
23. 'Report of the Preparatory Committee on the Establishment of an International Criminal Court', UN Doc. A/CONF.183/2/Add.1, 14 April

1998, p. 27, available at *http://daccess-ods.un.org/TMP/9079310.html* (accessed 5 May 2008).
24. It is acknowledged that different definitions created obstacles in reaching international agreements on terrorism. See Jacqueline Ann Carberry, 'Terrorism: A Global Phenomenon Mandating a Unified International Response', *Indiana Journal of Global Legal Studies*, vol. 6 (2), 1999, pp. 710–11.
25. Rohan Gunaratna, *Inside Al-Qaeda* (London: Hurst & Company, 2002), p. 10.
26. '2001 ASEAN Declaration on Joint Action to Counter Terrorism'. Text is available at *http://www.aseansec.org/5620.htm* (accessed 6 May 2008).
27. Jonathan T. Chow, 'ASEAN Counterterrorism Cooperation since 9/11', *Asian Survey*, vol. 45 (2), 2005, p. 308.
28. 'Declaration on Terrorism by the 8th ASEAN Summit'. Text is available at *http://www.aseansec.org/13154.htm* (accessed 6 May 2008).
29. For other regions, there has been Arab Convention on the Suppression of Terrorism, signed at a meeting held at the General Secretariat of the League of Arab States in Cairo on 22 April 1998; Convention of the Organization of the Islamic Conference on Combating International Terrorism, adopted at Ouagadougou on 1 July 1999; European Convention on the Suppression of Terrorism, concluded at Strasbourg on 27 January 1977; OAS Convention to Prevent and Punish Acts of Terrorism Taking the Form of Crimes Against Persons and Related Extortion That are of International Significance, concluded at Washington, D.C., on 2 February 1971; OAU Convention on the Prevention and Combating of Terrorism, adopted at Algiers on 14 July 1999; SAARC Regional Convention on Suppression of Terrorism, signed at Kathmandu on 4 November 1987 and Treaty on Cooperation among States Members of the Commonwealth of Independent States in Combating Terrorism, signed at Minsk on 4 June 1999. Texts of most of the above treaties are available at *http://untreaty.un.org/English/Terrorism.asp* (accessed 5 May 2008).
30. Ong Yen Nee, 'International Responses to Terrorism: The Limits and Possibilities of Legal Control of Terrorism by Regional Arrangement with Particular Reference to Asean', IDSS Working Paper No. 29, July 2002 (Institute of Defence and Strategic Studies, Nanyang Technological University, Singapore), p. 20. For further reference, see Gregory Rose and Diana Nestorovska, 'Towards an ASEAN Counter-Terrorism Treaty', *Singapore Year Book of International Law*, vol. 9, 2005, pp. 157–89.
31. Article 1 of the Convention. Text is available at *http://www.aseansec.org/19250.htm* (accessed 21 May 2008).
32. Article 2 of the convention.
33. For historical background on piracy in Southeast Asia, see Robert C. Beckman, Carl Grundy-Warr and Vivian L. Forbes, 'Acts of Piracy in the Malacca and Singapore Straits', *IBRU Maritime Briefing*, vol. 1 (4), 1994, pp. 1–4.
34. They are (1) the Strait of Malacca, (2) the northern tip of Sumatra, near the Benaaten Strait, (3) the Phillip Channel and waters near the Riau Islands of Indonesia, (4) the South China Sea, near the Anambas Islands, (5) the South

China Sea, east of Pulau Tioman, near Mangkai, (6) the South China Sea, near Pedra Branca/Pulau Batu Puteh and (7) the Bangka Strait. SNSA, Press Release, May 1992; cited in Beckman et al, supra note 33, p. 13.

35. 'Pirate Attacks Jumped 28% in First Quarter', *The Shipping Times* (Singapore), 10 May 2002.
36. According to statistics, 24 incidents took place in the second quarter of 2008. See Jane Chan, 'Southeast Asia Maritime Security Review, 2nd Quarter 2008 (S. Rajaratnam School of International Studies, Nanyang Technological University, Singapore), p. 1, available at *http://www.rsis.edu.sg/research/PDF/Southeast_Asia_Maritime_Security_Review-2ndQtr08.pdf* (accessed 21 July 2008).
37. Stanley B. Weeks, 'Sea Lines of Communications (SLOC) Security and Access', in Michael Stankiewicz (ed.), *Maritime Shipping in Northeast Asia: Law of the Sea, Sea Lanes, and Security*, IGCC Policy Paper No. 33 (Institute on Global Conflict and Co-operation, University of California, February 1998), p. 55.
38. Hal Olson, 'Marine Traffic in the South China Sea', *Ocean Yearbook*, vol. 12, 1996, p. 137.
39. As is said, 'a pirate, under the law of nations, is an enemy of the human race; being the enemy of all, he is liable to be punished by all'. Appendix to *United States v. Smith*, Wheaton (U.S.), vol. 5 (153), 1820, pp. 7–8; quoted in the Harvard Draft Convention, *American Journal of International Law*, Supplement, vol. 26 (4), 1932, p. 764.
40. Article 101 of the LOS Convention. United Nations, *The Law of the Sea: United Nations Convention on the Law of the Sea with Index and Final Act of the Third United Nations Conference on the Law of the Sea* (New York: United Nations, 1983), p. 34.
41. On 3 October 1985, a group of Palestinian guerrillas hijacked the Italian cruise ship *Achille Lauro* within the Egyptian territorial waters. The hijackers demanded the release of 50 Palestinians held by Israel in return of the release of the passengers. They ordered the ship to sail to Syria, which refused them port entry. On 8 October, the hijackers killed an American passenger. Several days later the four hijackers surrendered before the Egyptian authorities. On 11 October, an Egyptian civilian aircraft was intercepted by United States military aircraft over the Mediterranean Sea and was instructed to land at an air base in Sicily. Four Palestinians on board were detained by the Italian authorities and were subsequently indicted and convicted in Genoa for offences related to the hijacking of the ship and the death of the American passenger.
42. IMB Piracy Reporting Centre, *Piracy and Armed Robbery against Ships*, Report for the Period of 1 January–30 June 1998, Kuala Lumpur, July 1998, p. 1.
43. Birgit S. Olsen, 'Piracy and the Law', paper presented to the IMO Seminar and Workshop on Piracy and Armed Robbery against Ships, Singapore, 3–5 February 1999, p. 2 (on file with the author).
44. For details, see Zou Keyuan, 'Piracy at Sea and China's Response', *Lloyd's Maritime and Commercial Law Quarterly*, August 2000, pp. 364–82.
45. 'Indonesian Foreign Minister: China Is Willing to Help Strengthen the Safety of the Malacca Straits', *Liaohe Zaobao* (in Chinese), 2 August 2005,

available at *http://www.zaobao.com/gj/yx050802_501.html* (accessed 2 August 2005).

46. 'Ship Owners Urged to Install Anti-Piracy Tracking Devices', Agence France-Presse, 8 May 2002.
47. 'ICC Report Sends Six Warships into Battle Against Pirates', available at *http://www.iccwbo.org/home/news_archives/2002/piracy.asp* (accessed 11 May 2002).
48. 'Singapore and Malaysia Discussed Air Surveillance over the Malacca Straits', *Liaohe Zaobao* (in Chinese), 30 July 2005, available at *http://www.zaobao.com/sp/sp050730_503.html* (accessed 30 July 2005).
49. 'Singapore, Malaysia and Indonesia Carry Air Patrol over the Malacca Straits from Next Month', *Liaohe Zaobao* (in Chinese), 3 August 2005, available at *http://www.zaobao.com/sp/sp050803_501.html* (accessed August 3, 2005).
50. ICC-IMB, *Piracy and Armed Robbery against Ships*, Annual Report, 1 January–31 December 1997, p. 2.
51. Article 3 of the ReCAAP. Text is available at *http://www.recaap.org/about/pdf/ReCAAP%20Agreement.pdf* (accessed 6 May 2008).
52. For details, see the ReCAAP ISC website: *http://www.recaap.org/index_home.html* (accessed 6 May 2008).
53. Texts of the convention and its two protocols are available at *http://www.uncjin.org/Documents/Conventions/dcatoc/final_documents_2/index.htm* (accessed 14 May 2008).
54. Article 3 of the Smuggling Protocol.
55. Article 3 (a) of the Trafficking Protocol.
56. See relevant provisions, particularly Articles 9, 10 and 11 of the Smuggling Protocol.
57. United Nations Office on Drugs and Crime (UNODC), *Trafficking in Persons: Global Patterns*, April 2006, p. 24, available at *http://www.unodc.org/unodc/en/human-trafficking/publications.html* (accessed 14 May 2008).
58. Eric Yong-Joong Lee, 'National and International Legal Concerns Regarding Recent North Korean Escapees', *International Journal of Refuge Law*, vol. 13 (1–2), 2001, p. 143.
59. Jiang Zhuqing, 'Japanese Snakehead Deported', *China Daily*, 18 August 2004, p. 2.
60. China has not yet acceded to the Trafficking Protocol or to the Smuggling Protocol.
61. Article 9 of the criminal law. An unofficial English version is available in Wei Luo, *The 1997 Criminal Code of the People's Republic of China with English Translation and Introduction* (Buffalo, New York: William S Hein & Co., Inc., 1998), pp. 23–226.
62. Articles 319–320 of the criminal law.
63. Text is reprinted in Peng Liming (ed.), *A Complete Collection of Existing Laws of the People's Republic of China* (Beijing: China Constructing Materials Industry Press, 1998) (in Chinese), pp. 470–2.
64. Article 6 of the 1994 supplementary rules.
65. Texts of these laws are reprinted in Peng, supra note 63, pp. 1913–20.

66. Article 4 of the Law on the Management of the Border Entry and Exit of Chinese Citizens.
67. 'ASEAN Declaration Against Trafficking in Persons Particularly Women and Children'. Text is available at *http://www.aseansec.org/16793.htm* (accessed 9 May 2008).
68. Text is available at *http://www.aseansec.org/16572.htm* (accessed 9 May 2008).
69. Text is available at *http://www.aseansec.org/18570.htm* (accessed 21 July 2008).
70. Jiang Zhuqing, 'China, ASEAN Fight Transnational Crime', *China Daily*, 5 July 2004, available at *http://www.chinadaily.com.cn/english/doc/2004-07/05/content_345535.htm* (accessed 5 July 2004).
71. E/CN.4/2005/SR.40 (24 August 2004), 11, paragraph 61; cited from Hu Qian, 'Chinese Practice in Public International Law: 2005 (I)', *Chinese Journal of International Law*, vol. 5 (2), 2006, pp. 473–4.
72. Susu Thatun, 'Mekong Sub-Region Committed to Ending Trafficking', available at *http://www.fmreview.org/text/FMR/25/10.doc* (accessed 6 May 2008).
73. The COMMIT MOU. Text is available at *http://www.no-trafficking.org/content/COMMIT_Process/COMMIT_pdf/final%20COMMIT%20mou.pdf* (accessed 7 May 2008).
74. Text is available at *http://www.unodc.org/unodc/en/treaties/psychotropics.html* (accessed 9 May 2008). The convention came into force on 16 August 1976. China and all ASEAN members are its signatories.
75. Text is available at *http://www.unodc.org/unodc/en/treaties/illicit-trafficking.html* (accessed 9 May 2008). The convention came into force on 11 November 1990.
76. Text is available at *http://www.aseansec.org/5731.htm* (accessed 7 May 2008).
77. 'Plan of Action on Drug Abuse Control'. Text is available at *http://www.aseansec.org/5735.htm* (accessed 9 May 2008).
78. They are the 1998 Joint Declaration for a Drug-Free ASEAN and the 2000 Bangkok Political Declaration in Pursuit of a Drug-Free ASEAN 2015. Texts are available at *http://www.aseansec.org/12698.htm* (accessed 14 May 2008).
79. Text is available in *People's Daily* (in Chinese), 19 February 2008, p. 14.
80. The updated plan of action (2005–10) is available at *http://www.accordplan.net/file/072006/28/Updated%20ACCORD%20Plan%20of%20Action%2022-6-06.pdf* (accessed 9 May 2008).
81. Ralf Emmers, 'International Regime Building in Southeast Asia: ASEAN Cooperation Against the Illicit Trafficking and Abuse of Drugs', IDSS Working Paper No. 106, February 2006 (Institute of Defence and Strategic Studies, Nanyang Technological University, Singapore), p. 13.
82. The Beijing Declaration. Text is available at *http://www.aseansec.org/17848.htm* (accessed 14 May 2008).
83. 'National Report of Drug Control, 2007', available at *http://www.china.com.cn/law/zhuanti/yldp/2007-06/02/content_8333483_10.htm* (accessed 7 May 2008).

84. On 19 December 2006, China and the Philippines jointly uncovered the very big 'Shao Chuntian' transnational trafficking case, destroying the drug factory of 3,000 square metres in the Philippines and arresting 20 suspects. See 'National Report of Drug Control, 2007', available at *http://www.china.com.cn/law/zhuanti/yldp/2007-06/02/content_8333483_10.htm* (accessed 7 May 2008). In 2007, the two countries jointly uncovered another similar big case. See 'China and the Philippines Joined Hands to Uncover the Extra Big Drug Case', *People's Daily* (in Chinese), 26 June 2007, p. 5.
85. For details, see 'Three Extra Big Transnatioanl Drug Cases Have Been Uncovered This Year', *People's Daily* (in Chinese), 26 June 2007, p. 5.
86. 'National Report of Drug Control, 2007', available at *http://www.china.com.cn/law/zhuanti/yldp/2007-06/02/content_8333483_10.htm* (accessed 7 May 2008).
87. mu is a land unit denominator used in China. One mu equals to about 667 m^2.
88. Song Wei, 'China Changed the "Golden Triangle"', *People's Daily* (in Chinese), 27 June 2007, p. 14.
89. 'ARF Symposium on Drug Prohibition Was Held in Xi'an', *People's Daily* (in Chinese), 22 September 2007, p. 4.
90. They came into force in September 2003, December 2005 and April 2002, respectively.
91. Song Yang, 'Money-laundering in China: A Policy Analysis', *Journal of Contemporary Criminal Justice*, vol. 18 (4), November 2002, p. 371.
92. Zhou Xiaochuan, 'Anti-Money Laundering in China: The Status Quo and Prospects', Speech at the first meeting of the Ministerial Joint Conference on AML, 27 August 2004, Beijing, available at *http://www.pbc.gov.cn/english/showaccdoc.asp?col=6500&id=55* (accessed 9 May 2008).
93. Text is available at *http://www.gov.cn/jrzg/2006-10/31/content_429245.htm* (accessed 9 May 2008).
94. Lai Hongyi, 'Regional Cooperation in Epidemic Prevention: China and ASEAN', in John Wong, Zou Keyuan and Zeng Huaqun (eds.), *China–ASEAN Relations: Economic and Legal Dimensions* (Singapore: World Scientific, 2006), p. 71.
95. For details, see Lai, ibid., pp. 59–73.
96. For details, see Srikanth Kondapalli, 'Tsunami and China: Relief with Chinese Characteristics', available at *http://www.niaslinc.dk/gateway_to_asia/Asia_insights/China%20%20Tsunami.doc* (accessed 10 May 2008).
97. Text is available at *http://www.aseansec.org/17579.htm* (accessed 10 May 2008).

8

Law governing the South China Sea issue

Geography of the South China Sea

The United Nations Convention on the Law of the Sea (the LOS Convention)[1] categorises the South China Sea as a semi-enclosed sea, which is defined under Article 122 as 'a gulf, basin, or sea surrounded by two or more States and connected to another sea or the ocean by a narrow outlet or consisting entirely or primarily of the territorial seas and exclusive economic zones of two or more coastal States'. The South China Sea is surrounded by six states – China (including Taiwan), Vietnam, the Philippines, Brunei, Malaysia and Indonesia. It has an area of 648,000 square nautical miles, twice that of the Sea of Japan.[2] There are hundreds of small islands in the South China Sea, along with several underwater features, namely, uninhabited islets, shoals, reefs, banks, sands, cays and rocks.[3] According to Workman, these islands mainly consist of coral reefs[4] and are mainly categorised into four groups: the Pratas Islands (*Dongsha Qundao* in Chinese), the Paracel Islands (*Xisha Qundao* in Chinese and *Hoang Sa* in Vietnamese), the Macclesfield Bank (*Zhongsha Qundao* in Chinese) and the Spratly Islands (*Nansha Qundao* in Chinese and *Truong Sa* in Vietnamese). It is interesting to note that, in Chinese, these groups of small islands have a big name 'qundao', which means archipelago in English. Such a nomenclature is questionable in law and/or in geography,[5] particularly for the Macclesfield Bank that is permanently submerged under water, though a common Chinese view considers the Scarborough Reef a part of the Macclesfield Bank.[6] If such a view were generally accepted, then the English name would have been changed to 'the Macclesfield Islands',[7] similar to that of the other three groups. However, a detailed discussion on it is beyond the scope of this chapter.

The geographical differences among the islands groups give rise to complications in their political situations, which lead to conflicts in national interests. The Pratas Islands are under the firm control of the Taiwan Chinese, where no competing claims exist under the current conception of 'one China'. For the Macclesfield Bank, the only claimant is China including Taiwan.[8] Nevertheless, if the Scarborough Reef were considered part of the Macclesfield, then Philippines would have lodged its territorial claim over the Reef, finally extending its claim over the Macclesfield. The Paracel Islands are under the firm control of China (though contested by the Vietnamese), which keeps the political situation around the Paracel Islands relatively calm and stable in comparison with that around the Spratly Islands. The dispute over the Spratly Islands is most complicated since these islands are claimed by as many as five states and six parties – Brunei, China, Malaysia, the Philippines, Taiwan and Vietnam. It is not usual in the history of international relations that so many countries make claims over such small islets and have physical presence there. As many predict, if the issue of the Spratly Islands is not handled well, it could pose a serious threat to the peace and security in the East Asian region. China views the issue on disputes over boundaries and sovereignty over areas of the South China Sea as one of the three main factors that might trigger military conflicts in the Asia-Pacific region.[9] It could also stimulate disharmony and tension in the overall China–ASEAN relations.

Territorial disputes over islands and maritime claims

Any territorial and maritime dispute centres on the key question of who owns the disputed land and its surrounding seas, and the South China Sea is no exception. Resorting to international law becomes indispensable to justify a country's sovereignty and jurisdiction over the disputed areas.

Traditional international laws allow states to acquire territorial sovereignty through any of the five defined methods, that is, 'accretion', 'occupation', 'prescription', 'conquest' and 'cession'. However, after the World War II, the United Nations Charter prohibits the illegal use of force; thus, forced cession and conquest are no longer valid methods of acquiring territorial sovereignty. Chinese scholars often cite three important cases concerning territory acquisition in international law: the Case of Palmas Island (between the United States and Holland) in 1924, the Case of

Clipperton Island (between France and Mexico) in 1931 and the Case of Eastern Greenland (between Denmark and Norway) in 1933.[10] These cases are significant in international law and also meaningful in the context of the territorial sovereignty over the South China Sea islands. On the one hand, China's claim to have discovered the South China Sea islands as early as in the Han Dynasty is a strong argument in its favour to acquire the sovereignty over the islands since according to modern international law, only discovery can satisfy the conditions of territorial acquisition.[11]

On the other hand, Chinese scholars have realised that it is not enough that the argument for China's sovereignty over the South China Sea islands rests only on China's discovery of these islands; under modern international law, effective occupation is much more crucial and forceful to justify and defend territorial sovereignty. Thus, attempts are being made to justify the effective occupation of ancient China over the South China Sea islands by listing Chinese activities in the sea, including economic development and operations, such as fishing, planting, house building, etc.; administrative jurisdiction; navy patrols; and astronomical surveys.[12] However, modern international law tends to recognise the recent practice of effective occupation over earlier or ancient state practice.

In addition, the Chinese scholars use the concept of intertemporal law as a legal argument in its favour. Intertemporal law refers to the collective response of international law to temporal disputes. Its rules and principles come from subsystems of international law such as the law of treaties and customary international law.[13] In the Island of Palmas Case, Judge Huber considered that 'the act creative of a right' has to be judged by the 'law in force at the time the right arises'. [14] In 1975, the Institut de Droit International adopted a resolution on 'the Intertemporal Problem in Public International Law' which calls upon the states to apply the principle that 'the temporal sphere of application of any norm of public international law shall be determined in accordance with the general principle of law by which any fact, action or situation must be assessed in the light of the rules of law that are contemporaneous with it'.[15] In the context of the South China Sea islands, any rules in international law applicable to them must be those which were valid at the time the rights of the state were created. This argument is favourable for China since it is the earliest country to discover these islands and to conduct relevant human activities in the South China Sea.

Another argument which may not be purely legal is concerning Vietnam's recognition of China's sovereignty over the South China Sea islands as early as in the 1950s and 1960s. However, after 1975, Vietnam reversed its position and claimed the Paracel and Spratly Islands. As criticised by the Chinese scholars, such behaviour is in violation of an international law principle called 'estoppel' or principle of preclusion. Since Vietnam has already recognised China's sovereignty over these two islands, it should not create disputes with China afterwards.[16]

Legal status of the Chinese U-shaped line

The U-shaped line is called the Chinese traditional maritime boundary line in China (hereinafter referred to as 'the line') and refers to the line with nine segments off the Chinese coast on the South China Sea, as displayed on the Chinese map. People may query what the line means and what its significance is. Does China claim all within the line as its national territory, including the islands, underwater rocks, the seabed as well as the water columns?

The line first appeared on the map in December 1914, which was compiled by Hu Jinjie, a Chinese cartographer, according to some known sources.[17] The maps published during the 1920s and 1930s continued to follow Hu's drawings.[18] The line at that time only included the Pratas and the Paracels. It began from the Sino-Vietnamese land boundary next to the Gulf of Tonkin, extending southeastwards along the offshore of the Vietnamese coast, then running eastwards to the west side of the Island of Luzon, then northeastwards along the east side of the Pratas, through the Taiwan Strait, and finally to meet the Chinese boundary line to the East China Sea and the Yellow Sea. The southernmost end of the demarcation was located at about 15° and 16° north latitude.[19] However, no reasons were given why the line was drawn as it was.

The year 1933 was an important time for the modification and emphasis of the line on the Chinese maps. In July that year, France, the then protector of Vietnam, occupied nine small islands of the Spratly Islands. In protest, China extended the line in the maps relating to the South China Sea further south to 7°–9° north latitude.[20] The intention was clear: to indicate that the Spratly Islands belonged to China. However, the James Shoal (Zengmu Ansha) was not included. While the line at that time on most of the maps were drawn between 7° and 9° north latitude, there was at least one atlas collection which included the James Shoal into the line, further extending it to 4° north latitude. This is the *New China's Construction Atlas* edited by Bai Meichu and published in 1936. Actually, in 1935, the Committee of Examining the Water and Land Maps of the Republic of China published the names of 132 islets and reefs of the four South China Sea 'archipelagos'. The publication had an annexed map that marked the James Shoal at about 4° north latitude and 112° east longitude, though there was no demarcation of the line on the map. It indicated that the then Chinese government considered the southernmost territory of China to be at 4° north latitude.[21] It is therefore clear that Bai had taken the above publication to be the basis for the line in his compilation.

It should be noted that all the atlases at that time were compiled by individuals. Thus, they were only indirect evidences to show the official position of the government. It was only in 1947, after the end of World War II, that the line was officially confirmed by the Chinese government. On 1 December 1947, the Chinese ministry of interior renamed the islands in the South China Sea and thus formally allocated them to the administration of the Chinese Hainan Special District.[22] Meanwhile, the same ministry prepared a location map of the islands in the South China Sea, which was then first released for internal use. In February 1948, the *Atlas of Administrative Areas of the Republic of China* was officially published, in which the above map was included. This was the first official map with the line for the South China Sea and it had substantial influence over the subsequent maps published by mainland China or by Taiwan. It had two general characteristics: the southernmost end of the line was set at 4° north latitude including the James Shoal; and the 11-segment line was drawn instead of the previous continuing line. According to the then official explanation, the basis for drawing the line was: '[t]he southernmost limit of the South China Sea territory should be at the James Shoal. This limit was followed by our governmental departments, schools and publishers before the anti-Japanese war, and it was also recorded on file in the Ministry of Interior. Accordingly it should remain unchanged'.[23] The explanation does not seem to be very clear because one may query whether the explanation is referred to the line or to the southernmost territory of China, and before the anti-Japanese war, there were a few atlases that marked the line at about 4° north latitude. It is thus hard to say that southernmost limit was consistently followed in practice. On the other hand, the explanation did not give reasons why the line was drawn this way. Despite all the above doubts, the line on the map has been accepted ever since in Chinese practice.

Chinese scholars face a dilemma on how to define this line in the legal and political context so as to defend China's rights and interests in the South China Sea. The crucial question is concerning the legal status of the line: is it a maritime boundary line like the land border lines or a line only indicating that the islands, not the waters, within the line belong to China? This question has been discussed on many academic occasions in China.

For example, in 2002, the Hainan Research Institute for the South China Sea (now renamed as National Institute for the South China Sea Studies) held a special conference on the U-shaped line in which the issue was thoroughly discussed. Though still debated, the majority of the Chinese scholars tend to recognise that the line is the one that only defines the islands and other territories within the line.[24] After China's publicising of its baselines encircling the Paracel Islands in 1996 and promulgation of the Law on the Exclusive Economic Zone and the Continental Shelf in 1998, there has been a decrease in the force that insists on arguing that the line is a maritime boundary line between China and its neighbouring countries. On the other hand, the Chinese Government never expressly states that this line has been abandoned as it always remains on the Chinese maps.

Debate on historic rights and historic waters

Closely related to the U-shaped line is the debate on whether the waters within the line are China's historic waters. The concept of historical waters is not definitive in international law. A scholarly definition was offered by Bouchez: 'Historic waters are waters over which the coastal State, contrary to the generally applicable rules of international law, clearly, effectively, continuously, and over a substantial period of time, exercises sovereign rights with the acquiescence of the community of States'.[25] The definition has not been formally adopted in the recent LOS Convention; however, a variant term of historic bay and historic title is mentioned in the convention relating to bays, delimitation of the territorial sea between states with opposite or adjacent coasts, and limitations and exceptions in the settlement of disputes.[26] According to the late O'Connell, there are three circumstances which could be considered as historic waters: (1) areas of claimed bays, which are greater in extent, or less in configuration, than standard bays; (2) areas of claimed waters linked to a coast by offshore features but which are not enclosed under the standard rules and (3) areas of claimed seas which would, but for the claim, be high seas as they are not covered by any rules concerning bays or delimitation of coastal waters (*maria clausa*).[27] Accordingly, the concept is usually applicable to bays and gulfs. Once established as historic waters, the waters in question are regarded as internal waters. There may be exceptions to this rule; that is, some historic waters claimed by states may not be bays or gulfs, but open seas, which could therefore be regarded as internal waters.

The International Law Commission of the United Nations discussed the concept of historic waters, and in 1962 its report on the juridical regime of historic waters, including historic bays, was released to the public. The report examined the elements of title to historic waters, the issues of burden of proof, the legal status of waters treated as historic waters and the settlement of disputes. However, it did not provide a conclusive concept of historic waters and the standard according to which this concept could be applied.[28] Thus, the theoretical problem in regard to the concept of historic waters has yet not been resolved. Because of the controversy around this concept, the Third UN Conference on the Law of the Sea simply kept the issue out of the discussion and left some wordings in the LOS Convention.[29] Generally, three conditions should be fulfilled to sustain a historic water claim. They are (1) the exercise of the authority over the area; (2) the continuity of this exercise of authority over time and (3) the attitude of foreign states to the claim.[30]

The concept of historic waters has been established, in practice, as a criterion to determine the jurisdictional waters of a coastal state. According to Churchill and Lowe, there are about 20 claims in the world over historic bays.[31] For example, the former Soviet Union claimed the Peter the Great Bay as its 'historic bay', and the length of the closing line was 108 nautical miles.[32] While the claim was opposed by the Western countries led by the United States, it was expressly recognised by China.[33] The most controversial example was set by Libya who claimed the Gulf of Sidra in 1974 as its historic bay with 296 nautical miles of closing line. The claim was challenged by the Western countries as well as the former Soviet Union, which later caused a severe conflict between Libya and the United States. Tonga's claim over a rectangle of the water areas in the high seas, with several groups of islands inside, as its 'historic waters' since 1887 may have some analogous effect upon the line in the South China Sea.[34] It is not clear whether Tonga's claim has ever been challenged since it is located in a relatively unnoticed area.

The issue of whether the water areas within the line are Chinese historic waters has been seriously discussed among the scholars in Taiwan. The Taiwan authorities gave the status of historic waters to the water areas within the U-shaped line in 1993 when it issued its South China Sea Policy Guidelines which stated that 'the South China Sea area within the historic water limit is the maritime area under the jurisdiction of the Republic of China, in which the Republic of China possesses all rights and interests'.[35] However, such a claim could not get a unanimous support even from Taiwanese scholars. In 1993, a round table discussion was held at the National Chengchi University, Taipei. The participants were divided into two groups based on their divergent views. One group supported the idea of historic waters and asserted that the water areas within the line were Chinese historic waters. The other group was rather dubious and cautious of the line, taking the view that it was difficult to establish such a claim in international law.[36]

Scholars in mainland China have also expressed their views upon the line. One scholar actively defended this line for his argument of historic waters,[37] and the other advocated claiming the waters in the South China Sea by its name.[38] A recent piece noted that the water within the U-shaped line was China's water of historic title, 'China's special EEZ, or historic EEZ', and it should be given the same status as the EEZ prescribed in the LOS Convention.[39] Yet, the author did not explain why the water within the U-shaped line should be China's 'historic EEZ'. Perhaps he had based his arguments on Article 14 of China's EEZ Law.

Generally speaking, whether a certain water area can be established as historic water depends upon whether it can satisfy certain preconditions as described above. In the South China Sea, the line provides the basis for a claim on historic waters. However, neither mainland China nor Taiwan has ever exercised enough authority over it; also, the authority focused on the islands within the line rather than on the water areas. The freedom of navigation and freedom of fishery do not seem to be affected by these exercises. Thus, a question is raised whether there is effective control over the area within the line so as to establish it as historic waters. It may be argued that the relative frequency of the exercise of authority should be considered vis-à-vis other claimant countries. Yet there are doubts how China could establish its claim of historic waters in the South China Sea.

Generally, two types of historic rights are recognised: one is exclusive with full sovereignty, such as historic waters and historic bays; and the other is non-exclusive without full sovereignty, such as historic fishing rights in the high seas. On 26 June 1998, China officially promulgated the Law on the Exclusive Economic Zone and the Continental Shelf in which Article 14 provides that 'the provisions of this Law shall not affect the historic rights enjoyed by the People's Republic of China'.[40] In this context, the provision seems to help the Chinese scholars end the debate on whether the waters within the U-shaped line are historic waters, since China mentions only 'historic rights' in its EEZ law.

Governing laws

International law requires states to solve their disputes through peaceful means. There are a number of mechanisms for the settlement of territorial and maritime disputes, including political means such as negotiation and consultation between the parties concerned, mediation, good offices, conciliation and investigation involving third parties, and judicial means such as arbitration and international adjudication, most of which are listed in the Charter of the United Nations.[41] Since China and all the ASEAN member states are UN members, they are obliged to comply with the requirements imposed by the UN Charter in terms of the settlement of their disputes. Other international organisations, whether universal or regional, can also play an active role in dispute settlement, as is seen through the ASEAN itself, which has played a key role in diffusing the tension in the South China Sea and solving such a tricky issue.

By 1992, China had physical presence in nine islets and this alarmed ASEAN. Under the pressure of some of the ASEAN members with interests in the South China Sea, ASEAN adopted the ASEAN Declaration on the South China Sea in July 1992, the first concerted step of the ASEAN members regarding their position towards the South China Sea issue. The declaration urges 'all parties concerned to exercise restraint with the view to creating a positive climate for the eventual resolution of all disputes', 'to explore the possibility of cooperation in the South China Sea relating to the safety of maritime navigation and communication, protection against pollution of the marine environment, coordination of search and rescue operations, efforts towards combating piracy and armed robbery as well as collaboration in the campaign against illicit trafficking in drugs', and 'to apply the principles contained in the Treaty of Amity and Cooperation in Southeast Asia as the basis for establishing a code of international conduct over the South China Sea'.[42] Though it was adopted by the initial six ASEAN members, it has been endorsed by the newer ASEAN members as well. While the declaration is only for the ASEAN members, it has implications for China as a major claimant in the South China Sea. It is significant that some of the contents in the declaration were later reflected in the 2002 Declaration on the Conduct of Parties in the South China Sea, which was adopted by China and all 10 ASEAN member states. It was also the first regional document that mentioned the adoption of a code of conduct for the South China Sea.

After the Mischief Reef incident in 1995, ASEAN foreign ministers issued a statement in March 1995, urging the claimants to refrain from exacerbating the South China Sea situation and to undertake cooperative activities which increase trust and confidence and promote stability in the area.[43] In the same year, China agreed to discuss with the ASEAN countries the dispute over the Spratly Islands, and in August that year China and the Philippines reached a code of conduct for self-restraint in the South China Sea.[44] However, this is only a bilateral document between

China and the Philippines. Later, ASEAN asked Philippines and Vietnam to prepare a regional code of conduct for the South China Sea, based on ASEAN–China documents, such as the five principles of peaceful coexistence; the 1976 Treaty of Amity and Cooperation in South East Asia; the ASEAN Declaration on the South China Sea of 1992; the ASEAN–China Joint Statement of 16 December 1997; the Joint Statement between the Philippines and the PRC on the South China Sea and Other Areas of Cooperation of August 1995; the code of conduct agreed upon between Vietnam and the Philippines in November 1995 and the Hanoi Plan of Action at the Sixth ASEAN Summit 1998.[45]

China rejected the ASEAN initiative for establishing a regional code of conduct in April 1999, since China regarded the South China Sea issue as a bilateral issue between itself and individual Southeast Asian countries. However, for undisclosed reasons, China changed its original position and agreed to consider the possibility of a regional code of conduct. According to some scholars, 'China's interest in the code was motivated by the need to prevent further American involvement in the area and to head off military exercises between ASEAN with the United States'.[46] The pressure from ASEAN is certainly an important factor which cannot be ignored. Finally, in March 2000, the first ASEAN–China Consultations on the code of conduct in the South China Sea were held in Thailand. In November 2002, the two sides reached the agreement on the Declaration on the Conduct of Parties in the South China Sea (the 2002 DOC).

The 2002 DOC

The 2002 DOC is not a lengthy document and contains only 10 points as the parties (1) 'reaffirm their commitment to the purposes and principles of the Charter of the United Nations, the 1982 UN Convention on the Law of the Sea, the Treaty of Amity and Cooperation in Southeast Asia, the Five Principles of Peaceful Coexistence, and other universally recognized principles of international law which shall serve as the basic norms governing state-to-state relations'; (2) 'are committed to exploring ways for building trust and confidence in accordance with the above-mentioned principles and on the basis of equality and mutual respect'; (3) 'reaffirm their respect for and commitment to the freedom of navigation in and overflight above the South China Sea as provided for by the universally recognized principles of international law, including the 1982 UN Convention on the Law of the Sea'; (4) 'undertake to resolve their territorial and jurisdictional disputes by peaceful means, without resorting to the threat or use of force, through friendly consultations and negotiations by sovereign states directly concerned, in accordance with universally recognized principles of international law, including the 1982 UN Convention on the Law of the Sea'; (5) 'undertake to exercise self-restraint in the conduct of activities that would complicate or escalate disputes and affect peace and stability including, among others, refraining from action of inhabiting on the presently uninhabited islands, reefs, shoals, cays, and other features and to handle their differences in a constructive manner', and 'undertake to intensify efforts to seek ways, in the spirit of cooperation and understanding, to build trust and confidence between and among them, including: a. holding dialogues and exchange of views as appropriate between their defense and military officials; b. ensuring just and humane treatment of all persons who are either in danger or in distress; c. notifying, on a voluntary basis, other Parties concerned of any impending joint/combined military exercise; and d. exchanging, on a voluntary basis, relevant information', pending the peaceful settlement of territorial and jurisdictional disputes; (6) 'explore or undertake cooperative activities including a. marine environmental protection; b. marine scientific research; c. safety of navigation and communication at sea; d. search and rescue operation; and e. combating transnational crime, including but not limited to trafficking in illicit drugs, piracy and armed robbery at sea, and illegal traffic in arms', pending a comprehensive and durable settlement of the disputes; (7) 'stand ready to continue their consultations and dialogues concerning relevant issues, through modalities to be agreed by them, including regular consultations on the observance of this Declaration, for the purpose of promoting good neighbourliness and transparency, establishing harmony, mutual understanding and cooperation, and facilitating peaceful resolution of disputes among them'; (8) 'undertake to respect the provisions of this Declaration and take actions consistent therewith'; (9) 'encourage other countries to respect the principles contained in this Declaration'; and (10) 'reaffirm that the adoption of a code of conduct in the South China Sea would further promote peace and stability in the region and agree to work, on the basis of consensus, towards the eventual attainment of this objective'.[47]

The document is significant in the sense that the South China Sea issue, which was originally bilateral, has now turned into a regional issue and should be solved under the framework of the China–ASEAN cooperation. As the Philippine President Gloria Arroyo Macapagal declared, the agreement represented a 'diplomatic breakthrough' for peace in the region and the first step in the implementation of the ASEAN Code of Conduct with China.[48]

After the signing of the 2002 Declaration, the ASEAN and China established two mechanisms in 2005 for the purpose of implementing the declaration: one is the 'ASEAN–China Senior Officials Meeting on the Implementation of the Declaration on the Conduct of Parties in the South China Sea (DOC)', and the other 'ASEAN–China Joint Working Group on the Implementation of the DOC'. While the first, which is ad hoc, reviews the progress of the implementation of the 2002 DOC and discusses the principles and methods thereof, [49] the second, which meets twice a year, functions under the direction of the ASEAN–China Senior Officials Meeting.

The ASEAN–China Senior Officials Meeting held in December 2004 adopted the terms of reference of the joint working group (JWG). According to the terms of reference, the main task of the JWG is 'to study and recommend measures to translate the provisions of the DOC into concrete cooperative activities that will enhance mutual understanding and trust'. The JWG can make recommendations regarding the guidelines and the action plan for the implementation of the 2002 DOC as well as regarding specific cooperative areas such as marine environmental protection, marine scientific research, etc. listed in the 2002 DOC.[50] The JWG meeting held in Sanya, China in February 2006 exchanged views on guidelines for the implementation of the 2002 DOC, discussed project proposals within the related areas of cooperation and issued the 2006 Working Plan.[51]

The LOS Convention

The 2002 DOC clearly endorses a number of legal principles and documents of international law and specifies the LOS Convention, which was concluded in 1982 and brought into force in 1994. The LOS Convention, consisting 320 clauses and nine annexes, is regarded as a constitution for oceans. As of June 2008, 155 states were party to the convention. China and most of the ASEAN states (except Cambodia and Thailand) have ratified and acceded to it. For non-parties to the LOS Convention, by signing the 2002 DOC, they have thus demonstrated their willingness to accept the principles and objectives of the convention in the context of the South China Sea issue.

As the South China Sea is a semi-enclosed sea, the states bordering it are required to cooperate under the LOS Convention in matters of common interest including the protection and conservation of marine living resources, protection of the marine environment and marine scientific research.[52] The convention also contains a chapter on dispute settlement through peaceful means, in accordance with the UN Charter. Provisions regarding maritime delimitation in the convention can provide legal guidelines for the states to delimit their overlapping maritime boundaries in the South China Sea. In 2000, China and Vietnam successfully reached an agreement on the delimitation of the maritime boundary in the Gulf of Tonkin,[53] which set a good example for maritime boundary delimitation in the South China Sea.

Nevertheless, the LOS Convention has its limitations in the settlement of maritime disputes: it only governs disputes over maritime zones and maritime activities, rather than disputes over the sovereignty of islands. That is why the 2002 DOC, while specifying the LOS Convention, mentions the whole body of general international law including customary international law for the dispute settlement in the South China Sea. In addition, the convention itself has complicated the South China Sea situation as a number of states such as Brunei and Malaysia have made use of the relevant provisions on EEZ in the convention in making claims over reefs in the South China Sea.

Joint development

In accordance with the LOS Convention, the parties to a dispute, in a spirit of understanding and cooperation, can 'make every effort to enter into provisional arrangements of a practical nature and, during this transitional period, not to jeopardize or hamper the reaching of the final agreement' on the delimitation of the EEZ and continental shelf.[54] It provides a legal basis for joint development in disputed maritime areas, pending the settlement of the maritime boundary delimitation. This legal norm has been reflected in many existing cases and can be applied to the South China Sea as well. However, the LOS Convention leaves other options open to the states concerned about whether they can enter into joint development agreements after the definite maritime boundary delimitation. It may be recalled that as early as in 1969 the International Court of Justice (ICJ) touched upon this issue in the North Sea Continental Shelf cases by stating that:

> if . . . the delimitation leaves to the Parties areas that overlap, there are to be divided between them in agreed proportions or failing agreement, equally, unless they decide on a regime of joint jurisdiction, use or exploitation for the zones of overlap or any part of them.[55]

China's rapid economic development has pushed the demand for energy, particularly oil and gas, to an all time high. Experts have predicted that, going by the present trend, China would be required to import more than 500 million tons of oil and over 100 billion m^3 of natural gas in 2020.[56] Security of energy reserves in the South China Sea has become a critical issue within the overall South China Sea issue. In the Spratly area, there are eight sedimentary basins with an area of 410,000 km^2, of which 260,000 km^2 is within China's unilaterally claimed U-shaped line. China estimates that these eight sedimentary basins contain 34.97 billion tons of petroleum reserves, including the 1.182 billion tons of oil and 8000 billion m^3 of gas that have been discovered. In addition, gas hydrate (also known as flammable ice) is present in huge quantity in the South China Sea.[57] Thus, the South China Sea is sometimes called the second 'Persian Gulf'.

Because of the disputes among the countries concerned, joint development becomes the most feasible option for them to cooperate in the exploration for and exploitation of oil and gas in the South China Sea. 'Joint development' refers to 'an agreement between two States to develop so as to share jointly in agreed proportions by inter-State cooperation and national measures the offshore oil and gas in a designated zone of the seabed and subsoil of the continental shelf to which both or either of the participating States are entitled in international law'.[58] It contains several characteristics: (a) it is an arrangement between two countries; (b) it concerns an overlapping boundary maritime area; (c) it is a provisional arrangement pending the settlement of the boundary delimitation disputes between the countries concerned and (d) it is designed to jointly develop the mineral resources in the disputed area. In East Asia, joint development agreements include, inter alia, the Japan–South Korean arrangement in the Sea of Japan and the East China Sea in the 1970s, the Malaysia–Thailand joint development area in the Gulf of Thailand and the Australian–Indonesia joint development zone for the Timor Gap.

Encouraged or triggered by all these developments in East Asia, China put forward the idea of joint development in the disputed sea areas. When Wu Bangguo, chairman of the Chinese National People's Congress, visited the Philippines in August 2003, he proposed to his Philippine counterpart to jointly develop petroleum drilling in the South China Sea.[59] According to China, a joint development among states claiming areas in the South China Sea is essential: (1) to stabilise the region in order to provide an environment conducive for social and economic development; (2) to make effective and rational use of South China Sea resources, which could be a prerequisite to peaceful resolution of the

South China Sea disputes and (3) to enhance and expand regional cooperation in other areas.[60] On 11 November 2003, the China National Offshore Oil Corporation (CNOOC) and the Philippine National Oil Company signed the letter of intent to jointly explore oil and gas in the South China Sea. A joint committee was set up to select the areas to be explored and to establish a program to 'review, assess and evaluate relevant geographical, geophysical and other technical data available to determine the oil and gas potential in the area'.[61] As a follow-up, the two state oil companies signed an agreement on joint seismic work in the Sino-Philippine disputed area in the South China Sea, which is the first joint development agreement for the disputed area.[62] Further developments took place when state-owned oil companies in China, the Philippines and Vietnam signed an unprecedented tripartite agreement on joint seismic surveying activities in the South China Sea on 14 March 2005. The size for cooperation is 143,000 km^2.[63] But the agreement was limited to seismic data collection, and the first stage of the operation was completed in November 2005.

Due to the fact that the South China Sea dispute is a multiparty dispute, a new model for potential joint development has been proposed, which comprises China (including Taiwan) as one party and ASEAN (including all 10 member states) as the other party. This model is based on the existing formula of the 2002 DOC. If this can stand, then bilateral cooperation between China and ASEAN in the South China Sea can be formulated.[64]

Conclusion

It is not easy to resolve the South China Sea issue between China and relevant ASEAN countries at least in the short run, firstly due to its complexity and multiparty involvement. The issue is further complicated by overlapping claims not only to territorial sovereignty of islands, but also to maritime zones in the South China Sea. Individual states do indulge in protests and unilateral actions from time to time even after the adoption of the 2002 DOC. For example, in November 2007, Vietnam lodged a protest against China's military exercise around the Paracel Islands in violation of Vietnam's sovereignty.[65]

Second, the 2002 DOC falls within the category of 'soft law'; it is only a political document without a legally binding force. It is even less persuasive than a code of conduct. For this reason, the 2002 DOC urges the states to negotiate on and adopt a code of conduct so as to further promote stability and peace in the South China Sea. It is therefore seen from the above that it is unlikely that China and ASEAN adopt a legally binding agreement on the South China Sea issue.

Third, though the 2002 DOC applies to the whole South China Sea, there is no express mention of its geographical coverage, which may lead to different interpretations. China may be very reluctant to apply the 2002 DOC to the whole South China Sea since this may harm China's territorial and maritime interests claimed within its U-shaped line and in its effectively occupied Paracel Islands which are also claimed by Vietnam. As for the principle of self-restraint, the 2002 DOC reflects it in point 5 above. However, as revealed, the ban proposed by the Philippines on erecting new structures was rejected during the negotiation.[66]

Fourth, the proposed joint development scheme for the South China Sea, particularly around the Spratly Islands, is an interim measure pending the settlement of territorial and maritime disputes. It would help to stabilise the status quo of the disputed area, and may finally lead to a permanent dispute resolution. Till then, the dispute prevents the effective implementation of any joint development arrangement. As seen in practice, there are obstacles in implementing the tripartite agreement signed by China, the Philippines and Vietnam, arising from their individual interests in the South China Sea as well as distrust in each other.

Fifth, the Taiwan factor in the South China Sea cannot be ignored as Taiwan (in the name of the Republic of China, ROC) has effectively occupied the largest island (the Taiping/Itu Aba Island) of the Spratly Islands since the early 1950s and claimed the whole South China Sea based on the historic facts of China. However, due to its special status in the international community, Taiwan is not eligible to join the treaties or sign international documents that only the sovereign states are entitled to. Thus, it is not a signatory to the LOS Convention or a party to the 2002 DOC. In recent years, Taiwan has intensified its activities in the Spratly Islands, leading to protests from other claimants. It built an airstrip on the Taiping Island in 2006, and its president visited the island in February 2008 to demonstrate Taiwan's sovereignty over the islands as well as its presence in the South China Sea. It is clear that Taiwan's motive is to catch the attention of the world community to its rights and interests in the South China Sea.[67] The ASEAN states and China need to accommodate Taiwan in the resolution of the South China Sea issue since Taiwan is now an important player in this regard.

Notes

1. The LOS Convention was adopted in the Third United Nations Conference on the Law of the Sea on 10 December 1982 and came into force on 16 November 1994. Text is reprinted in *International Legal Materials*, vol. 21, 1982, p. 1261.
2. J. R.V. Prescott, *The Maritime Political Boundaries of the World* (London: Methuen, 1985), p. 209.
3. According to Hungdah Chiu, there are 127 islands in the South China Sea based upon a survey conducted during 1946–7 sponsored by the then Chinese ministry of internal affairs. Hungdah Chiu, 'South China Sea Islands: Implications for Delimiting the Seabed and Future Shipping Routes', *China Quarterly*, vol. 72, 1977, p. 756.
4. D.R. Workman, 'The South China Sea Basin, Its Mineral Resources and Their Exploitation', in R.D. Hill, N.G. Owen and E.V. Roberts (eds.), *Fishing in Troubled Waters, Proceedings of an Academic Conference on Territorial Claims in the South China Sea* (Hong Kong: Centre of Asian Studies, University of Hong Kong, 1991), p. 9.
5. According to Article 46 (b) of the LOS Convention, 'archipelago' means a group of islands, including parts of islands, interconnecting waters and other natural features which are so closely interrelated that such islands, waters and other natural features form an intrinsic geographical, economic and political entity, or which historically have been regarded as such. Clearly, the '*qundao*' in the South China Sea cannot be fitted into this definition.
6. Jun Jiwu, 'Zhongsha Archipelagos in the Middle South China Sea', in Xin Yejiang (ed.), *China's South China Sea Islands* (Haiko: Hainan International Information Publishing Centre, 1996) (in Chinese), p. 131.
7. The Chinese name of the Scarborough Reef is *Huangyan Dao*. It is located 164 miles southeast from the Macclesfield Bank. Such a wide distance between them may defeat the argument that it is part of the Macclesfields by geographical standards.
8. A main reason that there is no other claimant for the Macclesfield Bank is that this bank is permanently submerged under the water. Otherwise, Vietnam or the Philippines might have claimed it as well.
9. The other two factors are: military confrontation in the Korean Peninsular region, and the controversial US–Japan military alliance and Taiwan's separatist activities. See Yan Xuetong, 'Co-operation Key to Regional Peace', *China Daily*, 27 March 1998, p. 4.
10. Wang Liyu, 'International Legal Norms Applicable to the Sovereignty Issue of the South China Sea Islands', in China Institute for Marine Development Strategy (ed.), *Selected Papers of the Workshop on the South China Sea Islands* (Beijing: China Institute for Marine Development Strategy) (in Chinese), March 1992, pp. 9–12.
11. See Wang, ibid., p. 24.
12. See Wang, ibid., pp. 24–6.
13. For relevant account, see T.O. Elias, 'The Doctrine of Intertemporal Law', *American Journal of International Law*, vol. 74, 1980, pp. 285–307.

14. Permanent Court of Arbitration. Sole Arbitrator: Huber. 2 R.I.A.A. 829 at 833.
15. 'The Intertemporal Problem in Public International Law', Session of Wiesbaden, 11 August 1975, available at *http://www.idi-iil.org/idiE/resolutionsE/1975_wies_01_en.pdf* (accessed 5 January 2006).
16. Zhao Lihai, *Studies on the Law of the Sea Issues* (Beijing: Peking University Press, 1996) (in Chinese), pp. 14–5.
17. The map was named as 'The Chinese territorial map before the Qianglong-Jiaqing period' (A.D. 1736–1820) of the Qing Dynasty in his compilation of *New Geographical Atlas of the Republic of China*. See Han Zhenhua (ed.), *A Compilation of Historical Materials on China's South China Sea Islands* (Beijing: Oriental Press, 1988) (in Chinese), p. 355.
18. 'The Chinese Map of Boundary Changes', in Tu Shichong (ed.), *The New Chinese Situation Atlas*, May 1927; 'The Chinese Map of Territorial Changes', in Chen Duo (ed.), *China's Model Atlas*, July 1933. Han, ibid., pp. 355–6.
19. Zhang Haiwen, *The Legal System Applicable to the Islands in the South China Sea*, Ph.D. dissertation (in Chinese), Peking University, 1995, p. 43 (on file with the author).
20. Chen Duo (ed.), *Newly-Made Chinese Atlas*, August 1934; Tan Lian and Chen Kaoji (eds.), *Civilised Geography of China*, September 1936; Ge Shuichen (ed.), *Newly-Made Large Hanging Atlas*, December 1939. See Han, supra note 17, pp. 356–9.
21. Zhang, supra note 19, p. 46.
22. Ministry of Interior, *An Outline of the Geography of the South China Sea Islands*, National Territory Series, 1947, Fig. 11, p. 861; as cited in J.K.T. Chao, 'South China Sea: Boundary Problems Relating to the Nansha and Hsisha Islands', in R.D. Hill et al. (eds.), supra note 4, p. 88.
23. Han, supra note 17, pp. 181–4.
24. Zhao Lihai, supra note 16, pp. 37–8. For further reference, see Li Jinming and Li Dexia, 'The Dotted Line on the Chinese Map of the South China Sea: A Note', *Ocean Development and International Law*, vol. 34, 2003, pp. 287–95.
25. Leo J. Bouchez, *The Regime of Bays in International Law* (Leyden: A.W. Sythoff, 1964), p. 281.
26. Articles 10 (6), 15 and 298 (1)(a)(i) of the LOS Convention.
27. D.P. O'Connell, *The International Law of the Sea* (Oxford: Clarendon Press, 1982), vol. 1, p. 417.
28. UN Doc. A/CN.4/143, 9 March 1962, entitled 'Juridical Regime of Historic Waters, Including Historic Bays', *Yearbook of the International Law Commission*, vol. 2, 1962, p. 6.
29. Some scholars assume that there are two possible reasons for this. First, the 12-mile territorial sea had generally been accepted by most coastal states, which made it possible to place the waters concerned under a state's sovereignty and jurisdiction. Second, the development of the legal regimes of the continental shelf, EEZ and archipelagic waters may bring about a gradual phasing out and eventual elimination of the phenomenon of 'historic' claims. See Yann-huei Song and Peter Kien-hong Yu, 'China's "Historic Waters" in

the South China Sea: An Analysis from Taiwan, R.O.C.', *The American Asian Review*, vol. 12 (4), 1994, p. 91.

30. UN Doc. A/CN.4/143, supra note 28, p. 13.
31. R.R. Churchill and A.V. Lowe, *The Law of the Sea* (Manchester: Manchester University Press, 1983), p. 37.
32. As a general rule, the accepted length of the closing line is 24 nm (nautical miles).
33. *People's Daily* (in Chinese), 23 September 1957.
34. O'Cornell, supra note 27, p. 418. (He seems to support Tonga's claim by saying that 'History might validate the claim to the rectangle, as an exception to the law relating to the high seas, but only as broadening of the area which could be claimed under the standard rules'.)
35. Kuan-Ming Sun, 'Policy of the Republic of China towards the South China Sea', *Marine Policy*, vol. 19, 1995, p. 408. Partly due to the differences reflected in the above discussion and partly due to Taiwan's domestic politics, the later developments have indicated that Taiwan has retreated from its 1993 Guidelines position. This can be seen from its 1998 Law on the Territorial Sea and the Contiguous Zone in which an original provision on 'historic waters' was dropped before its promulgation.`
36. 'Legal Regime of China's Historic Waters in the South China Sea', *Issues and Studies* (Chinese edition), vol. 32 (8), 1993, pp. 1–12.
37. Pan Shiying, 'South China Sea and the International Practice of the Historic Title', paper presented to the American Enterprise Institute Conference on the South China Sea, Washington, 7–9 September 1994, p. 5.
38. Wu Fengbing, 'Historical Evidence of China's Ownership of the Sovereignty over the Spratly Islands', in China Institute for Marine Development Strategy (ed.), *Selected Papers of the Conference on the South China Sea Islands* (Beijing: Ocean Press, 1992) (in Chinese), p. 111.
39. Jiao Yongke, 'No Question of Re-demarcation in the South China Sea', *Ocean Development and Management* (in Chinese), vol. 17 (2), 2000, p. 52.
40. *People's Daily* (in Chinese), 30 June 1998. An unofficial English version of the Law is appended to Zou Keyuan, *China's Marine Legal System and the Law of the Sea* (Leiden/Boston: Martinus Nijhoff, 2005), pp. 342–5.
41. Article 33 (1) of the UN Charter. Text is available at *http://www.un.org/aboutun/charter/index.html* (accessed 9 June 2008).
42. See the ASEAN Declaration on the South China Sea, available at *http://www.aseansec.org/3634.htm* (accessed 5 June 2008).
43. 'Recent Developments in the South China Sea', 18 March 1995, available at *http://www.aseansec.org/5232.htm* (accessed 9 June 2008).
44. Text is appended to Nguyen Hong Thao, 'Vietnam and the Code of Conduct for the South China Sea', *Ocean Development and International Law*, vol. 32, 2001, pp. 125–6.
45. Nguyen Hong Thao, ibid., p. 114. The draft is appended to Nguyen Hong Thao, ibid., pp. 127–9.
46. Leszek Buszynski and Iskandar Sazlan, 'Maritime Claims and Energy Cooperation in the South China Sea', *Contemporary Southeast Asia*, vol. 29 (1), 2007, p. 154.

47. Text is available at *http://www.aseansec.org/13163.htm* (accessed 9 June 2008).
48. See *Star Maritime*, 15 March 2005; cited in Leszek Buszynski and Iskandar Sazlan, supra note 46, p. 164.
49. 'Database on the Cooperation Progressing in the ASEAN Plus Three and ASEAN Plus One Cooperation Frameworks' as of 11 January 2008, p. 81, available at *http://www.aseansec.org/* (accessed 20 May 2008).
50. 'Terms of Reference of the ASEAN–China Joint Working Group on the Implementation of the Declaration on the Conduct of Parties in the South China Sea', available at *http://www.aseansec.org/16885.htm* (accessed 9 June 2008).
51. Ibid.
52. See Article 123 of the LOS Convention.
53. Zou Keyuan, 'The Sino-Vietnamese Agreement on Maritime Boundary Delimitation in the Gulf of Tonkin', *Ocean Development and International Law*, vol. 36, 2005, pp. 13–24.
54. See Articles 74(3) and 83(3) of the LOS Convention.
55. *North Sea Continental Shelf Cases*, Judgment of 20 February 1969, [1969] ICJ Rep 53.
56. *CCH Asia China E-News Alert*, no. 43, February 2004.
57. Wu Shicun and Hong Nong, 'The Energy Security of China and the Oil and Gas Exploitation in the Disputed South China Sea Area', in Myron H. Nordquist, John Norton Moore and Kuen-chen Fu (eds.), *Recent Developments in the Law of the Sea and China* (Leiden/Boston: Martinus Nijhoff, 2006), p. 148.
58. British Institute of International and Comparative Law, *Joint Development of Offshore Oil and Gas: A Model Agreement for States for Joint Development with Explanatory Commentary* (London: British Institute of International and Comparative Law, 1989), p. 45.
59. 'Wu Bangguo Proposes a Multiple Cooperation for Oil in the Spratly Islands', *Lianhe Zaobao* (in Chinese) (Singapore), 1 September 2003.
60. Li Guoqiang, 'Preliminary Discussion on Joint Development in the South China Sea', in Zhong Tianxiang, Han Jia and Ren Huaifeng (eds.), *Proceedings of the South China Sea Workshop 2002* (Hainan, Hainan Institute for the South China Sea, 2002) (in Chinese), p. 134.
61. 'Chinese, Philippine Firms Join Forces to Look for Oil in South China Sea', Agence France Presse, 13 November 2003.
62. 'China and the Philippines for the First Time Jointly Explore South China Sea Resources Without Drilling and Exploitation', *Jinghua Shibao* (Beijing-China Times) (in Chinese), 4 September 2004, p. A02.
63. 'China, Philippines and Vietnam Sign Agreement to Explore Oil in the South China Sea', *Lianhe Zaobao*, 15 March 2005, available at *http://www.zaobao.com/gj/yx501_150305.html* (accessed 15 March 2005).
64. Zou Keyuan, 'Joint Development in the South China Sea: A New Approach', *International Journal of Marine and Coastal Law*, vol. 21 (1), 2006, pp. 83–109.
65. 'China's Military Exercise in the Hoang Sa Archipelago is a Violation of Vietnam's Sovereignty', 11 November 2007, available at *http://www.mofa.gov.vn/en/tt_baochi/pbnfn/ns071126152905* (accessed 9 June 2008).

66. Nguyen Hong Thao, 'The 2002 Declaration on the Conduct of Parties in the South China Sea: A Note', *Ocean Development and International Law*, vol. 34, 2003, p. 281.
67. For relevant discussions on how Taiwan can play a role in the South China Sea, see Yann-huei Song, 'The Potential Marine Pollution Threat from Oil and Gas Activities in the Disputed South China Sea/Spratly Area: A Role that Taiwan Can Play', *Ocean Development and International Law*, vol. 39, 2008, pp. 150–77.

Part III
Bilateral relations between China and individual ASEAN countries

9

China's possible role in Myanmar's national reconciliation[1]

Historical link

China and Myanmar are neighbouring countries and their contact with each other dates back to 122 A.D.[2] Since that time, the Burmese have had intermittent tributary relations with the Chinese empire, which was severed by the invasion of the Western colonialists into the Asian region in the nineteenth century. After the founding of the People's Republic of China (PRC) in 1949, the Sino-Myanmar relations were generally stable, except for the anti-Chinese riots that occurred in the late 1960s. The two countries established formal diplomatic relations on 8 June 1950. In the 1950s, China and Myanmar jointly adopted the Five Principles of Peaceful Coexistence, namely, mutual respect for territorial integrity and sovereignty, mutual non-aggression, non-interference in each other's internal affairs, equality and mutual benefit, and peaceful coexistence.[3] With a spirit of mutual understanding and accommodation through friendly consultation, the two countries took the lead in working out a satisfactory solution to their border issues which had until then persisted as an unresolved historical legacy. This set a good example for the settlement of border issues between China and other neighbouring countries.

Leaders of China and Myanmar have a tradition of exchanging visits. Many Chinese leaders of the older generation, including Chairman Liu Shaoqi, Premier Zhou Enlai and Vice-Premier Chen Yi, paid visits to Myanmar while the Myanmar leaders, such as Chairman U Ne Win, President U San Yu and Prime Minister U Maung Maung Kha, reciprocally visited China on several occasions. Premier Zhou Enlai's nine visits to Myanmar and Chairman U Ne Win's 12 visits to China became a much-told tale between the two nations. Because of the traditional friendship, the people of the two countries always call each other 'Paukphaw' which means brother.

China's basic foreign policy

China's foreign policy has changed several times since the founding of the PRC.[4] The current policy is fundamentally based on the Five Principles of Peaceful Coexistence as mentioned above. China has pledged to pursue an independent foreign policy, which is designed to defend China's independence, state sovereignty and territorial integrity, to create a favourable international environment for economic reform and opening up to the outside world and for the modernisation drive of the nation, and to maintain world peace and promote common development. China has vowed not to establish a military bloc, join in the arms race nor seek military expansion.[5] China's previous experiences in joining the communist bloc have left a bitter memory.

China regards sovereignty to be a fundamental virtue in the formulation and existence of a nation-state. China has zealously defended its sovereignty due to the fact that China is still a relatively weak country, though big, and because it was exploited blatantly by Western powers in the past.[6] China claims that the main thrust of its foreign policy is to oppose hegemony and to safeguard world peace. It holds that all countries are equal members of the international community irrespective of their being big or small, strong or weak, rich or poor. All countries should settle their disputes and conflicts through peaceful consultations, instead of resorting to force or the threat of force. No country should interfere in the internal affairs of another country under any pretext, bully the weak country, or invade and subvert other countries.

China holds that the diversity of the world should not be an obstacle to the development of relations between various countries but should serve as an impetus to mutual exchange, complementarity and enrichment. All countries are entitled to choose their own social systems, development strategies and lifestyle that suit their particular conditions. The affairs of a country should be settled upon by its own people. On this basis, China strongly opposes any form of intervention. China criticised NATO's intervention in Kosovo in 1999, stating that NATO's action was a violation of the principle of non-interference in the internal affairs of a sovereign country and the principle of finding a peaceful solution to international disputes.[7] This attitude is also reflected in

China's stance towards the Iraq War launched by the American–British forces in March 2003. Since non-intervention is, in China's eyes, a fundamental principle in international relations, China itself has to abide by it. It is recalled that in the Mao era, China exported a 'communist revolution' to Southeast Asian countries. However, since the Deng Xiaoping reform era, China has adopted a more pragmatic diplomacy and no longer provided support for armed rebellion by communist parties in other countries.

China has improved its relations with the neighbouring countries as an important component of its foreign policy, taking firm steps towards settling the longstanding disputes with them. Strengthening China's solidarity and cooperation with the other developing countries is the basic framework of China's foreign policy since it shares common historical experiences with the developing countries and is confronted with the same goal of safeguarding national independence and developing the economy.[8]

China no longer regards the Association of Southeast Asian Nations (ASEAN) as a 'jackal' of the imperialist West. Recently, China's own economic reform brought it closer to its neighbouring countries in terms of interdependent and common development. As commented, China's policy within Southeast Asia is now largely governed by a rational ordering of national priorities in the context of interdependent economic interests and continuing tensions with the United States and Japan.[9] The Southeast Asian region seems to be China's backyard and is therefore critical to its vital interest and strategic security. Stabilising the surrounding areas (*wending zhoubian*) is one of the top priorities in China's current foreign policy. Recently, China further appeased the ASEAN countries by signing joint agreements on economic cooperation and integration and, remarkably, the Declaration on the Conduct of Parties in the South China Sea in November 2002.[10]

In addition, China takes part in multilateral diplomatic activities. The Chinese government has realised the importance of human rights and acceded to 17 international human rights conventions. China signed the International Covenant on Economic, Social and Cultural Rights and the International Covenant on Civil and Political Rights in October 1997 and October 1998 respectively, and ratified the first one in February 2001. However, China attaches more importance to economic rather than political and other rights, and views basic human rights as a possible trigger to social unrest in China. That is why China has so far not yet ratified the International Covenant on Civil and Political Rights.

Developments in Sino-Myanmar relations

Over a long period of time, the bilateral relations between China and Myanmar have witnessed steady development as both sides adhere to good neighbourly friendship and pursue a path of cooperation in both international and regional affairs. In June 1999 when Secretary-1 of the State Peace and Development Council (SPDC) Lt-Gen Khin Nyunt visited China, leaders of both sides reached a consensus on working towards a sustainable, stable, good-neighbourly and mutually trusted friendly cooperation relationship oriented towards the twenty-first century. They also exchanged in-depth views on further strengthening economic and trade cooperation between the two countries. Since then, the bilateral relations have achieved a positive momentum of development.[11]

Over the years, the two countries have continued to exchange high-level visits. This is attested by the visits to Myanmar of State Councillor and Secretary-General of the State Council Luo Gan (in January 1991), State Councillor and Foreign Minister Qian Qichen (in February 1993), Premier Li Peng (in December 1994), Chairman Li Ruihuan (in March 1997) and Vice-Premier Wu Bangguo (in October 1997), Vice-President Hu Jingtao (in July 2000), Li Lanqing (in January 2003 and Vice-Premier Wu Yi (in March 2004). The Myanmar leaders, including Chairman of the State Law and Peace Restoration Council Saw Maung (in August 1991), Secretary-1 of SPDC Khin Nyunt (in September 1994 and June 1999), Deputy Secretary-2 of SPDC Tin Oo (in November 1994), Chairman of the SPDC Senior General Than Shwe (in January 1996 and April 2005), Vice-Chairman of the SPDC General Maung Aye (in October 1996), and Prime Minister Soe Win (in February 2006) paid their respective visits to China. The foreign ministries of both countries have maintained sound cooperation. Diplomatic consultations at the vice-ministerial level have been held three times since the diplomatic consultation system was established in 1992. In January 1998, when Vice-Foreign Minister Tang Jiaxuan visited Myanmar for diplomatic consultation, the two sides signed the Agreement on Mutual Exemption of Visa for Diplomatic and Service Passport Holders. In 1993, both sides agreed to reopen their consulates-general; consequently, the Myanmar consulate-general in Kunming and Chinese consulate-general in Mandalay reopened in September 1993 and in August 1994 respectively.

Stable military ties have been maintained between the armed forces of both countries. In recent years, military leaders of both sides have sustained a momentum of exchange visits. Deputy Chief of General Staff He Qizong (in November 1991), Defence Minister Chi Haotian (in 1995),

Chairman of the Military Commission of CPC Central Committee Zhang Wannian (in April 1996) and Chief of General Staff Fu Quanyou (in April 2001) paid their visits to Myanmar. Similarly, Lt-Gen Than Shwe (in October 1989), Chief of the Army Lt-Gen Tin Oo (in December 1989 and November 1994) and Deputy Commander-in-Chief Senior General Maung Aye (in October 1996) visited China.[12]

The establishment of diplomatic relations have brought about economic and technological cooperation, resulting in steady progress in the economic and trade relations between China and Myanmar. The first trade agreement between the two countries was signed in 1954. A renewed trade agreement signed in 1971 stipulated that each side should give the most-favoured-nation treatment to the other side. Since December 1988, when the two countries started border trade, the annual bilateral trade volume has increased by a wide margin, rising from US$40 million to US$760 million in 1995. However, it decreased owing to the impact of Asian financial crisis, dropping to US$640 million and US$ 580 million in 1997 and 1998 respectively. While in 2000 the trade between the two countries reached US$620 million,[13] the bilateral trade volume in 2006 increased to US$1460 million. China's main exports to Myanmar include textiles, chemical raw materials, instruments and meters, machinery, medicines etc., while main imports from Myanmar include timber, local products, jades, livestock products etc. China has aided in constructing 22 commercial projects including Yangon–Thanlyin bridge, a sugar-processing plant, a textile factory, a plywood plant, a rice mill, a coal-fired power plant, a gymnasium, theatre etc. By the end of 1997, 183 contracts for labour services and construction projects were signed by the Chinese companies in Myanmar, the total contract value of which reached US$398 million.[14] In 1998, 103 more contracts were signed and the contract value totalled US$523 million. Chinese companies have invested US$31.55 million in Myanmar.[15] Table 9.1 shows China's investments in Myanmar from 1995 to 2001.

Culturally, both China and Myanmar are Buddhist countries. In 1994 and 1996, relics of Buddha's bones and teeth, which are China's national treasures, were sent twice to Myanmar for worship; this gesture was warmly hailed by the Myanmar government and people from all walks of life.

Since the State Law and Order Restoration Council (SLORC), recently renamed the State Peace and Development Council (SPDC), came into power in 1988, Myanmar has played the 'China card'. According to one commentator, the military junta in Rangoon actually abandoned the non-alignment policy and cultivated close ties with China. Thus, by the

Table 9.1 China's investments in Myanmar

Year	Investment (in US$ million)
1995–96	0.150
1996–97	23.100
1997–98	0.500
1998–99	2.662
1999–2000	–
Apr. 2000–Dec. 2001	28.980
Total	55.402

Source: adapted from S.D. Muni, *China's Strategic Engagement with the New ASEAN: An Exploratory Study of China's Post-Cold War Political, Strategic and Economic Relations with Myanmar, Laos, Cambodia and Vietnam* (Institute of Defence and Strategic Studies, Nanyang Technological University, Singapore, 2002), p. 108.

mid-1990s, Myanmar 'seemed to be drawn increasingly into a Chinese sphere of influence'.[16] Myanmar began its open economic policy after 1988, practicing the reform path China had embarked upon in the late 1970s. The Myanmar leaders shared the same view as the Chinese leaders that an open economy could enhance the country's stability and increase the nation's economic strength.[17] The pro-China policy resulted in a number of significant positive results for the Rangoon regime. First, China helped the Myanmar government to stabilise the internal situation and consolidate the power of the military junta. After the SLORC came to power, particularly after over-riding the results of the general election held in 1990, Myanmar faced hard economic sanctions from Western countries and international aid agencies. However, China provided substantial support to it. As China is a permanent member of the UN Security Council, any attempt to pass a resolution through the council to impose sanctions on Myanmar failed without the support of China. In addition, China stopped supporting the Myanmar Communist Party and persuaded the old communist party leaders to go to China for a comfortable retirement.[18] Meanwhile, Myanmar took a flexible policy towards the ethnic and communist rebels. Between March 1989 and May 1997, the military government signed peace agreements with 19 minority anti-government armed groups.[19]

China helped Myanmar to strengthen its capability of national defence and security through three means: (1) provision of advanced weapons; (2) assistance in building military installations and (3) facilitating the

Table 9.2 Arms sales to Myanmar

Weapon	Type	Units	Ordered/Delivered
Fighter	F-7	4	1996/1998
Ground Attack		21	1996/1998
Trainer	K-8	4	1996/1998
		4	1998/2000
Frigate	Mod.	2	1994/1998
	Jianghu		
APC	Type-85	150	1991/1996
MBT	Type-69	50	1993/1996

Note: APC, armoured personnel carrier; MBT, main battle tank.

Source: adapted from S.D. Muni, *China's Strategic Engagement with the New ASEAN: An Exploratory Study of China's Post-Cold War Political, Strategic and Economic Relations with Myanmar, Laos, Cambodia and Vietnam* (Institute of Defence and Strategic Studies, Nanyang Technological University, Singapore, 2002), p. 78.

peace dialogue between the military government and the anti-government armed groups using its own influence.[20] China has become the largest provider of weapons for Myanmar (see Table 9.2). It should be pointed out here that the Burmese junta may possibly turn these weapons against its own people. China's provision of armed might for the Burmese junta promoted the militarisation process within the Burmese society.[21]

One significant event that attracted the world's attention was China's assistance to Myanmar in establishing naval bases in the Hianggyi Island in the Irrawaddy River Delta and in the Great Coco Island in the Indian Ocean, approximately 30 nautical miles from India's Andaman Islands.

From an economic perspective, the cross-border trade between China and Myanmar has expanded dramatically. The two countries concluded the Border Trade Agreement on 5 August 1988 so as to open the border for Sino-Burmese trade. According to statistics, the trade increased to RMB¥ 2.569 billion and 3.084 billion in 1993 and 1994 respectively.[22] In February 1996, Myanmar set up the Myanmar–China Economic Enhancement Committee to promote economic cooperation with China. An extreme view taken by a commentator is that 'the net consequence of the free border trade with China has been a Chinese takeover of Upper Burma'.[23] Nevertheless, owing to the Asian financial crisis, the Sino-Burmese border trade met with some difficulties. For example, the trade in the border town of Ruili in Yunnan province decreased from RMB¥ 110 million in 1996 to RMB¥ 40 million in 1997.[24]

In the diplomatic area, Myanmar, with the support of China, broke through the diplomatic blockade made by the West, particularly the United States. ASEAN decided to carry out a constructive engagement policy towards Myanmar. Japan provided large loans to Rangoon. India tried to pull Myanmar into the sphere of nascent association for Bangladesh–India–Sri Lanka–Thailand Economic Cooperation (BIST-EC) after it had witnessed China's growing influence in the Bay of Bengal.[25]

In short, China has helped Myanmar substantially, arguably to the extent that without China's help, the military regime in Rangoon could not have survived to date.

The ASEAN mechanism

Since the inclusion of Myanmar into ASEAN in 1997, the involvement of the ASEAN in the Myanmar issue is inevitable provided that the principle of non-intervention in domestic affairs of member states is complied with. The ASEAN mechanism includes (1) an annual meeting of foreign ministers; (2) a standing committee under the chairmanship of the host country; (3) ad-hoc committees and permanent committees of specialists and officials on specific subjects and (4) a national secretariat in each member country. In 1993, the ASEAN countries agreed that ASEAN should consider the establishment of a regional human rights mechanism. They realised that the lack of an ASEAN mechanism provides the ASEAN countries with few opportunities to take stock of human rights developments. The establishment of an ASEAN mechanism with government support could help redress such an unfavourable situation so that the ASEAN perspective would be better understood by outsiders. For this purpose, a working group for an ASEAN human rights mechanism formulated a policy initiative for the ASEAN governments in 1998. The working group made the following suggestions: (1) to promote and support human rights activities, in particular, those in commemoration of the 50th anniversary of the Universal Declaration of Human Rights; (2) to regularise its contacts with the working group and acknowledge it as an important catalyst for the promotion of human rights in ASEAN, and to sustain the momentum for the eventual creation of a regional human rights commission and (3) to create a task force to examine the issues of form, substance and procedure related to the establishment of a regional human rights commission.[26] The newly adopted ASEAN Charter requires the future establishment of a human rights body within ASEAN. Though the mechanism has not yet come into being, the human rights situation in Myanmar is no doubt of common concern to the ASEAN member countries. Since Myanmar is a member of ASEAN, it is obliged to have dialogues relating to human rights within the framework of ASEAN.

On the other hand, ASEAN has established a number of basic principles to govern their relationships and resolve any of their differences. By upholding these principles, other ASEAN countries agree not to interfere in the domestic affairs of Myanmar, although they seek to promote a dialogue between the military regime and the opposition forces. Unlike the approach taken by the West led by the United States, which applied sanction measures, the ASEAN members conducted a constructive engagement with Rangoon. Further, they admitted Myanmar's participation in ASEAN. In ASEAN's view, constructive engagement and supported economic development contributes more to advance democracy and improve human rights conditions than can be achieved by an isolationist and retributionist approach.[27] Constructive engagement is also an avenue of influence. Aung San Suu Kyi's release from prison was viewed by ASEAN as a positive step both towards dialogue and reconciliation between the two adversaries as well as for the democratisation of Myanmar, and an achievement of its constructive engagement policy.[28] Furthermore, ASEAN attempted to show its independence and the 'ASEAN way' of dealing with issues within this region. It does not subject itself to the pressure from the West led by the United States. In this respect, the ASEAN's stance is quite similar to China's. The role of ASEAN is evident in the appointment of a special UN envoy to Myanmar for a dialogue between the United Nations and Rangoon on democracy and human rights, since the envoy was from Malaysia, an ASEAN member country. Owing to the pressure from ASEAN, Myanmar forwent the assigned chairmanship for 2006 in July 2005. This is seen by some as the association's move beyond its traditional non-intervention policy.[29]

China's possible role

Myanmar's national reconciliation is a necessary step towards democratisation of the country and has been at the heart of its democracy movement since 1988. There are two main components of the national reconciliation: (a) reconciliation between the military junta and the democratic forces led by Aung San Suu Kyi and (b) reconciliation between Burmese and ethnic groups. The ethnic reconciliation began in December 1990 when the Karen National Union agreed to the formation of the National Coalition Government of the Union of Burma (NCGUB) in Karen territory. Since then, several agreements were concluded in this respect, including the 1991 Manerplaw Agreement to establish a Federal Union of Burma; the 1997 Mae Tha Raw Hta Agreement regarding ceasefire and work with democracy movement and the 1998 Toemwe Khaloe Agreement regarding ethnic and pro-democracy groups agreeing to work together to restore democracy and establish a federal system of government. However, there has been a stalemate for the dialogue between the pro-democratic forces and the military government, despite the call from the United Nations for tripartite dialogue to resolve Myanmar's political future.[30] The secret talks between the two sides since October 2000 have not produced any fruitful results. In order to push forward the democratic process in Myanmar, the pro-democratic groups, supported by foreign funding, launched the National Reconciliation Programme in May 1999,[31] but so far there have been no substantial achievements. It should be realised that without the financial support of the government, such a programme can hardly be implemented in practice. On the other hand, the recent secret talks between the military junta and the National League for Democracy (NLD) annoyed the ethnic groups. They regarded such a dialogue 'as a meeting between two factions of Burmans' to redistribute the state power.[32] They fear that their interest and rights might be compromised by such a secret dialogue without their participation. Thus, national reconciliation would be out of question without the involvement of the ethnic minorities.

National reconciliation, in China's eyes, is entirely Myanmar's domestic affair. To follow the principle of non-intervention in state-to-state relations, China will not express any view about how the Myanmar regime should launch a dialogue with the opposition forces. China should not and will not have the right to interfere. This is China's basic stand.

China has shared the same view as Myanmar with regard to bilateral relations, international situations, human rights and Western values. They were both invaded and exploited by Western colonialists and are highly averse to the Western ideology. Both countries strongly oppose any interference in the domestic affairs of other countries on the pretext of religion or human rights. They have supported each other in the meetings of the UN Commission on Human Rights. China strongly protested

NATO's military intervention in Kosovo, regarding it as a grave violation of international law and a source of human disaster. However, on the other hand, China acknowledges the positive result of dialogues on human rights issues. China itself has such dialogues regularly with the United States and the European Union. On 20 November 2000, China signed a memorandum of understanding with the Office of the UN High Commissioner for Human Rights to strengthen cooperation on human rights protection. Vice-Primer Qian Qichen reiterated China's consistent willingness to participate in international cooperation in this field and stressed that the dialogue was the only way to solve disputes relating to human rights issues.[33] For this reason, China does not oppose Rangoon's dialogue with other countries regarding the human rights issues in Myanmar. Likewise, China holds the same attitude towards the dialogue between the military regime and the opposition forces in Myanmar.

China's view about Aung San Suu Kyi is likely to be quite similar to the position it holds on the military junta in Rangoon. China usually regards the Nobel Prizes in peace and literature as political instruments of the West to humiliate or insult the countries despised by the West. Hence, such prizes, once given, contain subversive elements. This has been well illustrated by the negative attitude of the Chinese towards the peace prize given to Dalai Lama in 1989 and the literature prize awarded to Gao Xingjian in 2000. Also, China does not regard Aung San Suu Kyi as a potential *minlawn* (contender to the throne) in Myanmar. In the view of a Chinese scholar, Aung San Suu Kyi does not command sufficient talents to accomplish her aims and is incapable of becoming the next leader of Myanmar. In her struggle, she faces not a few military leaders, but a strong, well organised, unified and experienced Myanmar army, which cannot be easily overthrown.[34] According to one scholar, even if the military junta were overthrown by an external power, no domestic political force would be able to take over the government.[35] For that reason, China is very reluctant to push forward the dialogue of reconciliation between the Rangoon government and Aung San Suu Kyi.[36] However, on the other hand, it should be noted that for the sake of regional stability as well as for the interest of China in Myanmar, China does not like to see any domestic turmoil within that country. A friendly and stable Myanmar is very important for China. Thus, China was the first country to offer its congratulations to the NLD immediately after it won the 1990 general elections.[37]

If the military junta shows its willingness to arrive at a compromise with the opposition forces, China would only be too glad and possibly provide some kind of assistance upon the request of the Myanmar government. As reported, the military government has been actively seeking advice from China and Vietnam on how to refashion itself into a more acceptable form.[38] The success of economic reform in China has encouraged the Rangoon regime to begin its own reform in recent years. The China model may be regarded by Rangoon as the most suitable for the economic reform in Myanmar, which can help develop economy on the one hand, and maintain authoritarian control on the other.

Furthermore, since China is a big regional power, its influence over the surrounding countries is inevitable and natural. In addition, owing to friendly relations between China and Myanmar, if China expresses its willingness to see the national reconciliation in Myanmar, it is more likely that the Myanmar government listens to China rather than yielding to pressures from other countries, particularly some Western hardliners.

There are other issues for China to consider. First, with regard to democratisation, China faces the same problem. China would think of the possible impact from Myanmar on China's own democratic process. Currently, in practice, China suppresses all the democratic movements, and political dissidents can only operate their activities outside China. There is no such person as Aung San Suu Kyi within the Chinese territory. The tolerance of Aung San Suu Kyi and the NLD in Myanmar may indicate the mercy of the military junta. In May 2002, Aung San Suu Kyi was released from home arrest and was allowed to visit places beyond the capital city of Myanmar, though harassment from the government occurs from time to time. In this sense, Myanmar is more democratic than China. On the other hand, whether Myanmar becomes democratic or not is purely a matter of domestic concern. According to China's pragmatic foreign policy, China will have to respect the choice of the people of Myanmar.

Second, if a mechanism were to be established within ASEAN in dealing with the issue of Myanmar, China would no doubt be willing to participate in the relevant process, as illustrated in the current ASEAN+3 and ASEAN+1 dialogues. China's attitude could be more supportive. Since the 1990s, the Sino-ASEAN relations have developed on a sound track with increasingly closer political ties. The year 1995 saw the establishment of the Senior Official Political Consultation mechanism, through which both China and ASEAN engage in talks to enhance mutual understanding and trust regarding political and security issues every year. The close ties between China and ASEAN may well indicate that China would prefer a dialogue regarding Myanmar within the framework of ASEAN. It is obvious that China has a stake in ASEAN. If the Myanmar issue hurts the relationship among the ASEAN members, it will also hurt the Sino-ASEAN relations.

Third, the 'China card' is undoubtedly important for the Rangoon regime. It has brought many benefits vis-à-vis the relations with the United States and ASEAN countries, particularly Thailand.[39] However, as stated by some scholars, Rangoon has now realised that it is placing too much reliance on China for political, military and economic support. To maintain its independence and diplomatic strategy, it has balanced the Chinese influence by using the 'ASEAN card' and the 'West card', particularly the Japanese card. Since Myanmar's accession to ASEAN and the Asian financial crisis, China's influence in Myanmar has been receding. At some point, Rangoon may seek to balance the influence by China by improving ties with India.[40] It is obvious that increased contacts with other members of the world community will lessen the dependence of the Rangoon regime on China. Myanmar may choose to return to the U Nu's old foreign policy of strict neutrality and non-alignment. In 1999, foreign observers reported a cooling of Beijing–Rangoon ties.[41] For this reason, China's role in Myanmar's national reconciliation is limited, though its influence in other areas is immense.

Prospects

The military junta in Rangoon still faces pressure both from inside and outside the country. The opposition forces will continue to voice their demand for democracy in Myanmar. The minority armed rebels, though having signed truce agreements with the government, may step up their demands. However, the most pressing matter is how to transfer the state power from the military junta to a civilian government. The military government in 1990 had promised that once the new constitution is formulated and the state order is restored, the power would be handed over to a civilian government. The developments in the 1990s showed that the military government was very reluctant towards such a handover. The demise of the Suharto regime in Indonesia may have had a heavy psychological blow to the Rangoon military regime because the latter had tried to follow the Indonesian model for its survival as well as development.[42] The military junta has to consider other alternatives. The new constitution was approved through a referendum held in May 2008, wherein the military junta promised to hold a general election in 2010, while continuing to play the leading role in the government. Hence, the domestic situation in Myanmar remains tense and uncertain unless a national reconciliation takes place soon.

The external pressure is, at present, largely coming from the United States. It has still maintained the economic sanctions against Myanmar, though whether the sanctions could play a critical role is unknown. The available data indicate that to date such a hardline approach has not been effective in pushing the Myanmar government to change its policy.[43] However, the pressure is strong enough to torment the Rangoon regime. Pressures may also come from other ASEAN member countries. In 1998, Thailand and the Philippines openly criticised Myanmar's violation of human rights.[44]

China continues its firm support to Myanmar. China criticised the United States' hegemonistic behaviour when it declared its second economic sanction against Myanmar in April 1997.[45] On the other hand, China was concerned whether Myanmar would yield to the American pressure. It is suggested that China should continue to reinforce its economic and trade cooperation with Myanmar to promote the friendly relationship between ASEAN and Myanmar, and to support the Myanmar government, particularly in the human rights field.[46] Economic cooperation can increase China's stake in Myanmar. As the commercial counsellor at the Chinese embassy to Myanmar admitted that the investment in Myanmar is not only based on commercial interests, but also on political considerations.[47] No doubt, China will continue to maintain the traditional friendly relationship with Myanmar.

From Myanmar's perspective, the close political, military and economic ties with China are a major source of comfort to the SPDC, particularly when it faced sanctions and isolation from the West. 'They are a critical factor in the government's belief that, in a worst case scenario, it would be able to survive, and indeed prosper, on the basis of its bilateral activities with that nation'.[48] One thing is clear: as long as the United States and possibly other countries continue to impose sanctions against Myanmar, this country will continue to choose to rely heavily on China. While we have seen the close relationship between the two countries, we should be aware that problems and issues exist in their relationship. It is reported that many Burmese view the Chinese 'as a new crop of colonists'.[49] One commentator has predicted that 'local resentment of immigrant Chinese is potentially a serious problem, and it could lead to a replay of the anti-Chinese riots of 1967'.[50] The author even concluded negatively that the Rangoon regime was playing with fire by having such close ties with China.[51]

While it may be argued whether these negative conclusions are well founded, it is to be admitted that potential problems and issues exist. Their resolution will depend on the wisdom and actions of the two countries. On the other hand, the Sino-Myanmar relations will continue to develop. A plan of 'Golden Quadrangle' encompassing Yunnan province of China, Upper Burma, northern Thailand and Laos has been discussed among the above four countries.[52] Once this plan comes to fruition, it will no doubt enhance the economic development of the region as well as the cooperation among the countries concerned. It should be noted that no matter who will be in power, the Sino-Myanmar relationship will be maintained and developed in a friendly and stable manner, as manifested by their historical transactions.

The national reconciliation is necessary for Myanmar, and dialogue is the only avenue of hope and success. We have to wait and see whether the military junta is willing to sit together with the NLD members and Aung San Suu Kyi as well as ethnic groups to build a democratic society in Myanmar. It may yet take some time to reach this goal.

Notes

1. It is gratefully acknowledged that this chapter is a revised and updated version of the paper with the same title published in *Copenhagen Journal of Asian Studies*, no. 17, 2003.
2. Lin Xixing, 'On the Formation of Burmese Overseas Chinese Economic Societies in the Early Time', *Southeast Asian Studies* (in Chinese), no. 4, 1998, p. 4.
3. They were contained in the Sino-Burmese Joint Declaration dated 29 June 1954, and adopted as guidelines of the bilateral relations between the two countries; see Wang Tieya (ed.), *International Law* (Beijing: Law Press, 1995) (in Chinese), p. 58.
4. John W. Garver, *Foreign Relations of the People's Republic of China* (New Jersey: Prentice-Hall, 1993).
5. See *http://www.fmprc.gov.cn* (accessed 18 November 2000).
6. Gerald Chan, *Chinese Perspectives on International Relations: A Framework for Analysis* (London: MacMillan Press, 1999), pp. 78–9.
7. Li Bian, 'NATO Challenges International Laws', *Beijing Review*, 26 April–2 May 1999, p. 7. The NATO intervention is regarded as an analogy of the aggression of the eight powers alliance against China in the late 1800s. See Ma Yuezheng, 'Diplomacy of the New China', *Hubei Social Sciences* (in Chinese), no. 6, 1999, p. 5.
8. See *http://www.fmprc.gov.cn* (accessed 18 November 2000).
9. Michael Leifer, 'China in Southeast Asia: Interdependence and Accommodation', in David S.G. Goodman and Gerald Segal (eds.), *China Rising: Nationalism and Interdependence* (London: Routledge, 1997), p. 168.
10. Text is available at *http://www.aseansec.org/13495.htm* (accessed 7 April 2002).
11. See *http://www.fmprc.gov.cn* (accessed 18 November 2000).

12. Ibid.
13. 'Real friends help each other', *Yanzhou Zhoukan*, 23–29 April 2001, p. 17.
14. The figure in 2006 was US$2630 million.
15. See *http://www.fmprc.gov.cn* (accessed 18 November 2000).
16. Donald M. Seekins, 'Burma–China Relations: Playing with Fire', *Asian Survey*, vol. 37 (6), 1997, p. 525.
17. Lin Xixing, 'Myanmar's Policy toward China after the Cold War', *Southeast Asian Studies* (in Chinese), no. 4, 1999, p. 28.
18. Ibid., p. 28. It is noted that China stopped its 'export of revolution' to Southeast Asia after 1978 except for the Burma Communist Party (to about 1988) and the Khmer Rouge (to 1991). See Harold C. Hinton, 'China as an Asian Power', in Thomas W. Robinson and David Shambaugh (eds.), *Chinese Foreign Policy: Theory and Practice* (Oxford: Clarendon Press, 1994), p. 352.
19. Lin Xixing, 'The Present Situation of Myanmar's Internal Politics and International Relations', *Southeast Asian Studies* (in Chinese), no. 3, 2000, p. 27.
20. Lin Xixing, supra note 16, p. 31.
21. Seekins, supra note 15, p. 539.
22. Lin Xinxing, supra note 16, p. 30.
23. Mya Maung, 'Burma's Economic Performance under Military Rule: An Assessment', *Asian Survey*, vol. 37 (6), 1997, p. 520.
24. Lin Xixing, 'Myanmar Loses Its Expectation on ASEAN in the Financial Crisis', *Southeast Asian Studies* (in Chinese), no. 1, 1999, p. 14.
25. James Guyot, 'Burma in 1997: From Empire to ASEAN', *Asian Survey*, vol. 38 (2), 1998, p. 191.
26. Working Group for an ASEAN human rights mechanism, 'Synopsis of a Policy Initiative for the Establishment of an ASEAN Human Rights Mechanism', reprinted in Miriam Defensor Santiago, *International Law with Philippine Cases and Materials and ASEAN Instruments* (Quezon City, Philippines: Central Professional Books, Inc., 1999), p. 389.
27. Thai Foreign Minister Surin Pitsuwan once proposed the concept of 'flexible engagement', a franker, more critical discussion of the internal problems of member states that challenged ASEAN's 30-year-old policy of strict non-interference. 'Flexible engagement' was rejected by a majority of foreign ministers attending the July 1998 ASEAN Summit in Manila, though Surin was supported by the host country's foreign minister, Domingo Siazon. See Donald M. Seekings, 'Burma in 1998: Little to Celebrate', *Asian Survey*, vol. 39 (1), 1999, p. 17.
28. Mya Maung, 'The Burma Road to the Past', *Asian Survey*, vol. 39 (2), 1999, p. 272. However, Mya Maung denied any positive effect resulting from the constructive engagement policy by stating that 'a constructive engagement policy can only lead to a prolongation of the military's stranglehold on power to the detriment, in this case, of the democracy movement led by Daw Suu Kyi and the NLD', ibid., p. 285.
29. Ruukun Katanyuu, 'Beyond Non-Interference in ASEAN: The Association's Role in Myanmar's National Reconciliation and Democratization', *Asian Survey*, vol. 46 (6), 2006, p. 845.

30. The United Nations urges the government of Myanmar to take urgent and meaningful measures to ensure the establishment of democracy in accordance with the will of the people as expressed in the democratic elections held in 1990 and to engage immediately and unconditionally in a genuine and substantive dialogue with the leaders of political parties and of ethnic minorities with the aim of achieving national reconciliation and the restoration of democracy. See UN DOC. E/CN.4/RES/2000/23 (Situation of human rights in Myanmar), 18 April 2000.
31. National Reconciliation Programme (revised November 1999), kindly provided by Mr. Harn Yawnghwe, Director of the European Office for the Development of Democracy in Burma, Brussels.
32. Barry Wain, 'Ethnic Conflict Clouds Myanmar', *Asian Wall Street Journal*, 20 April 2001, p. 6.
33. 'Human Rights Memorandum Signed with UN', *China Daily*, 21 November 2000.
34. Mu Sheng, 'Aung San Suu Kyi's Role in the Present Burmese Politics', *Southeast Asian Studies* (in Chinese), no. 1, 1997, p. 20.
35. Li Chenyang, 'China–Myanmar Relations since 1988', in Lai Hongyi and Lim Tin Seng (eds.), *Harmony and Development: ASEAN–China Relations* (Singapore: World Scientific, 2007), p. 60.
36. It should be noted that China has never openly criticised Aung San Suu Kyi, and the latter has never done that either, though she once complained about China's support of the Rangoon regime. It seems that both sides maintain some degree of flexibility for future dialogue.
37. Harn Yawnghwe, 'EU–ASEAN Relations: A Burmese/Myanmar Perspective', *Panorama*, vol. 2, 2000, p. 80.
38. Allen L. Clark, 'Myanmar's Present Development and Future Options', *Asian Survey*, vol. 39 (5), 1999, p. 787.
39. Li Xixing, supra note 16, p. 32.
40. John W. Garver, *Protracted Contest: Sino-Indian Rivalry in the Twentieth Century* (Seattle: University of Washington Press, 2001), p. 274.
41. Antony Davis, 'China's Shadow', *Asiaweek*, 28 May 1999, pp. 30–4.
42. As is pointed out, Soeharto's resignation in May 1998 may have exposed the bankruptcy of the 'Indonesian model' of army-directed state building, which the National Convention incorporated into its new constitution. Seekins, supra note 26, p. 18.
43. Clark, supra note 37, p. 783.
44. Li Chenyang, 'An Analysis of the Impact of Southeast Asian Financial Crisis on Myanmar', *Southeast Asian Studies* (in Chinese), no. 1, 1999, p. 17.
45. Zuo Xiao'an et al., 'The Influence of American Sanctions against Myanmar on Southeast Asian Situation', *Southeast Asian Studies* (in Chinese), no. 4, 1997, p. 18.
46. Ibid., p. 19.
47. 'Real friends help each other', supra note 12, p. 17.
48. Clark, supra note 37, p. 786.
49. Denny Roy, *China's Foreign Relations* (Lanham: Rowman & Littlefield, 1998), p. 174.
50. Seekins, supra note 15, p. 530.

51. He listed three reasons. First, abandonment of Burma's traditional neutrality may draw the country into conflicts with China and other Asian countries by the beginning of the next century. Second, Chinese involvement in, and even domination of the domestic economy, especially in Upper Burma, may spark communal violence similar to the anti-Chinese riots of 1967, or mob attacks on Burmese Muslims in 1997. Third, China's large-scale contributions to SLORC's armed might, in the form of weapons, infrastructure aid and training promote the ongoing militarisation of Burmese society, which will only lead to more violence and instability as the generals turn away from non-violent alternatives that alone can bring the country social peace and development, Ibid., p. 539.
52. Yang Xiaohui, 'An Analysis of the Quadrilateral Economic Cooperation Program of Mainland China, Laos, Myanmar and Thailand', *Southeast Asian Studies* (in Chinese), no. 2, 1999, pp. 25–30, 35.

Appendixes[1]

1. Treaty of Amity and Cooperation in Southeast Asia

Treaty of Amity and Cooperation in Southeast Asia Indonesia, 24 February 1976

The High Contracting Parties:

CONSCIOUS of the existing ties of history, geography and culture, which have bound their peoples together;

ANXIOUS to promote regional peace and stability through abiding respect for justice and the rule or law and enhancing regional resilience in their relations;

DESIRING to enhance peace, friendship and mutual cooperation on matters affecting Southeast Asia consistent with the spirit and principles of the Charter of the United Nations, the Ten Principles adopted by the Asian-African Conference in Bandung on 25 April 1955, the Declaration of the Association of Southeast Asian Nations signed in Bangkok on 8 August 1967 and the Declaration signed in Kuala Lumpur on 27 November 1971;

CONVINCED that the settlement of differences or disputes between their countries should be regulated by rational, effective and sufficiently flexible procedures, avoiding negative attitudes which might endanger or hinder cooperation;

[1] It is acknowledged that all the documents reprinted here are from the website of the ASEAN Secretariat: www.aseansec.org.

BELIEVING in the need for cooperation with all peace-loving nations, both within and outside Southeast Asia, in the furtherance of world peace, stability and harmony;

SOLEMNLY AGREE to enter into a Treaty of Amity and Cooperation as follows:

Chapter I: Purpose and Principles

Article 1

The purpose of this Treaty is to promote perpetual peace, everlasting amity and cooperation among their peoples which would contribute to their strength, solidarity and closer relationship.

Article 2

In their relations with one another, the High Contracting Parties shall be guided by the following fundamental principles:

a. mutual respect for the independence, sovereignty, equality, territorial integrity and national identity of all nations;
b. the right of every State to lead its national existence free from external interference, subversion or coercion;
c. non-interference in the internal affairs of one another;
d. settlement of differences or disputes by peaceful means;
e. renunciation of the threat or use of force;
f. effective cooperation among themselves.

Chapter II: Amity

Article 3

In pursuance of the purpose of this Treaty the High Contracting Parties shall endeavour to develop and strengthen the traditional, cultural and historical ties of friendship, good neighbourliness and cooperation which bind them together and shall fulfill in good faith the obligations assumed under this Treaty. In order to promote closer understanding among them, the High Contracting Parties shall encourage and facilitate contact and intercourse among their peoples.

Chapter III: Cooperation

Article 4

The High Contracting Parties shall promote active cooperation in the economic, social, technical, scientific and administrative fields as well as in matters of common ideals and aspirations of international peace and stability in the region and all other matters of common interest.

Article 5

Pursuant to Article 4 the High Contracting Parties shall exert their maximum efforts multilaterally as well as bilaterally on the basis of equality, non-discrimination and mutual benefit.

Article 6

The High Contracting Parties shall collaborate for the acceleration of the economic growth in the region in order to strengthen the foundation for a prosperous and peaceful community of nations in Southeast Asia. To this end, they shall promote the greater utilisation of their agriculture and industries, the expansion of their trade and the improvement of their economic infrastructure for the mutual benefit of their peoples. In this regard, they shall continue to explore all avenues for close and beneficial cooperation with other States as well as international and regional organisations outside the region.

Article 7

The High Contracting Parties, in order to achieve social justice and to raise the standards of living of the peoples of the region, shall intensify economic cooperation. For this purpose, they shall adopt appropriate regional strategies for economic development and mutual assistance.

Article 8

The High Contracting Parties shall strive to achieve the closest cooperation on the widest scale and shall seek to provide assistance to one another in the form of training and research facilities in the social, cultural, technical, scientific and administrative fields.

Article 9

The High Contracting Parties shall endeavour to foster cooperation in the furtherance of the cause of peace, harmony, and stability in the region. To this end, the High Contracting Parties shall maintain regular contacts and consultations with one another on international and regional matters with a view to coordinating their views actions and policies.

Article 10

Each High Contracting Party shall not in any manner or form participate in any activity which shall constitute a threat to the political and economic stability, sovereignty, or territorial integrity of another High Contracting Party.

Article 11

The High Contracting Parties shall endeavour to strengthen their respective national resilience in their political, economic, socio-cultural as well as security fields in conformity with their respective ideals and aspirations, free from external interference as well as internal subversive activities in order to preserve their respective national identities.

Article 12

The High Contracting Parties in their efforts to achieve regional prosperity and security, shall endeavour to cooperate in all fields for the promotion of regional resilience, based on the principles of self-confidence, self-reliance, mutual respect, cooperation and solidarity which will constitute the foundation for a strong and viable community of nations in Southeast Asia.

Chapter IV: Pacific Settlement of Disputes

Article 13

The High Contracting Parties shall have the determination and good faith to prevent disputes from arising. In case disputes on matters directly affecting them should arise, especially disputes likely to disturb regional peace and harmony, they shall refrain from the threat or use of force and shall at all times settle such disputes among themselves through friendly negotiations.

Article 14

To settle disputes through regional processes, the High Contracting Parties shall constitute, as a continuing body, a High Council comprising a Representative at ministerial level from each of the High Contracting Parties to take cognizance of the existence of disputes or situations likely to disturb regional peace and harmony.

Article 15

In the event no solution is reached through direct negotiations, the High Council shall take cognizance of the dispute or the situation and shall recommend to the parties in dispute appropriate means of settlement such as good offices, mediation, inquiry or conciliation. The High Council may however offer its good offices, or upon agreement of the parties in dispute, constitute itself into a committee of mediation, inquiry or conciliation. When deemed necessary, the High Council shall recommend appropriate measures for the prevention of a deterioration of the dispute or the situation.

Article 16

The foregoing provision of this Chapter shall not apply to a dispute unless all the parties to the dispute agree to their application to that dispute. However, this shall not preclude the other High Contracting Parties not party to the dispute from offering all possible assistance to settle the said dispute. Parties to the dispute should be well disposed towards such offers of assistance.

Article 17

Nothing in this Treaty shall preclude recourse to the modes of peaceful settlement contained in Article 33(l) of the Charter of the United Nations. The High Contracting Parties which are parties to a dispute should be encouraged to take initiatives to solve it by friendly negotiations before resorting to the other procedures provided for in the Charter of the United Nations.

Chapter V: General Provision

Article 18

This Treaty shall be signed by the Republic of Indonesia, Malaysia, the Republic of the Philippines, the Republic of Singapore and the Kingdom of Thailand. It shall be ratified in accordance with the constitutional procedures of each signatory State. It shall be open for accession by other States in Southeast Asia.

Article 19

This Treaty shall enter into force on the date of the deposit of the fifth instrument of ratification with the Governments of the signatory States which are designated Depositories of this Treaty and the instruments of ratification or accession.

Article 20

This Treaty is drawn up in the official languages of the High Contracting Parties, all of which are equally authoritative. There shall be an agreed common translation of the texts in the English language. Any divergent interpretation of the common text shall be settled by negotiation.

IN FAITH THEREOF the High Contracting Parties have signed the Treaty and have hereto affixed their Seals.

DONE at Denpasar, Bali, this twenty-fourth day of February in the year one thousand nine hundred and seventy-six.

2. Framework Agreement on Comprehensive Economic Co-Operation between ASEAN and China

Framework Agreement on Comprehensive Economic Co-Operation Between ASEAN and the People's Republic of China
Phnom Penh, 5 November 2002

PREAMBLE

We, the Heads of Government/State of Brunei Darussalam, the Kingdom of Cambodia, the Republic of Indonesia, the Lao People's Democratic

Republic ('Lao PDR'), Malaysia, the Union of Myanmar, the Republic of the Philippines, the Republic of Singapore, the Kingdom of Thailand and the Socialist Republic of Viet Nam, Member States of the Association of South East Asian Nations (collectively, 'ASEAN' or 'ASEAN Member States', or individually, 'ASEAN Member State') and the People's Republic of China ('China'),

Recalling our decision made at the ASEAN-China Summit held on 6 November 2001 in Bandar Seri Begawan, Brunei Darussalam, regarding a Framework on Economic Co-operation and to establish an ASEAN-China Free Trade Area ('ASEAN-China FTA') within 10 years with special and differential treatment and flexibility for the newer ASEAN Member States of Cambodia, Lao PDR, Myanmar and Viet Nam ('the newer ASEAN Member States') and with provision for an early harvest in which the list of products and services will be determined by mutual consultation;

Desiring to adopt a Framework Agreement on Comprehensive Economic Co-operation ('this Agreement') between ASEAN and China (collectively, 'the Parties', or individually referring to an ASEAN Member State or to China as a 'Party') that is forward-looking in order to forge closer economic relations in the 21st century;

Desiring to minimise barriers and deepen economic linkages between the Parties; lower costs; increase intra-regional trade and investment; increase economic efficiency; create a larger market with greater opportunities and larger economies of scale for the businesses of the Parties; and enhance the attractiveness of the Parties to capital and talent;

Being confident that the establishment of an ASEAN-China FTA will create a partnership between the Parties, and provide an important mechanism for strengthening co-operation and supporting economic stability in East Asia;

Recognising the important role and contribution of the business sector in enhancing trade and investment between the Parties and the need to further promote and facilitate their co-operation and utilisation of greater business opportunities provided by the ASEAN-China FTA;

Recognising the different stages of economic development among ASEAN Member States and the need for flexibility, in particular the need to facilitate the increasing participation of the newer ASEAN Member States in the ASEAN-China economic co-operation and the expansion of their exports, including, inter alia, through the strengthening of their domestic capacity, efficiency and competitiveness;

Reaffirming the rights, obligations and undertakings of the respective parties under the World Trade Organisation (WTO), and other multilateral, regional and bilateral agreements and arrangements;

Recognising the catalytic role that regional trade arrangements can contribute towards accelerating regional and global liberalisation and as building blocks in the framework of the multilateral trading system;

Have agreed as follows:

Article 1

Objectives

The objectives of this Agreement are to:

a. strengthen and enhance economic, trade and investment co-operation between the Parties;
b. progressively liberalise and promote trade in goods and services as well as create a transparent, liberal and facilitative investment regime;
c. explore new areas and develop appropriate measures for closer economic co-operation between the Parties; and
d. facilitate the more effective economic integration of the newer ASEAN Member States and bridge the development gap among the Parties.

Article 2

Measures For Comprehensive Economic Co-operation

The Parties agree to negotiate expeditiously in order to establish an ASEAN-China FTA within 10 years, and to strengthen and enhance economic co-operation through the following:

a. progressive elimination of tariffs and non-tariff barriers in substantially all trade in goods;
b. progressive liberalisation of trade in services with substantial sectoral coverage;
c. establishment of an open and competitive investment regime that facilitates and promotes investment within the ASEAN-China FTA;
d. provision of special and differential treatment and flexibility to the newer ASEAN Member States;

e. provision of flexibility to the Parties in the ASEAN-China FTA negotiations to address their sensitive areas in the goods, services and investment sectors with such flexibility to be negotiated and mutually agreed based on the principle of reciprocity and mutual benefits;

f. establishment of effective trade and investment facilitation measures, including, but not limited to, simplification of customs procedures and development of mutual recognition arrangements;

g. expansion of economic co-operation in areas as may be mutually agreed between the Parties that will complement the deepening of trade and investment links between the Parties and formulation of action plans and programmes in order to implement the agreed sectors/areas of co-operation; and

h. establishment of appropriate mechanisms for the purposes of effective implementation of this Agreement.

PART 1

Article 3

Trade In Goods

1. In addition to the Early Harvest Programme under Article 6 of this Agreement, and with a view to expediting the expansion of trade in goods, the Parties agree to enter into negotiations in which duties and other restrictive regulations of commerce (except, where necessary, those permitted under Article XXIV (8)(b) of the WTO General Agreement on Tariffs and Trade (GATT)) shall be eliminated on substantially all trade in goods between the Parties.

2. For the purposes of this Article, the following definitions shall apply unless the context otherwise requires:

   a. 'ASEAN 6' refers to Brunei, Indonesia, Malaysia, Philippines, Singapore and Thailand;

   b. 'applied MFN tariff rates' shall include in-quota rates, and shall:

      i. in the case of ASEAN Member States (which are WTO members as of 1 July 2003) and China, refer to their respective applied rates as of 1 July 2003; and

      ii. in the case of ASEAN Member States (which are non-WTO members as of 1 July 2003), refer to the rates as applied to China as of 1 July 2003;

   c. 'non-tariff measures' shall include non-tariff barriers.

3. The tariff reduction or elimination programme of the Parties shall require tariffs on listed products to be gradually reduced and where applicable, eliminated, in accordance with this Article.
4. The products which are subject to the tariff reduction or elimination programme under this Article shall include all products not covered by the Early Harvest Programme under Article 6 of this Agreement, and such products shall be categorised into two Tracks as follows:
   a. *Normal Track*: Products listed in the Normal Track by a Party on its own accord shall:
      i. have their respective applied MFN tariff rates gradually reduced or eliminated in accordance with specified schedules and rates (to be mutually agreed by the Parties) over a period from 1 January 2005 to 2010 for ASEAN 6 and China, and in the case of the newer ASEAN Member States, the period shall be from 1 January 2005 to 2015 with higher starting tariff rates and different staging; and
      ii. in respect of those tariffs which have been reduced but have not been eliminated under paragraph 4(a)(i) above, they shall be progressively eliminated within timeframes to be mutually agreed between the Parties.
   b. *Sensitive Track*: Products listed in the Sensitive Track by a Party on its own accord shall:
      i. have their respective applied MFN tariff rates reduced in accordance with the mutually agreed end rates and end dates; and
      ii. where applicable, have their respective applied MFN tariff rates progressively eliminated within timeframes to be mutually agreed between the parties.
5. The number of products listed in the Sensitive Track shall be subject to a maximum ceiling to be mutually agreed among the Parties.
6. The commitments undertaken by the Parties under this Article and Article 6 of this Agreement shall fulfil the WTO requirements to eliminate tariffs on substantially all the trade between the Parties.
7. The specified tariff rates to be mutually agreed between the Parties pursuant to this Article shall set out only the limits of the applicable tariff rates or range for the specified year of implementation by the Parties and shall not prevent any Party from accelerating its tariff reduction or elimination if it so wishes to.

8. The negotiations between the Parties to establish the ASEAN-China FTA covering trade in goods shall also include, but not be limited to the following:

   a. other detailed rules governing the tariff reduction or elimination programme for the Normal Track and the Sensitive Track as well as any other related matters, including principles governing reciprocal commitments, not provided for in the preceding paragraphs of this Article;

   b. Rules of Origin;

   c. treatment of out-of-quota rates;

   d. modification of a Party's commitments under the agreement on trade in goods based on Article XXVIII of the GATT;

   e. non-tariff measures imposed on any products covered under this Article or Article 6 of this Agreement, including, but not limited to quantitative restrictions or prohibition on the importation of any product or on the export or sale for export of any product, as well as scientifically unjustifiable sanitary and phytosanitary measures and technical barriers to trade;

   f. safeguards based on the GATT principles, including, but not limited to the following elements: transparency, coverage, objective criteria for action, including the concept of serious injury or threat thereof, and temporary nature;

   g. disciplines on subsidies and countervailing measures and anti-dumping measures based on the existing GATT disciplines; and

   h. facilitation and promotion of effective and adequate protection of trade-related aspects of intellectual property rights based on existing WTO, World Intellectual Property Organization (WIPO) and other relevant disciplines.

Article 4

Trade In Services

With a view to expediting the expansion of trade in services, the Parties agree to enter into negotiations to progressively liberalise trade in services with substantial sectoral coverage. Such negotiations shall be directed to:

a. progressive elimination of substantially all discrimination between or among the Parties and/or prohibition of new or more discriminatory measures with respect to trade in services between the Parties, except for measures permitted under Article V(1)(b) of the WTO General Agreement on Trade in Services (GATS);

b. expansion in the depth and scope of liberalisation of trade in services beyond those undertaken by ASEAN Member States and China under the GATS; and

c. enhanced co-operation in services between the Parties in order to improve efficiency and competitiveness, as well as to diversify the supply and distribution of services of the respective service suppliers of the Parties.

Article 5

Investment

To promote investments and to create a liberal, facilitative, transparent and competitive investment regime, the Parties agree to:

a. enter into negotiations in order to progressively liberalise the investment regime;

b. strengthen co-operation in investment, facilitate investment and improve transparency of investment rules and regulations; and

c. provide for the protection of investments.

Article 6

Early Harvest

1. With a view to accelerating the implementation of this Agreement, the Parties agree to implement an Early Harvest Programme (which is an integral part of the ASEAN-China FTA) for products covered under paragraph 3(a) below and which will commence and end in accordance with the timeframes set out in this Article.

2. For the purposes of this Article, the following definitions shall apply unless the context otherwise requires:

   a. 'ASEAN 6' refers to Brunei, Indonesia, Malaysia, Philippines, Singapore and Thailand;

   b. 'applied MFN tariff rates' shall include in-quota rates, and shall:

      i. in the case of ASEAN Member States (which are WTO members as of 1 July 2003) and China, refer to their respective applied rates as of 1 July 2003; and

ii. in the case of ASEAN Member States (which are non-WTO members as of 1 July 2003), refer to the tariff rates as applied to China as of 1 July 2003.

3. The product coverage, tariff reduction and elimination, implementation timeframes, Rules of Origin, trade remedies and emergency measures applicable to the Early Harvest Programme shall be as follows:

a. Product Coverage

i. All products in the following chapters at the 8/9 digit level (HS Code) shall be covered by the Early Harvest Programme, unless otherwise excluded by a Party in its Exclusion List as set out in Annex 1 of this Agreement, in which case these products shall be exempted for that Party:

Chapter	Description
01	Live Animals
02	Meat and Edible Meat Offal
03	Fish
04	Dairy Produce
05	Other Animals Products
06	Live Trees
07	Edible Vegetables
08	Edible Fruits and Nuts

ii. A Party which has placed products in the Exclusion List may, at any time, amend the Exclusion List to place one or more of these products under the Early Harvest Programme.

iii. The specific products set out in Annex 2 of this Agreement shall be covered by the Early Harvest Programme and the tariff concessions shall apply only to the parties indicated in Annex 2. These parties must have extended the tariff concessions on these products to each other.

iv. For those parties which are unable to complete the appropriate product lists in Annex 1 or Annex 2, the lists may still be drawn up no later than 1 March 2003 by mutual agreement.

b. Tariff Reduction and Elimination

i. All products covered under the Early Harvest Programme shall be divided into three product categories for tariff reduction and elimination as defined and to be implemented in accordance with the timeframes set out in Annex 3 to this Agreement. This paragraph shall not prevent any Party from accelerating its tariff reduction or elimination if it so wishes.

ii. All products where the applied MFN tariff rates are at 0%, shall remain at 0%.

iii. Where the implemented tariff rates are reduced to 0%, they shall remain at 0%.

iv. A Party shall enjoy the tariff concessions of all the other parties for a product covered under paragraph 3(a)(i) above so long as the same product of that Party remains in the Early Harvest Programme under paragraph 3(a)(i) above.

c. Interim Rules of Origin

The Interim Rules of Origin applicable to the products covered under the Early Harvest Programme shall be negotiated and completed by July 2003. The Interim Rules of Origin shall be superseded and replaced by the Rules of Origin to be negotiated and implemented by the Parties under Article 3(8)(b) of this Agreement.

d. Application of WTO provisions

The WTO provisions governing modification of commitments, safeguard actions, emergency measures and other trade remedies, including anti-dumping and subsidies and countervailing measures, shall, in the interim, be applicable to the products covered under the Early Harvest Programme and shall be superseded and replaced by the relevant disciplines negotiated and agreed to by the Parties under Article 3(8) of this Agreement once these disciplines are implemented.

4. In addition to the Early Harvest Programme for trade in goods as provided for in the preceding paragraphs of this Article, the Parties will explore the feasibility of an Early Harvest Programme for trade in services in early 2003.

5. With a view to promoting economic co-operation between the Parties, the activities set out in Annex 4 of this Agreement shall be undertaken or implemented on an accelerated basis, as the case may be.

PART 2

Article 7

Other Areas Of Economic Co-operation

1. The Parties agree to strengthen their co-operation in five priority sectors as follows:
   a. agriculture;
   b. information and communications technology;
   c. human resources development;
   d. investment; and
   e. Mekong River basin development.
2. Co-operation shall be extended to other areas, including, but not limited to, banking, finance, tourism, industrial co-operation, transport, telecommunications, intellectual property rights, small and medium enterprises (SMEs), environment, bio-technology, fishery, forestry and forestry products, mining, energy and sub-regional development.
3. Measures to strengthen co-operation shall include, but shall not be limited to:
   a. promotion and facilitation of trade in goods and services, and investment, such as:
      ii. standards and conformity assessment;
      iii. technical barriers to trade/non-tariff measures; and
      iv. customs co-operation;
   b. increasing the competitiveness of SMEs;
   c. promotion of electronic commerce;
   d. capacity building; and
   e. technology transfer.
4. The Parties agree to implement capacity building programmes and technical assistance, particularly for the newer ASEAN Member States, in order to adjust their economic structure and expand their trade and investment with China.

PART 3

Article 8

Timeframes

1. For trade in goods, the negotiations on the agreement for tariff reduction or elimination and other matters as set out in Article 3 of this Agreement shall commence in early 2003 and be concluded by 30 June 2004 in order to establish the ASEAN-China FTA covering trade in goods by 2010 for Brunei, China, Indonesia, Malaysia, the Philippines, Singapore and Thailand, and by 2015 for the newer ASEAN Member States.
2. The negotiations on the Rules of Origin for trade in goods under Article 3 of this Agreement shall be completed no later than December 2003.
3. For trade in services and investments, the negotiations on the respective agreements shall commence in 2003 and be concluded as expeditiously as possible for implementation in accordance with the timeframes to be mutually agreed: (a) taking into account the sensitive sectors of the Parties; and (b) with special and differential treatment and flexibility for the newer ASEAN Member States.
4. For other areas of economic co-operation under Part 2 of this Agreement, the Parties shall continue to build upon existing or agreed programmes set out in Article 7 of this Agreement, develop new economic co-operation programmes and conclude agreements on the various areas of economic co-operation. The Parties shall do so expeditiously for early implementation in a manner and at a pace acceptable to all the parties concerned. The agreements shall include timeframes for the implementation of the commitments therein.

Article 9

Most-Favoured Nation Treatment

China shall accord Most-Favoured Nation (MFN) Treatment consistent with WTO rules and disciplines to all the non-WTO ASEAN Member States upon the date of signature of this Agreement.

Article 10

General Exceptions

Subject to the requirement that such measures are not applied in a manner which would constitute a means of arbitrary or unjustifiable discrimination between or among the Parties where the same conditions prevail, or a disguised restriction on trade within the ASEAN-China FTA, nothing in this Agreement shall prevent any Party from taking and adopting measures for the protection of its national security or the protection of articles of artistic, historic and archaeological value, or such other measures which it deems necessary for the protection of public morals, or for the protection of human, animal or plant life and health.

Article 11

Dispute Settlement Mechanism

1. The Parties shall, within one year after the date of entry into force of this Agreement, establish appropriate formal dispute settlement procedures and mechanism for the purposes of this Agreement.
2. Pending the establishment of the formal dispute settlement procedures and mechanism under paragraph 1 above, any disputes concerning the interpretation, implementation or application of this Agreement shall be settled amicably by consultations and/or mediation.

Article 12

Institutional Arrangements For The Negotiations

1. The ASEAN-China Trade Negotiation Committee (ASEAN-China TNC) that has been established shall continue to carry out the programme of negotiations set out in this Agreement.
2. The Parties may establish other bodies as may be necessary to co-ordinate and implement any economic co-operation activities undertaken pursuant to this Agreement.
3. The ASEAN-China TNC and any aforesaid bodies shall report regularly to the ASEAN Economic Ministers (AEM) and the Minister of the Ministry of Foreign Trade and Economic Co-operation (MOFTEC) of China, through the meetings of the ASEAN Senior Economic Officials (SEOM) and MOFTEC, on the progress and outcome of its negotiations.
4. The ASEAN Secretariat and MOFTEC shall jointly provide the necessary secretariat support to the ASEAN-China TNC whenever and wherever negotiations are held.

Article 13

Miscellaneous Provisions

1. This Agreement shall include the Annexes and the contents therein, and all future legal instruments agreed pursuant to this Agreement.
2. Except as otherwise provided in this Agreement, this Agreement or any action taken under it shall not affect or nullify the rights and obligations of a Party under existing agreements to which it is a party.
3. The Parties shall endeavour to refrain from increasing restrictions or limitations that would affect the application of this Agreement.

Article 14

Amendments

The provisions of this Agreement may be modified through amendments mutually agreed upon in writing by the Parties.

Article 15

Depositary

For the ASEAN Member States, this Agreement shall be deposited with the Secretary-General of ASEAN, who shall promptly furnish a certified copy thereof, to each ASEAN Member State.

Article 16

Entry Into Force

1. This Agreement shall enter into force on 1 July 2003.
2. The Parties undertake to complete their internal procedures for the entry into force of this Agreement prior to 1 July 2003.
3. Where a Party is unable to complete its internal procedures for the entry into force of this Agreement by 1 July 2003, the rights and obligations of that Party under this Agreement shall commence on the date of the completion of such internal procedures.
4. A Party shall upon the completion of its internal procedures for the entry into force of this Agreement notify all the other parties in writing.

IN WITNESS WHEREOF, we have signed this Framework Agreement on Comprehensive Economic Co-operation between the Association of South East Asian Nations and the People's Republic of China.

DONE at Phnom Penh, this 4th day of November, 2002 in duplicate copies in the English Language.

3. Joint Declaration of ASEAN and China on Cooperation in the Field of Non-Traditional Security Issues

Joint Declaration of ASEAN and China on Cooperation in the Field of Non-Traditional Security Issues
6th ASEAN-China Summit
Phnom Penh, 4 November 2002

We the Heads of State/Government of Brunei Darussalam, the Kingdom of Cambodia, the Republic of Indonesia, the Lao People's Democratic Republic, Malaysia, the Union of Myanmar, the Republic of the Philippines, the Republic of Singapore, the Kingdom of Thailand and the Socialist Republic of Viet Nam and the People's Republic of China, gathered in Phnom Penh, Cambodia for the Sixth ASEAN-China Summit,

Recalling the Joint Statement of the Meeting of the Heads of State/ Government of the Member States of ASEAN and of the People's Republic of China in 1997 which contains the commitment to strengthening dialogue and cooperation in all fields with the aim to enhance mutual understanding, expand mutual benefit and consolidate and substantiate the partnership of good neighbourliness and mutual trust;

Deeply concerned over the increasingly serious nature of non-traditional security issues such as trafficking in illegal drugs, people-smuggling including trafficking in women and children, sea piracy, terrorism, arms-smuggling, money-laundering, international economic crime and cyber crime, which have become important factors of uncertainty affecting regional and international security and are posing new challenges to regional and international peace and stability;

Recognising the complexity and deep-rooted background of the non-traditional security issues and the need to address them with an integrated approach that combines political, economic, diplomatic, legal, scientific and technological and other means;

Believing that regional and international cooperation needs to be strengthened to address non-traditional security issues and that ASEAN and China are close neighbours and share extensive common interests in coping with these issues;

Noting with satisfaction the cooperation conducted between ASEAN and China and results achieved in the non-traditional security security field, including the Plan of ASEAN and China Cooperative Operations in Response to Dangerous Drugs in 2000, the four-nation ministerial conference on drug control cooperation held by China, Laos, Myanmar and Thailand in 2001 and the resultant Beijing Declaration and the bilateral cooperation between ASEAN member states and China;

Welcoming the Statement of the ASEAN Ministerial Meeting on Transnational Crime (AMMTC) in 1997, the 2001 ASEAN Declaration on Joint Action to Counter Terrorism adopted by ASEAN Leaders, the Joint Communique of Special ASEAN Ministerial Meeting on Terrorism, the Agreement on Information Exchange and Establishment of Communication Procedures by Cambodia, Indonesia, Malaysia and the Philippines in 2002;

Confirming that cooperation should be conducted on the basis of observing the Five Principles of Peaceful Coexistence and other universally recognised norms of international law, which are embodied in the Charter of the United Nations and the Treaty of Amity and Cooperation in Southeast Asia, and respecting the legal systems of all countries;

Determined to further strengthen and deepen cooperation in the field of non-traditional security issues, we task our Ministers concerned to follow up on the implementation of this Declaration by understanding the following:

I. Objectives

In light of the shared needs of all sides, measures and modalities for cooperation in the field of non-traditional security issues will be formulated to enhance their capacity in dealing with non-traditional security issues, promote their stability and development and safeguard regional peace and security.

II. Priority and Form of Cooperation

1. The priorities at the current stage of cooperation are combating trafficking in illegal drugs, people-smuggling including trafficking in women and children, sea piracy, terrorism, arms-smuggling, money-laundering, international economic crime and cyber crime.
2. On the basis of deepening the existing multilateral and bilateral cooperation,
   a) to strengthen information exchange;
   b) to strengthen personnel exchange and training and enhance capacity-building;
   c) to strengthen practical cooperation on non-traditional security issues;
   d) to strengthen joint research on non-traditional security issues; and
   e) to explore other areas and modalities of cooperation.

III. Participation and Organisation

1. ASEAN and China will use existing mechanisms, as far as possible, such as the ASEAN Ministerial Meeting on Transnational Crime and Senior Officials Meeting on Transnational Crime to pursue the cooperation. Long-term and mid-term cooperation plans will be formulated based on the purposes and principles of the Joint Declaration to serve as guidance for cooperation.
2. Ad-hoc working groups will be established for cooperation in relevant fields to implement the plans of action through the above-mentioned mechanism supported by the competent authorities in ASEAN member countries and China.

IV. Others

To implement this Joint Declaration, action plans may be formulated in accordance with the purposes and principles of the Joint Declaration.

We, the Leaders of ASEAN member countries and the People's Republic of China, pledge to remain seized with the matter and call on other regions and countries to work with us in strengthening the cooperation in the field of non-traditional security issues.

4. Memorandum of Understanding between the Governments of the Member Countries of ASEAN and the Government of China on Cooperation in the Field of Non-Traditional Security Issues

Memorandum of Understanding Between the Governments of the Member Countries of the Association of Southeast Asian Nations (ASEAN) and the Government of the People's Republic of China on Cooperation in the Field of Non-Traditional Security Issues Bangkok, 10 January 2004

The Governments of the Member Countries of the Association of Southeast Asian Nations (ASEAN) and the Government of the People's Republic of China, (hereinafter referred to as 'the Parties');

DESIRING to strengthen the friendly cooperation among the Parties;

PURSUANT to the Joint Declaration of ASEAN and China on Cooperation in the Field of Non-traditional Security Issues adopted on 4th November 2002;

DETERMINED to deepen cooperation in the field of non-traditional security issues among the Parties;

Have agreed as follows:

Article 1

Objectives

The Parties shall develop practical strategies in accordance with their national laws and regulations to enhance the capacity of each individual country and the region as a whole in dealing with such non-traditional security issues as trafficking in illegal drugs, people smuggling including trafficking in women and children, sea piracy, terrorism, arms smuggling, money laundering, international economic crime and cyber crime.

Article 2

Areas of Cooperation

The Parties have identified the following fields of common interest for mid and long-term cooperation:

1. Information Exchange
   a. The Parties shall establish a compilation of their national laws and regulations pertaining to such fields as mentioned in Article 1.
   b. The Parties shall establish a collection of international conventions pertaining to such fields as mentioned in Article 1, to which they are parties, and a collection of bilateral agreements signed among them where appropriate.
   c. The Parties shall, subject to their respective national laws and policies, exchange intelligence on the non-traditional security issues referred to in Article 1.
   d. The Parties shall, subject to their respective national laws and policies, exchange information on special equipment and techniques applied in the prevention and investigation of the non-traditional security issues referred to in Article 1.
2. Personnel Exchange and Training
   a. The Parties shall promote personnel contact and exchange among their law enforcement officers and experts.
   b. China shall organise workshops to promote exchange of law enforcement experiences among the Parties in combating terrorism, trafficking in illegal drugs, sea piracy and international economic crime.
   c. China shall hold training courses to upgrade the level of capacity of each Party and the region as a whole in drug control, forensic sciences, immigration administration, road traffic control and the investigation of cyber crime. To ensure the quality of the training courses, China shall invite regional and international experts to give lectures.
   d. The Parties shall promote exchange and cooperation among institutions.
3. Law Enforcement Cooperation
   a. The Parties shall encourage and offer each other the fullest law enforcement cooperation possible in accordance with their respective

national laws and on the basis of mutual respect for sovereignty, equality and mutual benefit.

b. The Parties shall promote cooperation in accordance with their national laws in such fields as evidence gathering, tracing of crime proceeds, apprehension and repatriation of criminal fugitives and return of crime proceeds; and encourage each other to enter into bilateral legal arrangements therein.

4. Joint Research

   a. The Parties shall support the joint research by their experts and scholars in the field of non-traditional security issues, and share the results of research between them.

   b. The Parties shall organise experts in relevant fields to provide short-term technical services and to make study tours.

Article 3

Implementation

1. The Parties agree that the implementing agencies for this Memorandum of Understanding are:

   a. the ASEAN Secretariat in coordination with the relevant national agencies of the ASEAN Member Countries; and

   b. the Ministry of Public Security for the People's Republic of China.

The implementing agencies of the Parties shall determine through consultation the details, schedule and arrangements for the implementation of the cooperation provided in this Memorandum of Understanding, and shall serve as coordinators for such cooperation.

2. ASEAN welcomes China's participation in the existing ASEAN cooperation pertaining to the fight against transnational crime, including the ASEAN Action Plan on the Fight against Transnational Crime and its Work Program.

3. The Parties shall hold meetings at working level once every year to exchange information on implementation of this Memorandum of Understanding, to brief each other on the progress of cooperation under various mechanisms, and to discuss the plans for future cooperation.

Article 4

Financial Arrangements

1. Expenses of workshops and training courses organised by China in accordance with this Memorandum of Understanding shall be covered by the Chinese side, including meals, accommodation and local transportation for the participants sent by ASEAN Member Countries during their stay in China and fees for inviting experts, while the expenses of international travel shall be covered by the sending Countries, except when it is agreed otherwise.
2. Expenses incurred in the implementation of other cooperative activities in accordance with this Memorandum of Understanding shall be covered by the Parties through consultation.
3. The activities mentioned in this Memorandum of Understanding shall be conducted subject to the availability of funds and personnel of the Parties.

Article 5

Confidentiality

1. Information, document, data, equipment or technology received in accordance with this Memorandum of Understanding shall not be disclosed or distributed to any third party except to the extent as authorised in written form to do so by the country providing it.
2. In the event of termination of this Memorandum of Understanding, the Parties have agreed that the provisions of this Article shall continue to apply.

Article 6

Suspension

Each Party reserves the right for reasons of security, public order or public health to suspend temporarily, either in whole or in part the implementation of this Memorandum of Understanding, suspension of which shall take effect immediately after notification has been given to the other Party through diplomatic channels.

Article 7

Revision and Amendment

The Parties may request in writing a revision, amendment or modification of all or any part of this Memorandum of Understanding. Any revision, amendment or modification shall be mutually agreed upon in written form by the Parties and shall form part of this Memorandum of Understanding. Such revision, amendment or modification shall come into force on such date as may be determined by the Parties.

Article 8

Settlement of Dispute

Any dispute or differences arising out of the interpretation/ implementation/application of the provisions of this Memorandum of Understanding shall be settled amicably through consultation/negotiation between the Parties without reference to any third party.

Article 9

Entry Into Force, Duration and Termination

1. This Memorandum of Understanding shall come into effect on the date of its signing and shall remain in force for a period of five years. Thereafter, it may be extended for additional periods subject to availability of funds and agreements of the Parties expressed by way of exchange of letters.
2. Each Party may give written notice to the other of its desire to terminate this Memorandum of Understanding, of which termination shall be effective thirty (30) days after written notification has been given to the other Party. The termination of this Memorandum of Understanding shall not affect the implementation of ongoing activities/programs.

IN WITNESS WHEREOF, the undersigned, duly authorised by the respective Governments of the ASEAN Member Countries and the People's Republic of China, have signed this Memorandum of Understanding.

This Memorandum of Understanding is signed in Bangkok, Thailand, on the 10th day of January of the year two thousand and four in two original copies in the English language.

5. Declaration on the Conduct of the Parties in the South China Sea

Declaration on the Conduct of Parties in the South China Sea

The Governments of the Member States of ASEAN and the Government of the People's Republic of China,

REAFFIRMING their determination to consolidate and develop the friendship and cooperation existing between their people and governments with the view to promoting a 21st century-oriented partnership of good neighbourliness and mutual trust;

COGNIZANT of the need to promote a peaceful, friendly and harmonious environment in the South China Sea between ASEAN and China for the enhancement of peace, stability, economic growth and prosperity in the region;

COMMITTED to enhancing the principles and objectives of the 1997 Joint Statement of the Meeting of the Heads of State/Government of the Member States of ASEAN and President of the People's Republic of China;

DESIRING to enhance favourable conditions for a peaceful and durable solution of differences and disputes among countries concerned;

Hereby declare the following:

1. The Parties reaffirm their commitment to the purposes and principles of the Charter of the United Nations, the 1982 UN Convention on the Law of the Sea, the Treaty of Amity and Cooperation in Southeast Asia, the Five Principles of Peaceful Coexistence and other universally recognised principles of international law which shall serve as the basic norms governing state-to-state relations.
2. The Parties are committed to exploring ways for building trust and confidence in accordance with the above-mentioned principles and on the basis of equality and mutual respect.
3. The Parties reaffirm their respect for and commitment to the freedom of navigation in and overflight above the South China Sea as provided for by the universally recognised principles of international law, including the 1982 UN Convention on the Law of the Sea.

4. The Parties concerned undertake to resolve their territorial and jurisdictional disputes by peaceful means, without resorting to the threat or use of force, through friendly consultations and negotiations by sovereign states directly concerned, in accordance with universally recognised principles of international law, including the 1982 UN Convention on the Law of the Sea.
5. The Parties undertake to exercise self-restraint in the conduct of activities that would complicate or escalate disputes and affect peace and stability including, among others, refraining from action of inhabiting on the presently uninhabited islands, reefs, shoals, cays, and other features and to handle their differences in a constructive manner.

   Pending the peaceful settlement of territorial and jurisdictional disputes, the Parties concerned undertake to intensify efforts to seek ways, in the spirit of cooperation and understanding, to build trust and confidence between and among them, including:

   a. holding dialogues and exchange of views as appropriate between their defense and military officials;
   b. ensuring just and humane treatment of all persons who are either in danger or in distress;
   c. notifying, on a voluntary basis, other Parties concerned of any impending joint/combined military exercise; and
   d. exchanging, on a voluntary basis, relevant information.
6. Pending a comprehensive and durable settlement of the disputes, the Parties concerned may explore or undertake cooperative activities. These may include the following:

   a. marine environmental protection;
   b. marine scientific research;
   c. safety of navigation and communication at sea;
   d. search and rescue operation; and
   e. combating transnational crime, including but not limited to trafficking in illicit drugs, piracy and armed robbery at sea and illegal traffic in arms.

   The modalities, scope and locations, in respect of bilateral and multilateral cooperation should be agreed upon by the Parties concerned prior to their actual implementation.

7. The Parties concerned stand ready to continue their consultations and dialogues concerning relevant issues, through modalities to be agreed by them, including regular consultations on the observance of this Declaration, for the purpose of promoting good neighbourliness and transparency, establishing harmony, mutual understanding and cooperation, and facilitating peaceful resolution of disputes among them.
8. The Parties undertake to respect the provisions of this Declaration and take actions consistent therewith.
9. The Parties encourage other countries to respect the principles contained in this Declaration.
10. The Parties concerned reaffirm that the adoption of a code of conduct in the South China Sea would further promote peace and stability in the region and agree to work, on the basis of consensus, towards the eventual attainment of this objective.

Done on the Fourth Day of November in the year two thousand and two in Phnom Penh, the Kingdom of Cambodia.

Selected bibliography

Acharya, Amitav, 'Seeking Security in the Dragon's Shadow: China and Southeast Asia in the Emerging Asian Order', *IDSS Working Paper No. 44*, Institute of Defense and Strategic Studies, Singapore, March 2003.

Asian Development Bank, *Emerging Asia: Changes and Challenges* (Manila: Asian Development Bank, 1997).

Beckman, Robert C., Carl Grundy-Warr and Vivian L. Forbes, 'Acts of Piracy in the Malacca and Singapore Straits', *IBRU Maritime Briefing*, vol. 1 (4), 1994.

Birnie, Patricia W. and Alan E. Boyle, *International Law and the Environment* (Oxford: Clarendon Press, 1992).

Blake, Gerald H., William J. Hildersley, Martin A. Pratt, Rebecca J. Ridley and Clive H. Schofield (eds.), *The Peaceful Management of Transboundary Resources* (London: Graham & Trotman/Martinus Nijhoff, 1995).

Blake, Gerald, Chia Lin Sien, Carl Grundy-Warr, Martin Pratt and Clive Schofield (eds.), *International Boundaries and Environment Security: Frameworks for Regional Cooperation* (London/The Hague: Kluwer Law International, 1997).

Boer, Ben, Ross Ramsay and Donald R. Rothwell, *International Environmental Law in the Asia Pacific* (London: Kluwer Law International, 1998).

Bolla, Alexander J. and Ted L. McDorman, *Comparative Environmental Law Anthology* (Durham, North Carolina: Carolina Academic Press, 1999).

Bouchez, Leo J., *The Regime of Bays in International Law* (Leyden: A.W. Sythoff, 1964).

Brans, Edward H.P., Esther J. de Haan, Andre Nollkaemper and Jan Rinzema (eds.), *The Scarcity of Water: Emerging Legal and Policy Responses* (London: Kluwer Law International, 1997).

British Institute of International and Comparative Law, *Joint Development of Offshore Oil and Gas: A Model Agreement for States for Joint Development with Explanatory Commentary* (London: British Institute of International and Comparative Law, 1989).

Brownlie, Ian, *Principles of Public International Law*, 5th ed. (Oxford: Clarendon Press, 1998).

Buszynski, Leszek and Iskandar Sazlan, 'Maritime Claims and Energy Cooperation in the South China Sea', *Contemporary Southeast Asia*, vol. 29 (1), 2007, pp. 143–71.

Cai, Kevin G., 'The ASEAN–China Free Trade Agreement and East Asian Regional Grouping', *Contemporary Southeast Asia*, vol. 25 (3), 2003, pp. 387–404.

Carberry, Jacqueline Ann, 'Terrorism: A Global Phenomenon Mandating a Unified International Response', *Indiana Journal of Global Legal Studies*, vol. 6 (2), 1999, pp. 685–720.

Chan, Gerald, *Chinese Perspectives on International Relations: A Framework for Analysis* (London: MacMillan Press, 1999).

Chen, Huiping, 'China–ASEAN Investment Agreement Negotiations: The Substantive Issues', *The Journal of World Investment and Trade*, vol. 7 (1), 2006, pp. 143–63.

Chen, Huiping, 'China–ASEAN FTA: An Investment Perspective', in John Wong, Zou Keyuan and Zeng Huaqun (eds.), *China–ASEAN Relations: Economic and Legal Dimensions* (Singapore: World Scientific, 2006), pp. 133–57.

Chen, Juliana W., 'Achieving Supreme Excellence: How China Is Using Agreements with ASEAN to Overcome Obstacles to Its Leadership in Asian Regional Economic Integration', *Chicago Journal of International Law*, vol. 7 (2), 2006–2007, pp. 655–74.

Chen, Li-hui, Zeng Zun-gu and He Da-ming, 'Coordinating the Relationships between Interested Parties in Development of the International River – A Case Study of Lancang-Mekong', *World Regional Studies* (in Chinese), vol. 12 (1), March 2003, pp. 71–8.

Chen, Wen, 'Are China and ASEAN Compete for FDI?', in John Wong, Zou Keyuan and Zeng Huaqun (eds.), *China–ASEAN Relations: Economic and Legal Dimensions* (Singapore: World Scientific, 2006), pp. 199–215.

Chow, Jonathan T., 'ASEAN Counterterrorism Cooperation Since 9/11', *Asian Survey*, vol. 45 (2), 2005, pp. 302–21.

Chung, Moon-Soo, 'China–ASEAN FTA and Korean FTA Policies', in John Wong, Zou Keyuan and Zeng Huaqun (eds.), *China–ASEAN Relations: Economic and Legal Dimensions* (Singapore: World Scientific, 2006), pp. 293–307.

Churchill, Robin R. and A.Vaughan Lowe, *The Law of the Sea* (Manchester: Manchester University Press, 1983).

Clark, Allen L., 'Myanmar's Present Development and Future Options', *Asian Survey*, vol. 39 (5), 1999, pp. 772–91.

Crawford, James and Donald R. Rothwell (eds.), *The Law of the Sea in the Asia-Pacific Region: Developments and Prospects* (Dordrecht: Martinus Nijhoff, 1995).

Desker, Barry, 'Is the ASEAN Charter Necessary?', *RSIS Commentaries 77/2008*, S. Rajaratnam School of International Studies, Nanyang Technological University, Singapore, 17 July 2008.

Dutt, Ashok K. (ed.), *Southeast Asia: A Ten Nation Region* (Dordrecht: Kluwer Academic Publishers, 1996).

Elias, Taslim O., 'The Doctrine of Intertemporal law', *American Journal of International Law*, vol. 74, 1980, pp. 285–307.

Emmers, Ralf, 'International Regime Building in Southeast Asia: ASEAN Cooperation Against the Illicit Trafficking and Abuse of Drugs', *IDSS Working Paper No. 106*, Institute of Defence and Strategic Studies, Nanyang Technological University, Singapore, February 2006.

Garver, John W., *Foreign Relations of the People's Republic of China* (New Jersey: Prentice-Hall, 1993).

Garver, John W., *Protracted Contest: Sino-Indian Rivalry in the Twentieth Century* (Seattle: University of Washington Press, 2001).

Goh, Evelyn, 'China in the Mekong River Basin: The Regional Security Implications of Resource Development on the Lancang Jiang', *IDSS Working Paper No. 69*, Institute of Defence and Strategic Studies, Nanyang Technological University, Singapore, July 2004.

Goodman, David S.G. and Gerald Segal (eds.), *China Rising: Nationalism and Interdependence* (London: Routledge, 1997).

Guyot, James, 'Burma in 1997: From Empire to ASEAN', *Asian Survey*, vol. 38 (2), 1998, pp. 190–5.

Halvorssen, Anita M., 'Climate Change Regime–Amending the Kyoto Protocol to Include Annex C and the Annex D Mitigation Fund', *Colorado Journal of International Environmental Law and Policy*, vol. 18 (2), 2007, pp. 247–65.

Han, Zhenhua (ed.), *A Compilation of Historical Materials on China's South China Sea Islands* (Beijing: Oriental Press, 1988) (in Chinese).

He, Daming and Hsiang-te Kung, 'Facilitating Regional Sustainable Development Through Integrated Multi-Objective Utilization, Management of Water Resources in the Lancang-Mekong River Basin', *Journal of Chinese Geography*, vol. 7 (4), 1997, pp. 9–21.

Hill, R.D., Norman G. Owen and E.V. Roberts (eds.), *Fishing in Troubled Waters*, Proceedings of the Academic Conference on Territorial Claims in the South China Sea (Hong Kong: Centre of Asian Studies, University of Hong Kong, 1991).

Hu, Qian and Chen Qiang, 'China's Extradition Law of 2000', *Chinese Journal of International Law*, vol. 1 (2), 2002, pp. 645–54.

International Bureau of the Permanent Court of Arbitration (ed.), *International Investments and Protection of the Environment: The Role of Dispute Resolution Mechanisms* (The Hague: Kluwer Law International, 2001).

Japan Environmental Council (ed.), *The State of the Environment in Asia 1999/2000* (Tokyo: Springer-Verlag, 2000).

Jennings, Robert and A. Watts (eds.), *Oppenheim's International Law*, 9th ed., vol. 1 (Oxford: Clarendon Press, 1992).

Katanyuu, Ruukun, 'Beyond Non-Interference in ASEAN: The Association's Role in Myanmar's National Reconciliation and Democratization', *Asian Survey*, vol. 46 (6), 2006, pp. 825–45.

Kog, Yue-Choong, 'Environmental Management and Conflict in Southeast Asia: Land Reclamation and Its Political Impact', *IDSS Working Paper No. 101*, Institute for Defence and Strategic Studies, Nanyang Technological University, Singapore, January 2006.

Lai, Hongyi, 'Regional Cooperation in Epidemic Prevention: China and ASEAN', in John Wong, Zou Keyuan and Zeng Huaqun (eds.), *China–ASEAN Relations: Economic and Legal Dimensions* (Singapore: World Scientific, 2006), pp. 59–73.

Lai, Hongyi and Lim Tin Seng (eds.), *Harmony and Development: ASEAN–China Relations* (Singapore: World Scientific, 2007).

Lam, Peng Er, 'China's Ties with Southeast Asia in the Post–Cold War Era: Japan's Response', in John Wong, Zou Keyuan and Zeng Huaqun (eds.), *China–ASEAN Relations: Economic and Legal Dimensions* (Singapore: World Scientific, 2006), pp. 309–25.

Lansdowne, Helen, Philip Dearden and William Neilson (eds.), *Communities in Southeast Asia: Challenges and Responses* (University of Victoria, British Columbia, Canada: Centre for Asia-Pacific Initiatives, 2002).

Li, Guoqiang, 'Preliminary Discussion on Joint Development in the South China Sea', in Zhong Tianxiang, Han Jia and Ren Huaifeng (eds.), *Proceedings of the South China Sea Workshop (2002)* (Hainan: Hainan Institute for the South China Sea, 2002) (in Chinese), pp. 114–41.

Li, Jinming and Li Dexia, 'The Dotted Line on the Chinese Map of the South China Sea: A Note', *Ocean Development and International Law*, vol. 34, 2003, pp. 287–95.

Li, Yiping and Zhuang Guotu (eds.), *International Relations of Southeast Asia Since the Cold War* (Xiamen: Xiamen University Press, 2005) (in Chinese).

Lu, Xixi 'Transboundary Environmental Issues of the Mekong River: Cooperation or Conflicts among the Riparian Countries', in John Wong, Zou Keyuan and Zeng Huaqun (eds.), *China–ASEAN Relations: Economic and Legal Dimensions* (Singapore: World Scientific, 2006), pp. 179–97.

Luo, Wei, *The 1997 Criminal Code of the People's Republic of China with English Translation and Introduction* (Buffalo, New York: William S Hein & Co., Inc., 1998).

Mahbubani, Kishore, *The New Asian Hemisphere: The Irresistible Shift of Global Power to the East* (New York: Public Affairs, 2008).

Maung, Mya, 'Burma's Economic Performance under Military Rule: An Assessment', *Asian Survey*, vol. 37 (6), 1997, pp. 503–24.

Mi, Liang (ed.), *Selected Economic and Trade Laws of the Lao People's Democratic Republic* (Beijing: China Legal System Press, 2006) (in Chinese).

Nguyen, Hong Thao, 'Vietnam and the Code of Conduct for the South China Sea', *Ocean Development and International Law*, vol. 32, 2001, pp. 105–31.

Nguyen, Hong Thao, 'The 2002 Declaration on the Conduct of Parties in the South China Sea: A Note', *Ocean Development and International Law*, vol. 34, 2003, pp. 279–85.

O'Connell, Daniel P., *The International Law of the Sea*, vol. 1 (Oxford: Clarendon Press, 1982).

Ong, Yen Nee, 'International Responses to Terrorism: The Limits and Possibilities of Legal Control of Terrorism by Regional Arrangement with Particular Reference to Asean', *IDSS Working Paper No. 29*, Institute of Defence and Strategic Studies, Nanyang Technological University, Singapore, July 2002.

Peng, Liming (ed.), *A Complete Collection of Existing Laws of the People's Republic of China* (Beijing: China Constructing Materials Industry Press, 1998) (in Chinese).

Perrez, Xaver, *Cooperative Sovereignty: From Independence to Interdependence in the Structure of International Environmental Law* (The Hague: Kluwer Law International, 2000).

Prescott, J.R.Victor, *The Maritime Political Boundaries of the World* (London: Methuen, 1985).

Ratner, Blake D., 'The Politics of Regional Governance in the Mekong River Basin', *Global Change*, vol. 15 (1), 2003, pp. 59–76.

Ravenhill, John, 'Is China an Economic Threat to Southeast Asia?', *Asian Survey*, vol. 46 (5), 2006, pp. 653–74.

Robinson, Thomas W. and David Shambaugh (eds.), *Chinese Foreign Policy: Theory and Practice* (Oxford: Clarendon Press, 1994).

Romano, Cesare P.R., *The Peaceful Settlement of International Environmental Disputes: A Pragmatic Approach* (The Hague: Kluwer Law International, 2000).

Rose, Gregory and Diana Nestorovska, 'Towards an ASEAN Counter-Terrorism Treaty', *Singapore Year Book of International Law*, vol. 9, 2005, pp. 157–89.

Roy, Denny, *China's Foreign Relations* (Lanham: Rowman & Littlefield, 1998).

Roy, Denny, 'Southeast Asia and China: Balancing or Bandwagoning?', *Contemporary Southeast Asia*, vol. 27 (2), 2005, pp. 305–22.

Sand, Peter H., *Marine Environment Law in the United Nations Environment Programme* (London: Tycooly Publishing, 1988).

Sand, Peter H., *Transnational Environmental Law: Lessons in Global Change* (The Hague: Kluwer Law International, 1999).

Santiago, Miriam Defensor, *International Law: With Philippine Cases and Materials and ASEAN Instruments* (Quezon, Philippines: Central Professional Books, Inc., 1999).

Seekins, Donald M., 'Burma–China Relations: Playing with Fire', *Asian Survey*, vol. 37 (6), 1997, pp. 525–39.

Severino, Rodolfo C. (comp.), *Framing the ASEAN Charter: An I SEAS Perspective* (Singapore: Institute of Southeast Asian Studies, 2005).

Severino, Rodolfo C., *Southeast Asia in Search of an ASEAN Community: Insights from the Former ASEAN Secretary-General* (Singapore: Institute of Southeast Asian Studies, 2006).

Severino, Rodolfo C., 'ASEAN Beyond Forty: Towards Political and Economic Integration', *Contemporary Southeast Asia*, vol. 29 (3), 2007, pp. 406–23.

Sievers, Eric W., 'Transboundary Jurisdiction and Watercourse Law: China, Kazakhstan, and the Irtysh', *Texas International Law Journal*, vol. 37 (1), 2002, pp. 1–42.

Song, Yann-huei, 'The Potential Marine Pollution Threat from Oil and Gas Activities in the Disputed South China Sea/Spratly Area: A Role That Taiwan Can Play', *Ocean Development and International Law*, vol. 39, 2008, pp. 150–77.

Stankiewicz, Michael (ed.), *Maritime Shipping in Northeast Asia: Law of the Sea, Sea Lanes, and Security*, IGCC Policy Paper No. 33, Institute on Global Conflict and Co-operation, University of California, February 1998.

Stuart-Fox, Martin, 'Southeast Asia and China: The Role of History and Culture in Shaping Future Relations', *Contemporary Southeast Asia*, vol. 26 (1), 2004, pp. 116–39.

Tao, Zhenghua and Rüdiger Wolfrum (eds.), *Implementing International Environmental Law in Germany and China* (London: Kluwer Law International, 2001).

Vatikiotis, Michael R.J., 'Catching the Dragon's Tail: China and Southeast Asia in the 21st Century', *Contemporary Southeast Asia*, vol. 25 (1), 2003, pp. 65–78.

Wang, Jiangyu, 'The International Legal Personality of ASEAN and the Legal Nature of the China–ASEAN FTA', in John Wong, Zou Keyuan and Zeng Huaqun (eds.), *China–ASEAN Relations: Economic and Legal Dimensions* (Singapore: World Scientific, 2006), pp. 111–31.

Wang, Li, 'Zheng He's Voyage and Solution of Pirates Issue', in Nanjing Zheng He Study Association (ed.), *Chinese Heading for the Sea* (Beijing: Sea Tide Publisher, 1996) (in Chinese), pp. 311–9.

Wang, Tieya (ed.), *International Law* (Beijing: Law Press, 1995) (in Chinese).

Williams, Paul R., 'International Environmental Dispute Resolution: The Dispute between Slovakia and Hungary Concerning Construction of the Gabcíkovo and Nagymaros Dams', *Columbia Journal of Environmental Law*, vol. 19 (1), 1994, pp. 1–57.

Williams, Paul R., *International Law and the Resolution of Central and East European Transboundary Environmental Disputes* (London: Macmillan Press, 2000).

Wong, John and Sarah Chan, 'China–ASEAN Free Trade Agreement: Shaping Future Economic Relations', *Asian Survey*, vol. 43 (3), 2003, pp. 507–26.

Wong, John, Zou Keyuan and Zeng Huaqun (eds.), *China–ASEAN Relations: Economic and Legal Dimensions* (Singapore: World Scientific, 2006).

Wu, Shicun and Hong Nong, 'The Energy Security of China and the Oil and Gas Exploitation in the Disputed South China Sea Area', in Myron H. Nordquist, John Norton Moore and Kuen-chen Fu (eds.), *Recent Developments in the Law of the Sea and China* (Leiden/Boston: Martinus Nijhoff, 2006), pp. 145–54.

Xin, Yejiang (ed.), *China's South China Sea Islands* (Haiko: Hainan International Information Publishing Centre, 1996) (in Chinese).

Yee, Herbert and Ian James Storey (eds.), *The China Threat: Perceptions, Myths and Reality* (London: RoutledgeCurzon, 2002).

Young, Reuven, 'Defining Terrorism: The Evolution of Terrorism as a Legal Concept in International Law and Its Influence on Definitions in Domestic legislation', *Boston College International and Comparative Law Review*, vol. 29, 2006, pp. 23–105.

Zeng, Huaqun, 'WTO Rules and China–ASEAN FTA Agreement', in John Wong, Zou Keyuan and Zeng Huaqun (eds.), *China–ASEAN Relations: Economic and Legal Dimensions* (Singapore: World Scientific, 2006), pp. 93–109.

Zeng, Lingliang, 'ASEAN–China Relations: An International Law Perspective', in John Wong, Zou Keyuan and Zeng Huaqun (eds.), *China–ASEAN Relations: Economic and Legal Dimensions* (Singapore: World Scientific, 2006), pp. 33–55.

Zhang, Haibing, 'China and Southeast Asian Cooperation: New Developments and Challenges', in John Wong and Lai Hongyi (eds.), *China into the Hu-Wen Era: Policy Initiatives and Challenges* (Singapore: World Scientific Publishing, 2006), pp. 541–56.

Zhang, Xizheng, 'Progress of, Obstacles and Outlets to China's Participation in the Cooperation of the Greater Mekong Sub-Region', *Southeast Asian Affairs* (bimonthly in Chinese), no. 3, 2007, pp. 1–10.

Zhao, Lihai, *Studies on the Law of the Sea Issues* (Beijing: Peking University Press, 1996) (in Chinese).

Zou, Keyuan, 'Territory in International Law', in Wang Tieya (ed.), *International Law* (Beijing: Law Press, 1995) (in Chinese), pp. 229–55.

Zou, Keyuan, 'Piracy at Sea and China's Response', *Lloyd's Maritime and Commercial Law Quarterly*, August 2000, pp. 364–82.

Zou, Keyuan, *China's Marine Legal System and the Law of the Sea* (Leiden/Boston: Martinus Nijhoff, 2005).

Zou, Keyuan, 'The Sino-Vietnamese Agreement on Maritime Boundary Delimitation in the Gulf of Tonkin', *Ocean Development and International Law*, vol. 36, 2005, pp. 13–24.

Zou, Keyuan, 'Joint Development in the South China Sea: A New Approach', *International Journal of Marine and Coastal Law*, vol. 21 (1), 2006, pp. 83–109.

Index

Note: "n" in italic has been assigned to the terms found in the Note sections.

Lightning Source UK Ltd.
Milton Keynes UK
04 March 2010

150915UK00001B/67/P